The Desert Queen

ALSO BY

DORIS LESLIE

Novels

Biographical Studies

DORIS LESLIE

The Desert Queen

HEINEMANN : LONDON

William Heinemann Ltd
15 Queen Street, Mayfair, London W1X 8BE

LONDON MELBOURNE TORONTO
JOHANNESBURG AUCKLAND

First published 1972
© Doris Leslie 1972

Printed in Great Britain by Cox & Wyman Ltd
London, Fakenham and Reading

To the memory of
Ralph Straus

CONTENTS

A 'DRAMATIS PERSONAE' OF THE CHIEF CHARACTERS

Lady Hester Stanhope
Lady Griselda Stanhope } Daughters of 'Citizen Stanhope', Earl Stanhope
Lady Lucy Stanhope

Earl Stanhope

Viscount Mahon
The Hon. Charles Stanhope } Sons of Lord Stanhope
The Hon. James Stanhope

William Pitt, First Lord of the Treasury, Prime Minister of England

Lord Camelford

Lord Granville Leveson-Gower

General Sir John Moore

Michael Bruce

Ann Fry
Elizabeth Williams } Personal maids to Lady Hester

Dr Charles Lewis Meryon, Personal physician to Lady Hester

Mehemet Ali, Viceroy of Egypt

Emir Bechir, 'Prince of the Mountain'

Mahannah el Fadel, Chief of the Anazè tribes

Emir Nasar, his son

Stratford Canning, Minister Plenipotentiary to the Sublime Porte

Henry Pearce, friend of Michael Bruce

Mr Barker, British agent in the Levant

Lascaris, *agent provocateur* to Napoleon Bonaparte in the Middle East

Captain Forster, R.N.

Captain Yorke, R.N.

General Loustenau, 'The Prophet'

Captain Loustenau, his son

Metta, steward to Lady Hester on Mount Lebanon

Mustafa Berber, in command of the pashalic troops

Burckhardt, a Swiss explorer

and

Lamartine, Marcellus, Prince Pückler Maukau, Governors of Malta and Gibralta, Bertrand, Beaudin, Georgio (Georgiaki), dragomen, interpreters, Arab and Syrian servants, slaves, etc.

FOREWORD

In presenting this biographical study of Lady Hester Lucy Stanhope I have adhered strictly to fact. None of the characters nor excerpts from letters is fictitious. The battle scenes in the desert tribal wars in which she took an active part are taken from her memoirs and correspondence, as is much of the dialogue dictated to her personal physician, Dr Meryon, meticulously recorded by him, and which are the main sources of all that we know of this remarkable woman explorer.

During this century we have had innumerable accounts of her incredible adventures in the Middle East when, a hundred years before Lawrence of Arabia, she too lived among the Arabs as one of them, disguised as an Arabian or Bedouin chief.

The savage tribes over whom she ruled named her Queen and Prophetess, but she was often taken for a beardless youth in the various native costumes she adopted.

That she was said to have married a sheik has never yet been proven, yet there is evidence enough of her amorous affair with the son of a Bedouin chief.

Of all the men who sought her favour, as niece of the bachelor Prime Minister, Pitt the Younger, when she acted as hostess at Downing Street, the only man whom she would have married was the one great love of her life, General Sir John Moore, killed at Corunna.

He was succeeded by Michael Bruce who lived with her in the desert for four years and whom she persistently refused to marry. We have invaluable proof of this relationship between the lovers in the numerous letters collected and edited by his direct descendant, Ian Bruce, in *The Nun of Lebanon*.

Of her indomitable courage and her firm belief that she was destined to free the subjugated Arab tribes from their overlords, the Turks, and of her passionate last romance with Captain Loustenau, the young French officer who fought under Bonaparte, let this true story of her life speak for her.

I have dedicated the book to the memory of Ralph Straus, one time literary critic of the *Sunday Times* who, when I wrote the first of my biographical studies, *Royal William* (life of William IV), suggested I should write of Lady Hester Stanhope. It has taken me many years to follow his advice.

Among the innumerable authorities, both living and dead, whom I have consulted in the compilation of this book, I am particularly indebted to: Frank Hamel: *Lady Hester Stanhope*; to her niece, the Duchess of Cleveland: *Life and letters of Lady Hester Stanhope*; to Joan Haslip: *Lady Hester Stanhope*; to Ian Bruce: *The Nun of Lebanon*; to the *Memoirs and Travels* of Dr Charles Meryon; and to G. M. Trevelyan: *British History in the Nineteenth Century*.

DORIS LESLIE

PART ONE
Democracy Hall

ONE

'I might as well,' she said, 'be put to mind the geese instead of turkeys as Papa is always saying we're a flock of geese and then I'd be his goose girl.'

Her two younger sisters, whose joint ages combined with her own barely totalled forty, received this, concurrently, with giggles.

'Goose girl! Goose girl!' chortled Griselda, a plain dumpy child with a large inquisitive nose, an inheritance from a long line of Pitt forbears. 'Papa will have to change his flock and then we'll have goose for Christmas and not turkey. I hate turkey.'

'You'll be lucky if you get cheese rinds and pigs' trotters for Christmas,' was the comfortless reply. 'Papa won't have any Christian, or what he calls Pagan, jollifying for Christmas or any other time – not since he's turned republican.'

'D'you mean what the Gospels call publicans and sinners?'

Lucy, the youngest of the three, had her hair cut short in accordance with her father's mandate that 'all fripperies and vanities must be taboo,' in consequence of which Lord Stanhope insisted that his daughters should wear, as Hester complained, 'coarse hideous clothes like sackcloth. Wonder it is he don't put ashes on our heads as well.' And:

'Not publican, idiot,' she gave answer to Lucy, whose light empty eyes stared out of an enchantingly pretty little face in a kind of dazed transparency, unlike the eyes of Hester. Hers were a dazzling blue, changing colour almost to black according to her mood that

3

swung between heights of volatile exuberance to exaggerated depths of despair, to find her fledgling wings clipped by parental harsh restriction. She had reached that age of exciting adolescence when life is either radiant or agonizing; when the swift ebb and flow of bewildering impressions would fade before the vision that accompanied contraband adventure. Thus we have it that before the catastrophic tumult which plunged France into bloody revolution, the French Ambassador, visiting Chevening Manor, Lord Stanhope's country seat in Kent, arrived with a retinue of servants, wives – and mistresses – of his attachés. Glittering with jewels, the epitome of elegance the like of which Hester never had beheld, filled her with amaze and curiosity.

The children, having been sent to Hastings to be out of the way and provide room for the visitors, she was inspired to see for herself this wondrous country where gentlemen – never mind the ladies, she had never cared for ladies – where the gentlemen conversed in rapid Parisian French, praised her eyes, '*A merveille*', were patched and powdered, perfumed; smelt delicious. How different from the smell of pigsties and farmyards that pervaded Chevening indoors and out. And their manners! How different again from the manners of the fox-hunting squires, her father's neighbours who were red-faced, loud-voiced, and very often drunk.

So, on a day when the children were conducted to the beach by their governess, Hester managed to escape temporary vigilance to see boats resting on the shingle. One, invitingly moored to a breakwater near to the edge of the narrow sea that divided England from France, offered temptation. Imbued with the adventurous spirit which later was to lead her, in defiance of custom or convention, to those far off lands where no English-woman had ever set foot before, she untied the moorings of the boat, no easy task, and, seizing the oars – she had learned to scull on the lake at Chevening – she set off for

France. Not then, however, to reach those enviable shores. A frenzied governess, sighting her manfully rowing the bobbing boat, entreated a fisherman to go after her. In a few minutes she was overtaken and hauled back to the beach.

Punishment summarily followed. She was strapped between hard boards, a fad of this particular 'Miss' who meted mutiny with deportment that her young well-developed body should be, as Hester described it, 're-duced to the shape of our puny "Miss" '.

She was reminded of that incident which had sent her careering off in search of the gallant gentlemen of France, as, rounding on Lucy, she repeated: 'Not publicans – *re*publicans which is what those wicked French are who hang the aristocrats – *aristos* they call them – on lamp-posts in the streets and cut off their heads because they happen to be Dukes and Marquises and Counts, and because Papa sides with them – those monsters who are Revolutionists – Uncle William calls him a traitor to his class.'

'But Papa is English not French, so why should Uncle William call him a traitor?'

This from Griselda, always argumentative.

'Because he's an earl, whether English or not, so that's why.' And as Griselda opened her mouth further to question she was peremptorily checked.

'Go along now, both of you, and don't bother me or Papa will cut off my head if these damn turkeys go straying.'

'Muss'n say damn!' gasped Lucy, 'that's swearing. Muss'n swear.'

'I'll swear me to hell if I like,' shockingly said Hester. 'Papa swears so why shouldn't I? And don't you tell me what I must or mustn't do, it's for me to tell you. So be off and keep away from Mamma. She's mad as a puss since Papa got rid of her carriage and horses that she has to walk in the mud. But she'll have them back. I've seen to that. I got a pair of stilts from the stable boy – you remember? – and went stumping down the lane on them and Papa as usual was spying through his glass, and when I came in he roared at me to know what the devil I was doing with those damn things. So I told him and he laughed like anything and now Mamma will have the horses and her carriage again.'

'Papa,' grumbled Griselda, 'always favours you more than us. And she's not our real mamma only our step-mamma and she don't care about us, not even the boys who are her real sons. So why should you care about her?'

'Because she's too great a fool to care for herself more than to have hairdressers brought from London every week to do up her hair and paint up her face that she may go gallivanting off to Town to buy dozens of gowns that she can't wear here. Papa won't let her. But she'll have to walk to London if I don't get back her carriage.'

'She won't give a thank you if you do,' cut in Griselda, hoping for the last word which was forestalled by being hustled off with Lucy.

'Stop gaggling and leave me be. I must chase after those turkeys or they'll be in the pond. So for goodness sake – go!'

They went reluctantly, sped by Hester with a final warning: 'And keep away from the lake. Papa is sailing his steam boat and you know what he'll do to you if you interrupt him.'

Yes, they knew. They had suffered spanking enough for coming upon their father when engrossed with his latest invention, a toy boat propelled by steam which this remarkable scientist, part genius, wholly despot, advocate of Liberty, Equality, Fraternity who, when presenting his invention to the Admiralty, had it rejected with jeers. Yet Stephenson, a shepherd lad tending sheep in Roxburgh and then but seven years old, was hailed some twenty years later as the great inventor of steam

6

for all posterity. Not for Lord Stanhope the credit of discovering those steam-driven giants, first sailed as toy boats on a lake, which were destined to sweep the formidable battle ships and all merchant sailing ships from the Seven Seas. Born a century before his time, his versatility as inventor, politician, mechanician, caused his peers to regard him as a lunatic. For his second wife he had no use save in his bed for the production of his heirs, and was viewed in the light of his supernormal intelligence as a superfluous nonentity.

His tyrannical autocracy exacted in his household eventually drove his wife and children from their home. All stood in greatest awe of him, save Hester. She alone dared to combat his suzerainty; but even she, the only one of them who was not cowed by his violent temper, might have echoed the words of Madame de Maintenon who, from the favourite mistress of Louis XIV became privately married to him and declared, that: 'She ruled in the farmyard where her reign began. . . .' But like the de Maintenon, Hester could not have possibly foreseen that she too would reign as queen, led by her intrepid explorations to a world as far removed from Chevening as Great Britain was from Mars.

That for the future; for the present she, having shooed the turkeys from the edge of the pond, sat on a boulder to eat the contents of a basket handed to her by the cook for her mid-day meal while guarding turkeys on the common. And between sharing her crusts of bread and cheese with her gobbling charges, she allowed her thoughts rebelliously to wander.

Must she always be treated as a menial, tending turkeys and made to wear clothes that a peasant girl would despise, alternately bullied and shouted at by her father as he would shout at his peers in the House of Lords ? . . . This she had learned from the gossip of stablemen.

According to Lord Stanhope's democratic principles, when the revolution in France was at its height, he dubbed himself 'Citizen Stanhope', and had his coronet and armorial bearings effaced from the gates of Chevening and renamed the Manor 'Democracy Hall'.

'His Lardship be fair crazed,' ran the verdict Hester heard when grooming her horse; this a manual labour again approved by her father, another of his idiosyncracies in that he allowed her and her sisters to ride, providing they attended to the grooming of their mounts themselves. A fearless horsewoman, she would ride to hounds, jump high hedges and five barred gates to the astonished admiration of the Field.

Continually dictated by her governesses, as commanded by his lordship to strictest surveillance, she was ordered: 'Must not do this', or 'must not say that': or, on rare occasions when her father would deign to acknowledge her existence, he would show some preference for her society rather than that of her sisters to be turned out of his room if they dared venture in.

It is possible that the crumbs her father let fall of his iconoclastic principles, as eagerly swallowed as a nestling devours the worms offered by the parent bird to its ever open maw, went far to mould that force of character which dominates her later life. But as we see her now, aged fourteen, she was concerned not with that predestined future which, even in her wildest dreams she could not have envisaged, but with her present, as unpalatable to her as the crusts of bread and stale cheese disgustedly gnawed as she sat on a boulder while she voiced aloud her grievances. For want of better audience she would often talk to herself.

'They are right, those oafs in the stables. Papa *is* crazed, and if I stay under his roof I'll be as crazed as he. I am born for something better than to chase after turkeys. . . . Go away, you great ugly brute!' She kicked out a leather rough-shod foot at a red-jowled cadger for cheese. 'Take it then,' she threw him a cheese rind, 'and may it choke you!'

8

The kick had dislodged the loosely laced clumsy shoe. Complacently she surveyed her bare foot, for the coarse woollen hose prescribed by her father chafed her skin so that she went stockingless. She was proud of her feet. 'It is a sign of good breeding,' she would tell her sisters, 'to have a high instep like mine.' But it irked her to be forced to wear these horrible clodhoppers. 'Why, oh why must I endure all this and – *you*!' She addressed the flock that, following example of their leader, were approaching with necks outstretched in greedy anticipation of more largesse. 'No more – you horrid bald-headed things. How could a God of love and beauty have made anything so revolting as you? . . . And to think we are fattening you up to eat! If it weren't for the girls and the boys I'd clear out. I would. But how can I? If I did, and it would be easy enough, I'd take coach for London and go to Uncle William. I've money enough saved from the tuppence a week Papa doles out to us. Mean as hell he is. But how can I leave Lucy and Grisel and Mahon and James and Charles? What'd they do without me? . . . Hey! Not you *again*!' She kicked out once more at a turkey who waddled away with gobbling clucks. 'I'd sooner mind pigs than you – I like pigs. . . . No, I can't run off and leave them. They are my responsibility. Papa shirks his. Even Mahon. I think he hates him. They always hate their heir. That's why the King is so nasty to the Prince of Wales. Poor little Mahon. I must see what I can do for him. Papa won't spend the money to send him and the other two to school. That nasty Mr Joyce is no good as a tutor, besides he is as mad as Papa – calls *him*self a republican, too. Get along with you – you ugly old baldhead or I'll wring your scraggy neck! . . . Very well then, *take* it, greedy-guts!'

She flung the last piece of her crust to the most insistent of the 'bald-heads', and continuing her voiced soliloquy, 'Anyway if I can get the boys sent to school and settle the girls somewhere, perhaps with Grandmama, I'll be able to show Papa a clean pair of heels.'

'And a very pretty pair they are, although not notice-ably clean.'

The voice and the silent approach of a horseman, un-heard until then on the tussocky turf, made her jump. She turned, saw, scrambled up and ran to him.

'Uncle! What a happy surprise. I was just thinking about you. How wonderful! 'Tis as if you had come from heaven!'

'Only from Downing Street, which is, at this present, less heaven than hell.'

Dismounting, he tethered his horse to the jutting snag of a thorn bush and taking her hands looked down at her who was looking up at him; her face, that had been shadowed, alight with the joy of this meeting.

'I didn't know you were coming. I wasn't told. No one tells me anything. Did you ride all the way from Lon-don? . . . How did you know where to find me? Are you staying with us for a week or two – Oh, do, do stay! Can you? Please!'

Stemming the eager torrent of words, this still youthful Prime Minister held her at arms' length to see his dead sister in her eyes. When ten years earlier at the age of twenty-four he ascended to head the Tory Ministry, his name was rung throughout Britain by his opponents in a contemptuous jingle as:

A sight to make surrounding nations stare
A Kingdom trusted to a schoolboy's care.

There were yet traces of the schoolboy in the pale, sensitive face of him who carried on too slender shoulders the heavy burden of State.

Answering in rotation her almost pauseless questions:

'They told me where to find you.' He cast an amused glance at the waddling turkeys scattered upon his arrival. 'I had to see your father on some tiresome business to do with one of his speeches in the Lords. I came from London by coach and hired this nag from the Inn. No, I can't stay

10

a week and for only half a night as I have to leave here at dawn.'

'Oh, must you?'

'I must, to be in the House by nine o'clock tomorrow. So you are still tending the *meleagris*.'

'The *what*?'

'It's the ornithological name for the common turkey, first introduced into Europe from Mexico and America by Sebastian Cabot in the early part of the sixteenth century.'

'Fancy!' murmured Hester, impressed as always by her uncle's knowledge on all sorts of subjects which he would impart to her as if she were forty instead of fourteen.

'I always thought they were called turkeys because they came from Turkey. Who was Sebastian Something-or-other?'

'He was an explorer but it is doubtful if it were he or one of his father's lieutenants who actually discovered the mainland of North America, but at all events Sebastian was one of the Merchant Adventurers who attempted to sail the North West passage in the reign of the boy king, Edward VI.'

Her eyes were dreamy.

'I'd like to be an adventurer and go sailing off to discover foreign lands!'

'I gather,' he told her with a twinkle, 'that you have already made an effort to do so – in a rowing boat.'

'Yes, but that was when I was very young. Oh, dear,' she sighed, 'I am so bothered as to what I am to do with Lucy and Grisel and the boys. No one cares about us here, and I, being the eldest, feel that I should look after them. The boys, especially Mahon, who is almost ten now, should go to school. And as for the girls . . .' Another sigh. 'It isn't as if we had a mother. I often think of her, but I can't properly remember her. What was my real Mamma like, Uncle?'

'She was very like you.'

'Was she pretty?'

'She was beautiful.'

Her white even teeth became visible in a gratified smile.

'Am I beautiful?'

'You might be – were you washed. Go and put on your shoes – or whatever they are, lying out there unless left by some vagabond tramp, and don't jump about on your bare feet or you will have thorns in your flesh.'

'I have thorns in my flesh, already. Papa is one of them!' She laughed up at him. 'And they *are* my shoes, or rather my clodhoppers. Miles too big for me but Papa makes us wear them. He calls us his *Sansculottes* which means without shoes, doesn't it?'

'Actually it doesn't. It means without breeches, but as you don't wear the breeks I presume he effects a compromise.'

She seized his hand that he had let fall.

'Uncle, I am going to leave these what-you-may-call-'em – mealy greases, and go back to the house with you. If they fall in the pond I can't help it. I'll send one of the stable boys to fetch them in. I'm not going to stay out here till sundown minding those wretched fowls when *you're* here and there's so much I have to say and so – let me ride home with you.'

Jogging back to Chevening on her uncle's hired mount, her arms clasping Pitt's waist, her legs dangling either side the saddle; and with her skirts pulled up, her head bent down to shout in his ear above the clip-clop of hooves on the rough hewn road that led from the common to the manor, it is likely the 'much she had to say' may have induced her uncle to exert himself on her behalf with more interest than hitherto.

He heard, besides her litany of neglect, abuse, and tyranny she and her brothers and sisters had suffered from their father, how the boys, between the inadequate tuition of one Jeremiah Joyce, were now apprenticed to a blacksmith and made to work in the forge. This, their

12

father's latest idiosyncracy, had doubtless been fired by example of the *sansculottes* in Paris who had handed to a shoemaker the guardianship of the Dauphin, son of the ill-fated Louis XVI.

'Isn't it cruel of Papa to treat us as if we were children of beggars!' Hester's voice rose to a squeak of tearful indignation. 'You don't *know* what we have to bear. As for our governesses, none of them stays more than a few weeks. We have a French one now. She has escaped from France and Papa says she's an *aristo*. So he calls her *Citoyenne* and has taken down from the walls all the tapestries – did you know that?' She gave his tie-wig a pull; he was hatless. 'Are you listening, Uncle? I said he takes down all the tapestries because he says they are too aristo*crat*ical. Could you believe it?'

He could believe it and was more than ever convinced that Stanhope's eccentricities verged upon dementia. As for that fellow Joyce engaged to tutor those boys, he was Stanhope's familiar, a rabid revolutionary and the worst possible influence on the young Mahon who would some day take his seat in the Lords as successor to his father.

'Uncle!' Another tug at the wig. 'Can't you do *some*-thing to help us? I want to go to London. Papa never lets us go to London. I ought to meet people, not just the squires and farmers around here who hunt – and the stablemen – they are the only men *I* ever meet. I'm rising fifteen and I ought to meet men because I want to be married and that's the only escape I can see for me and Grisel and Lucy, only they are too young at present. I'm not. Girls are often married at fifteen. But if I go on living here I'll never be married, not if I were fifteen or fifty.' She brought her face round to his again: '*You* live in London and know everyone from the King downward and you aren't married, not yet, although you aren't fifty – or are you?'

A grin hovered over his lips that regressed him to the 'schoolboy' of the broadsides as he answered her:

'No, I'm not married, nor am I fifty; and as for know-ing everyone from the King downward, it's a wise man who knows even his own father – in London. Not that I have a father now, but he was the greatest man of politics in these last hundred years and he scarcely knew me, his son; yet I stand in the House where once he stood.' Then as he sensed a further volley of questions, in especial re-garding his marriage to be or not to be, he cut in with: 'As for your father and a possible exodus from him for you if not for your young sisters, to London's marriage market...'

She pounced on that.

'Do they have marriage markets in London? I have heard that in eastern countries they have markets where women are sold as slaves but never, surely, as wives?'

'Women,' he told her dryly, 'are often sold here in the markets for marriage, which can, in some cases, be slavery.'

'Yes,' she nodded, 'I see what you mean.'

In an unchildish flash of perception she did see what he meant, and:

'I don't think, after all, that I want to be married,' said she.

Whether Pitt's business with his brother-in-law was confined to criticism of Stanhope's speech in the Lords that had electrified his peers to the exclusion of his treat-ment to his children, is debatable; but in after years Hester confessed in her memoirs,* dictated to her doctor that: 'Nobody saw much of me until Lord Romney's review, so I was obliged to play a trick on my father to get there.'

It is likely that the 'trick' she played on her father as recalled in the *Memoirs* was that she told him she wished 'to visit the Miss Crumps or some such name'.

She most certainly could not have visited the Miss

* *Memoirs*: Meryon. Vol. II.

Crumps, whoever they were if they existed at all, in the awful garments she was made to wear while tending turkeys or performing the menial tasks imposed upon her by 'Citizen Stanhope'. We might therefore assume that if she did see the review she could have taken her horse and ridden the few miles to the Romneys' house in Kent in her shabby riding kit. But if truth, which Hester was not particular to tell were told, this incredible tale as recounted to her sisters was received by Griselda with marked scepticism and by Lucy with simple gullibility.

'How you could dare do it!' she gasped. 'Weren't you afraid of Papa finding out?'

'How could he have found out,' with scathing disbelief from Griselda, 'if it never happened? She's making it all up.'

'I tell you,' Hester blandly replied, 'that it's gospel truth. I *did* go to the review. And I *did* go properly dressed in a brand new riding habit Uncle Pitt gave me. I never went to the Miss Thing-me-bobs —'

'Of course you didn't. There's no such persons.'

'I had to tell Papa something to account for my absence for a whole day. And anyway he doesn't know the names of all the old maids in the neighbourhood.'

'So you went to Lord Romney's house,' Griselda looked down her long nose, 'rigged up to the nines in a brand new riding habit which Uncle Pitt never gave you – and what else? You met the King and Queen and all the Court and dined with Royalty at their table. Do you expect us to believe that?'

'I don't expect you to believe anything you don't want to believe, but if you *don't* believe it you can ask Uncle William. He was there and he arranged it all.'

Griselda's mouth slid sideways.

'Oh yes?'

'Yes. Go and ask him. He'll tell you.'

'Likely, isn't it,' sniggered Griselda, 'that I can go off to Downing Street to bother him about a pack of lies.'

Hester showed her teeth in something less than a smile.

'He is used to hearing a pack of lies in Parliament.' And goaded by Griselda's derision – there were frequent rows with this younger sister who, unlike the gentle Lucy, nursed resentment against the dominant Hester, so much prettier, cleverer, and altogether everything that Griselda was not – Hester's quick temper rose. A hand shot out to land smartly on Griselda's ear. 'Call me a liar, do you? Then take that – you little beast!'

And they were at it claw and fist with Hester the victor and immediately contrite.

'There, there – I'm sorry. But you do rile me.'

Griselda rubbed her reddened ear and, moderately subdued having countered attack with a vicious scratch on Hester's bare arm, told her sulkily:

'Go on with your tale. Lucy'll believe it if I don't.'

So on with her tale Hester went.

'Uncle Pitt was very pleased at the way the King and Queen received me. I was a success with Lord and Lady Romney and all the Dukes and courtiers —'

'I'll wager you were – not.' *Sotto voce* from Griselda. And, undaunted by discouragement Hester, inexcusably pursued: 'The King came after me when I was talking to the Dukes.'

'What Dukes?' Again from Griselda.

'How should I know what Dukes? I was presented to so many. I wish you wouldn't keep on interrupting.'

'Yes, Grisel, don't keep on interrupting,' echoed the dutiful Lucy. 'What did the King say?'

'He said —' A pause here to reimburse invention while she remembered descriptions of His Majesty's appearance as retailed by Lady Stanhope on those few occasions of her visits to London and to Court, and with intent to impress her step-daughters of her own importance, having none at Chevening.

'He said, "What, what." The King says everything twice, is goggle-eyed and stumpy and has rolls of fat dis-

16

appearing into the lace of his cravat,' (according to Lady Stanhope) 'and he is covered in orders and Garters and things.'

'Garters?' gasped Lucy. 'Do you mean like this?'

She lifted her petticoat to show a worn ribbon binding her thick woollen hose.

'Not like that, silly. *The* Garter. Almost all the gentlemen wore Garters too, great shining stars on their chests and lots of medals. And the King came puffing up to me while I talked to the Dukes and he kept saying, "Where is she? Where is Lady Hester?" And then he invited me into his coach with the Queen and said he would take me away from Democracy Hall —'

'Fancy the King knowing Chevening is called that,' put in the credulous Lucy.

'Kings know everything,' said Hester loftily. 'Do stop sniffing, Grisel – you ought to have been christened Thomasina.'

'Why should she?' from Lucy.

'Feminine of doubting Thomas. So then the Queen, she's a prim old thing, she said that as I had not my maid with me it were best I stayed behind.'

Grisel stuck her tongue in her cheek.

'As if you'd ever had a maid! So you did stay behind and rode all the way back in your grand new riding habit that Uncle Pitt gave you!'

'No, I didn't ride, I was offered to be driven home by' – invention may have flagged – 'by, um, one of the gentlemen whose name I – oh, yes, I know who it was. Lord Howick,* very handsome in a corbeau coloured coat.'

It is likely she had heard her father mention the name of this brilliant young Parliamentarian who, some forty years later, rose to be head of the Whig Ministry; and straightway she enlarged. 'He wanted me to leave my horse and to drive me here in his coach, but I said I had my groom with me' – Griselda snorted – 'and so I rode

* Afterwards Earl Grey.

back alone and came in at the North Lodge. Nobody saw me.'

'Which is not surprising,' Griselda remarked as of a Greek chorus, 'since you were not there to be seen.'

Disdaining denial of this she welcomed Lucy's wide-eyed question: 'What did you do with the fine habit Uncle Pitt gave you?'

'I hid it in one of the attics,' was the unblushing reply.

'Will you show it to us? Oh, do show it to us.'

'I will when I wear it again . . . some day.'

As for wearing that habit, imaginatively supplied by her Uncle Pitt, it was several years later, even if, on the flimsiest fabrication, she could have worn it to show to her sisters, 'some day'.

She was barely out of her teens when launched upon London society under the auspices of her uncle, the ex-Prime Minister, who had been superseded by the ineffectual Addington.

During the interim between Addington's fall and Pitt's return to power, he was able to devote more time to Hester, his favourite niece. He had eventually persuaded Lord Stanhope to allow her to be presented to the social sphere that was hers by right of birth, and to which her father unwillingly agreed in the hope she would find a suitable husband that he might be relieved of this most troublesome of his brood.

He was, however, rid of the other two girls long before he could be relieved of Hester. Lucy, at barely sixteen, was the first to go and with none other than the apothecary who attended the children at 'Democracy Hall'. He was a personable young man, this Mr Taylor, for whom Lucy had conceived a girlish passion that seems to have been as passionately returned.

The news of Lucy's flight from the parental roof reached Hester in London to bring her post-haste to Chevening, after a frantic appeal from Elizabeth Williams who had succeeded the governesses as attendant on the girls.

Notwithstanding Lord Stanhope's republican principles he had taken hardly this revolt of the youngest, prettiest, most docile of his daughters whom he hoped to have made a good match. When Hester arrived she found him in a brainstorm, Griselda in hysterics, and the maid, Williams, in tears.

'His lordship blames *me*!' she wailed. 'How could I have known that Lady Lucy would run away like this!'

How Hester heard that Lucy had run away like that was told her by Griselda restored from the vapours, caused less by concern for Lucy than from jealousy that she had dared where Griselda had dared not to escape from their odious fold.

As Hester had it from Griselda a rope had been found dangling from Lucy's bedroom window. Down this she must have climbed to meet her enamoured swain where he waited at the manor gates. . . . 'Just fancy! The cunning little devil!' Griselda exhibited envy. 'I wish it had been me. Not that I'd have wanted to run off with Taylor who, for all his good looks, is only an apothecary, not even a proper doctor; yet I can't see myself living here for the rest of my life. But I suppose now Lucy has gone with the only man within miles who ever comes near us, that I shall stay in this prison till I die.'

'We'll see about that.'

And Hester, who had secretly championed Lucy's defiance, did make every effort to see about that, aided by their Uncle Pitt.

Thanks to her persuasions Griselda was provided with a cottage on the Chatham estate, and soon after with a husband. A slight social improvement on an apothecary, he was a naval officer but still, in Lord Stanhope's opinion and despite his democratic views, no match for any one of his daughters.

19

'Papa is such a mass of contradictions,' Hester complained to her uncle. 'He professes to despise titles, wealth, pomp, everything – including the House of Lords, and yet he has set his heart on us all marrying into the peerage. But he keeps the boys drudging in the smithy and won't let Mahon go to a university. I'll have to see about him next.'

She had planned to 'see about him next', but in the meantime she had all to do to see about herself.

During this eighteenth century *fin de siècle* London welcomed with open doors those *emigrés* from France who had fled the guillotine. At the salons of eminent hostesses such as the lovely Georgiana, Duchess of Devonshire, Lady Melbourne of Holland House, and other leaders of fashion where Whig and Tory met and mingled irrespective of their politics, Hester, as the niece of the Tory ex-Prime Minister, was much in evidence and the subject of criticism, not always in her favour. One, however, much in favour with the *ton* was a gentleman who named himself 'Brothers', a fashionable fortune-teller often in demand among the ladies who sought his advice and prophecies – always to their, and his, considerable advantage.

Hester had met this 'Brothers' at one of the soirées, probably at Devonshire House, and was greatly intrigued to learn from him that she would travel in distant lands, would be acclaimed Queen of the Desert, and, more surprisingly, Queen of the Jews.

That her knowledge of Jews was confined solely to purveyors of old clothes who infrequently strayed into the sacred precincts of Mayfair and Belgravia, and a dim association with Shylock offered to her by one of the few English governesses who had suffered her employment at Chevening for more than a month and introduced her and her sisters to *The Merchant of Venice*, did not at all discredit her belief in this augury, no matter how far-fetched. But she was not to be reminded of it for many years later. . . .

Among those who, in their memoirs, give first hand accounts of this daughter of Stanhope who had been severely censured for his eccentricities and, above all, as a 'traitor to his class', we have the opinion of Madame la Comtesse de Boigne. Contrary to other ladies of her kind she was fulsome in praise of Lady Hester, whom she describes as 'a handsome girl, fond of dancing, tall, well made, something of a flirt, a very decided character and of striking originality. And for a Stanhope' (here some words are tactfully suppressed) 'she is prudence itself.'

We hear from this same source how Mr Pitt, chaperoning Hester, would stay up till all hours in the early mornings at balls and functions which must have bored him to extinction. . . . 'I have often seen him,' says Madame la Comtesse, 'sitting in a corner waiting with exemplary patience until Lady Hester should be pleased to end his sufferings.'

Pitt's sufferings on these occasions may have been somewhat over-estimated, as in *loco parentis* he would surely have been gratified to see his protegée the centre of attraction with the men, if not with the women.

The Duchess de Gontaut is less appreciative of Hester's charms than is Madame de Boigne, for we are told that Madame la Duchesse found her behaviour most unsuitable to a niece of Mr Pitt. His reflected glory does not seem to have descended upon Hester.

It was at a masquerade held in the gardens of Lady Stafford's house on the Thames in midsummer when we hear from Madame la Duchesse* that Hester behaved like a hoyden and wore a costume 'which had nothing feminine about it except the mask'. . . . As to why a mask should be more feminine than her costume we are not enlightened unless it were that Hester chose to appear as

* *Memoirs*, Duchess de Gontaut, translated by J. W. Davies, 1894.

a Tudor page. She always had a fancy to dress as a boy as did her notorious contemporary, Lady Caroline Lamb.

It is possible the censure of Madame la Duchesse passed upon the niece of Mr Pitt may have been prompted by the fact that the young lady, although eulogistic in her opinion of Madame as: 'A woman quite admirable, so full of resources and so well dressed, that it was a pity,' added *en haut voix* for the ears of la Duchesse, 'she had to turn washerwoman and go to parties in a hackney coach!' An unkind allusion to her impoverished state as a refugee from France that brought an immediate riposte also *en haut voix*, that: *'La jeune fille est un peu franchement candide*, and too *indépendante* to be *comme il faut. Enfin!* What could one expect from the daughter of the (unmentionable) Lord Stanhope?'

It proved to be a momentous afternoon for Hester. If she had made an enemy of Madame la Duchesse she had also made a friend, or one who was to be more than a friend in a succession of young men with whom this 'something of a flirt' became continually involved: none other than her cousin, Lord Camelford.

Descended from the Pitts on the distaff side, Thomas Pitt, this second Baron Camelford, Hester had never met and only known by name if mentioned at all, below breath. His vicissitudes and moral depravity outrivalled the most advanced set of Carlton House. He had inherited from a remote grand-uncle, one 'Diamond' Pitt, a fortune which had come to his father, the first Lord Camelford.

In direct contradiction to his disreputable son, he, a Latin scholar, devoted to the arts, a mild gentle gentleman, died leaving his heir to enjoy the wealth of the Indies left by this Thomas ('Diamond') Pitt, one time Governor of St George.

Launched at an early age on a carefree life of dissipation, this second Baron Camelford joined the navy and was sent to the West Indies as a midshipman. There he became the instigator of brawls inciting his fellow cadets to insubordination, fought with and fatally shot a superior officer and was court martialled. But as a relative of William Pitt, the Prime Minister, he was eventually acquitted of murder on the doubtful evidence that his victim had been killed in attempted mutiny, and from being discharged from the navy with dishonour, Camelford discharged himself with no blemish on his character more than that he had undertaken to quell a mutiny among the younger officers by asserting authority to which he had no right.

On his return to London the trail of smoke from this questionable affair pursued him. He often went incognito among the city's dregs, frequented all the taverns in the town, consorted with drunken sailors no less drunk than he, would fight any with his fists to champion the oppressed, and lavished much of his fortune on the undeserving. Thieves, gamblers, rogues, vagabonds, prostitutes, none who came to him with hard luck stories left him empty handed.

As a peer of the realm with unlimited wealth, he was loaded with invitations from matrons of marriageable daughters; also from the more unconventional hostesses who followed the example of Georgiana, Duchess of Devonshire, and her sister, Lady Bessborough. In their diverse pageants of exquisite frivolities, the pleasure-greedy satellites of that greatest of Corinthians at Carlton House, ignored the spectre of doom swift-dawning from the howling bloodstained streets of Paris. Sheltered in their tight little island by the silver cliffs of Dover, none in that joyous hedonistic whirligig gave a fleeting thought to the fear of invasion from France, nor of the pending war led by a little corporal who in the next thirteen years would bestride the whole of Europe.

Certainly neither Hester, nor he whose acquaintance she may first have made on that day of a masquerade, could have known or guessed that, at this nearing turn of the century, they and all of an older generation would

23

find their world drawn into the vortex which was to end at Waterloo.

So, while Hester, smarting under Madame's thrust with that cut at her father and which, in loyalty, however much she disliked him she would not tolerate, counter-charged above the braying of a band and of a donkey tethered on the lawn, repeating with smiles: 'Hee-haw! Yes! These good ladies are more stupid than that ass.'

This was followed by a loud guffaw behind her, and as she turned from one good lady who, at boiling pitch, prepared to challenge that impertinence, she was confronted by a swarthy young giant whose eyes full of laughter stared down into hers out of a sunburnt face.

'So, ho! Young cousin,' he boisterously applauded, 'go to't! Give her as good as you are given. These Frenchies from t'other side of the Channel take all from us and give back nothing while they batten on our charity which should begin at home!'

Disregarding an explosive: *'Diable! Quel perfide abominable!'* from the outraged Duchesse, Hester in her turn stared up at him to wonder at this common – and un-common – young man in a shabby gold-laced uniform and cocked hat, whose blue chin was in sore need of a shave and who dared claim cousinship with her.

'Who are you?' she demanded, 'and *what* are you?'

Moving from earshot of Madame la Duchesse, he ranged himself beside her, swept his hat to his knees in a bow that held a hint of mockery, to tell her:

' "What I am and what I would are to your ears divinity. To any other" ' – with a glance over his shoulder at the mortified Duchess – ' "profanation." '

Hester, believing this quotation to be extempore, was at once intrigued.

They were now lost in that crowded *mise en scène* where a variety of costume promenaded: nymphs, satyrs, columbines and knights, troubadours and Pompadours.

24

Here and there a disciple of Brummel in swallow tails and starched shirt front, the Beau's latest fashion, and women, especially the French, in their bouffant robes as worn at the Court of the murdered Marie Antoinette; or girls in high waisted muslins damped to make them cling, their hair cropped *à la victime* with a narrow scarlet ribbon round their throats fashionably reminiscent of *la Guillotine*.

The sparkling waters of the Thames wound like an iridescent snake between the river's banks, while the braying of the donkey and the band, subdued by distance, made it possible to speak and to be heard in a comparative silence broken only by bird song above a far off elfin chorus of voices and the sound of their footsteps in the grass.

'What is your name?' Hester asked of him who walked beside her measuring his long stride to hers.

'My name is Camelford, Thomas Pitt, at your service,' he answered, cutting with his stick at a clump of meadowsweet, 'and your name is Stanhope. My father was a Pitt. Your mother was a Pitt. She was a sister, as you know, of William Pitt, your uncle, and my father's cousin. Shall we sit?'

They had come to an arbour on the edge of the water where a pair of white swans, their necks proudly uplifted, sailed by. At the splash of some unseen water rat, one of the pair slewed an eye disdainfully round at the two creatures above him whose only excuse for existence was a likely bonus. This Camelford supplied, diving in his pocket to produce and fling at them pieces of cake purloined from the refreshment buffet.

Hester, watching with amusement, inquired:

'Do you carry largesse about with you for indiscriminate distribution?'

'I give to any who may need it whether fish, flesh, or fowl.' He shied another piece of cake at their expectant majesties. 'I saw this couple while I was dodging those' –

25

he jerked his head in the direction of the company they had deserted – 'the donkeys and geese as separated from the swans.'

She glanced aside at him where he sat, leaning forward, a frown between his jutting brows, like little shelves she thought them.

'I have heard of you,' she told him, 'and nothing to your credit, not even the feeding of swans or – sparrows that fall to the ground.'

'That you've heard nothing to my credit is certain,' he spoke not to her but to the retreating swans that, having haughtily imbibed his offerings, had sailed on their way. 'My name stinks among you of the *haut monde* who gather mud from the cesspools of scandal to sling at me.'

She eyed him coolly.

'Your name carries neither weight nor mud with me, and although I have heard nothing much to your credit, what I have learned of your exploits is not entirely discreditable. That is in my opinion for what 'tis worth and which is of no account.'

'Of all account to me.' His eyes came round to meet hers from which they seemed to find it difficult to disengage. 'You, too, I take it, are a rebel against *l'ancien régime*, as just now,' he chuckled, 'I have witnessed. I am also a rebel but not to the extent as is your father whose orations in the Upper House make him an object of ridicule; yet,' he pursued, preventing her attempt to circumvent this, 'he is to be applauded for the courage of his convictions, or rather those of Tom Paine whose revolutionary apostle he professes to be.'

She who had no knowledge of Tom Paine but was not greatly averse to this opinion of her father's convictions, slid another look at him whose hands, coarse, hairy-backed, were clasped between his knees. He still addressed not her but the rippling waters, emptied now of swans. 'I also,' he went on, 'am entitled to speak in the House of Lords but' – his mouth, senuous under a two days' growth

26

of dark bristle on his upper lip – 'I do not avail myself of that privilege. So,' and he turned to stare full at her, 'you and I are not only of one kin but of one mind, since we are both rebels.'

'I am not,' she contradicted, 'a rebel in your sense, if there is any sense in either your or my father's convictions. I am only rebellious against the injustice suffered by those who have *not*, from the oppression of those who *have*.'

'Then we —,' he cried, to cause a fish to jump – 'there goes a fine fat roach – I wish I had my rod. I was about to say' – (will he never have done talking? she inwardly inquired) – 'that we, being so closely allied in mind and kin should see more of each other, little cousin.' A swift unexpected smile flashed out to illumine his unhandsome but not unattractive face, 'and not so little neither.' His bold scrutiny raked her top to toe as if he would strip her to her bones, appraising the long lithe legs encased in boyish hose to meet the wide Tudor breeches. A scarlet tunic with slashed sleeves and an open-throated white shirt – she had discarded the ruff for coolness – completed her page's costume. Her hatless head revealed her hair, the colour of dark mahogany, and was clubbed under to fall either side her fair-skinned cheeks that were tanned from exposure to sun and all weathers at Chevening.

'You,' he continued after having made and approved his inspection, 'are less girl than boy and more boy than Ganymedes.'

'Ganymedes?' she echoed. 'Who or what is he or it?'

' "It" might be more appropriate. He was a beautiful epicene goatherd seduced by Jupiter who found him tending his father's flocks.'

'I used to tend my father's flocks but they aren't goats,' she laughed up at him, 'they are turkeys. And what do you mean by epicene?'

'Epicene,' he drew near to her, his eyes half closed as a

painter who examines his work, 'is both male and female in one, as was Adam until the Lord God performed that surgical operation on man to divide him into woman and which makes you what you are and what I – want.'

He seized her savagely forcing his mouth on hers.

For a moment she fought against the upsurge of response to him, and was then dissolved and yielded to the storm she had aroused.

He wrenched his lips from hers to say:

'I've had a hundred women but never have I wanted any one of them as I want you! And so —'

'And so!' She dragged herself free of his arms. Fury intermingled with a sense of shame that he, in his arrogance, had taken her momentary surrender as a permanent conquest, further inflamed her. 'You are too sure! Too sure of yourself to want me or anything other than – you!' Her hand shot out to land full on his blue-chinned jaw. 'Be damned for your braggart's boast of a hundred women! I'll wager any one of them'd be in beggarly want of a man to want *you*! You're naught but a braying ass who brays too loud!'

'And you too free of your asinine comparisons! But I can bray as loud as that jackass tethered yonder who protests to his confinement, or louder still than others who fear to tread where I would take. Why do you, so desirable' – his impudent grin lent fuel to her fire – 'stay single still, unmarried and unwooed? There's something wanting in you to account for it, I'll warrant!'

She had sprung to her feet, her face scarlet as she glowered down at him who had not risen while he hurled that at her. And she, who had held herself in now let herself out, with what little breath was left to her, in a tempestuous torrent of words.

'I'd have you know that if I'm unwed in this my first entry to your cesspool of scandal, that 'tis of *my* choice and *my* will! I could have been married fifty times according to the gossips of what you call *l'haut monde* which is no higher than the gutter to which *you* belong. And,' flourishing invention, 'I've been run away with once, but never with such a one as you. God forbid! Look at yourself, unmannerly, unshaven, unwashed. Our herdsman is more cleanly and appetizing than you, *Lord* Camelford!' Her tone spurned his title. 'And do you claim kinship with me that you take advantage to – to —' her breath dwindled on this wave of indignation as he, risen to his feet, interrupted with a shout of laughter and taking her hands he clapped them together punctuating each clap to his version of:

'Patty-cake, patty-cake, citizen's man,
I take what I want and I take where I can!

So I'll be the next one to run away with you and bring a hornet's nest about our ears if you'll come with me and be my love – as the poet has it.'

'To be the hundred and first of your hundred women? Let me go!' She was struggling to free herself. 'I tell you – let me *go*!'

'I'll never let you go, I'll —' his words were halted at the sudden appearance of a dandified young gentleman who had come, looking to right and left until, sighting the couple in evident combat, he hastened his steps calling in a high pitched scandalized voice:

'Lady Hester! Your chaperone, Lady Suffolk, has been searching for you everywhere. Her ladyship bids me advise you that she leaves for London at once. The carriage is waiting to take you to Mr Pitt's house at Putney.'

He had now reached the pair of whom one, released from her retainer, was sufficiently collected to say:

'You are come most opportunely, sir. My cousin here was attempting to persuade me to, er, to go with him, to, er . . .'

'To Richmond,' was Camelford's contribution to this impromptu, 'there to sup at the Star and Garter hostelry.'

'And being somewhat over tired,' Hester amplified, 'I am glad of the chance not to extend this afternoon's festivities but to return to my uncle's house and – and rest.'

'So you reside with your uncle *pro tem*?' said Camelford. 'I did not know he now lives at Putney.'

'Until he returns to Downing Street.'

'As he surely will,' suggested the young gentleman with an emphasis that defined him an ardent disciple of the ex-and-future Premier.

'You may be right in your prophecy,' Camelford still addressed Hester as if it were she who had spoken. 'A return of Pitt to head a Tory Government can only be an improvement on Addington, the present encumbrance who leads them. . . . Will you be staying indefinitely with your uncle? If so may I hope to call on you at Putney?'

'You may hope,' said she, turning a shoulder and taking the young gentleman's arm, 'but I shall not be at Putney with my uncle after tomorrow when I return to Chevening.'

'Then I'll be seeing you at Chevening,' Camelford doggedly persevered. 'It is time I became acquainted with your family to whom I am so closely allied.'

'An alliance,' she threw back, 'that has yet to be acknowledged.'

'*Touché!*' He chuckled, and swept her a bow that still held more of mockery than elegance.

'Goodbye,' she bade him curtly; and he, calling after her:

'You won't be rid of me so easily, young cousin. *Au revoir!*'

*   *   *

A frantic letter from Mahon telling Hester he could no longer endure the misery of his life at Chevening and his father's tyranny implored her to help his escape from his 'odious situation'. This decided her to forego the excite-

ladies from Bath on an outing with cavaliers who pulled up their mounts to watch Camelford in the midst of the fray. He had taken his whip and was applying it to the bawling turnpike's backside. The ladies, resorting to vinaigrettes and pretty palpitations, entreated their swains to ride on and halt at the nearest tea gardens for restoratives with 'chaney' tea and Bath buns.

Meantime Camelford, having left his victim yelling curses at him, returned to his seat beside Hester to whom he had handed the reins and had all to do in keeping the startled horses in check, her attention being halved by the fight.

'Are you out of your mind?' she cried, when he took the reins from her. 'Coming to fisticuffs with the toll-keeper on the King's highway! Wonder 'tis the horses didn't bolt. My arms are almost out of their sockets trying to hold them in.'

'I can't apologize enough,' said he as he urged on his horses with one hand while with the other he staunched blood from his nose, 'for involving you in this interruption to our idyllic afternoon.'

'About as idyllic,' she sourly rejoined, 'as the rout of the Gadarene swine!'

'And swine he is, believe me.' Camelford removed a gory handkerchief from his nostrils, and slid an eye round at her with a grin. 'He changed me a handful of bad pence. These blackguards keep a store of 'em to pass on to some poor devil of a carter or journeyman who've naught but the pittance from the sale of their wares or the miserable wage earned by the carters for their supper of bread and cheese. That'll teach him,' he chuckled. 'And I wish I'd lost him more than a tooth!'

The cheek nearest him showed a dimple.

'It looks like he is all but lost you an eye! It's already blue and will be black tonight.'

'Tomorrow, which will give them at the Assembly Rooms a mouthful of gob to spit at me.'

'I don't mind their – gob,' Hester said, slightly shying at the word. 'It may come back at them, full measure, if you let fly.'

That he did not 'let fly' when he appeared the next evening at the Assembly Rooms with Hester on his arm, and his eye a royal purple, kept conjecture busy hoping for a rift between this much discussed pair and expectant of a scandal.

No scandal, however, was disappointingly attached to the name of Lady Hester and Lord Camelford. She, determined on a capture, gave out by way of her maid, Williams, who in turn passed it to other abigails attendant on their ladies, that her ladyship and his lordship were engaged.

He, in mud-bespattered breeches, one eye a fading mauve, the other bloodshot, came fuming to Hester.

'You!' he hurled at her, pointing his riding crop, 'have had the impudence to broadcast that you – that we – that I —' he halted on a hiccup; he'd been drinking, 'that we – hic – are to marry. Not on your life, young Hester! Think'ee that I'd be tied to you for ever to be hag-ridden in Holy Matrimony.' He mouthed the words with a fleck of spittle on his lip. ' 'Tis I who'd be your master and you-hic-my mistress, or as good or as bad – were we wed.'

She had whitened, and now rushed at him to wrench the riding crop from his hand and flourish it within twelve inches of his nose, while chokingly she told him:

'You're drunk! Go souse your head! There'd be as much of holiness were we to wed as t'would be were Satan to take Jezebel to wife. I'd sink myself to hell were I wived with one as near to gallow's meat as makes no matter! No, keep off!' As he made to snatch the riding crop, 'or you'll have *two* black eyes!'

To that he let forth a huge guffaw, and slapping his thigh: 'God's truth!' he roared delightedly, 'you've hooked me, line and sinker. You're all I've wished for in a woman and never found – till now. One who can beat me at my own game – hah! And so we'll wed and rear a brood of your fine mettle mixed with mine which makes for sturdy stallions. How say you?'

'I say—' it took all her damaged pride to reassert herself, for she was drawn to him as no man heretofore had so physically attracted her. His bold coarse speech, his total lack of affectation, very different from the dandies of St James's or here at Bath with their mincing drawl and mannered pose, appealed to her against her will, but: 'I say – no! You are too late in crowing on your dungheap, my mettlesome gamecock! To share the marriage bed with you would find me on a bed of red hot cinders for my comfort! I've had enough of you and *your* fine mettle, Camelford – No, wait!' As he made attempt to speak. 'I've not done yet. There's too much of each other in *our* mettlesome make-up to pull in double harness. So it's no, and no, and *no* again! Go back to your stews and your other hundred women. Go back to your fellows, those who aren't still in Newgate or hanging on the gallow's tree at Tyburn. Go back to your thieves' dens where you mate with rogues and vagabonds – yes, you, the archhigh vagabond! But don't come back to *me*!'

While, during this tirade he had stood agape, the laughter dead in his throat, his reddened gills paling, she ran to the bell-rope and pulled it with such force that the tassel came off in her fist.

To the man at the door:

'His lordship is leaving,' she bade him. 'Show him out.'

He made a step forward; head in air she passed him by, dropped at his feet his riding crop, and without another word or look was gone.

TWO

The end of the war with the French Republic culminating in the Treaty of Amiens, though highly advantageous to Napoleon, was received with national rejoicing in England. Not, at that time realizing the implications less advantageous to Britain than to Bonaparte, the First Consul's representative was greeted by rapturous crowds who drew his carriage through London's streets in cheering welcome.

The continent, now purged of war, the élite of England flocked abroad to France, Italy, Germany, regardless of the hovering Napoleonic Eagle prepared to pounce upon and seize the whole of Europe.

Hester, among others of those who had followed the fashion, was delighted to obtain her grandmother's permission to travel under the chaperonage of a Mr and Mrs Egerton. Not so delighted were they as was Hester to brave the danger of travelling through France, despite an apparently peaceful reception from the 'French Cannibals'.

Her brother Mahon met her with the Egertons at Lyons and went on with them to Florence. She found him vastly different from the uncouth downtrodden youth, apprentice to the village blacksmith. A year or two at the University of Erlanger had given him poise and self-assurance, perhaps too much self-assurance for Hester's approval who had hitherto dominated if not a trifle tyrannized over her father's younger brood, and especially over Mahon. He, now very conscious of his status as the future Earl of Stanhope, resented his sister's scathing remarks on his foppishness, his boastful knowledge of primitive Tuscan art and the history of the Italian Renaissance on which Mahon presumed to be an authority. He let her know she bored him with her perpetual allusions to the conquests of her numerous admirers and of her enthusiasm for her Uncle Pitt whom she continuously quoted. The result being they parted company after leaving Florence; nor was she at all responsive to Mahon's contrite apology written from Leghorn regretting their disagreements.

'His conduct,' she wrote in a letter to one of her numerous young men, 'disgusted me extremely, and I am happy to know that the few English at Leghorn have taught him he is *not* the prodigy he thought he was'.

On her return to Burton Pynsent she was met with the news of the death of her grandmother, Lady Chatham, and of her father's refusal to have anything to do with her. Lord Stanhope would never forgive her part in the flight of his sons. And Hester, who had been received as if she were a minor royalty abroad because of her close relationship with Pitt, found the gates of 'Democracy Hall' closed against her, and she without a roof to shelter her at home.

One door alone remained open to her: a door that had never been closed. No longer would she be the talk of the Town for her many flirtations, her defiance of social conventions, or for her friendship – reputed to be more than friendship – with her disreputable cousin, Lord Camelford. The downfall of Addington had turned fortune's wheel in her favour, with William Pitt reinstated as First Lord of the Treasury, Prime Minister of England.

It was to be the corner stone of her astonishing career.

At Downing Street she was in her natural element; courted, fêted, feared for her caustic tongue, too often levelled at the expense of the Opposition Ministers who visited her uncle, and in particular his brilliant rival, Fox, for which she gained as many enemies as friends.

It is possible that Hester, who idolized her uncle, was jealous of the popularity accorded to the leader of the Whigs, first favourite at Carlton House and also with the Devonshire House crowd led by the lovely Georgiana.

The masterly statesmanship and dynamic personality of Charles James Fox outweighed the many scandals of high play, deep drink, and unsavoury intrigues attached to his name, in direct contrast to that of the cold and calculating Pitt, whose whole life, since his early twenties, had been devoted to his country's cause. He would have scorned to gather votes as did Fox, by presenting the electorate with a jovial familiarity, mixing with them in the stews of St Giles on the same terms as with the habitués of Boodles' and Brooke's. Yet it might have surprised Pitt's adversaries to have seen him in his home circle. Whether at Walmer Castle facing France, a bare five and twenty miles across the English Channel, or at Putney where he rented a villa to be nearer Westminster Hall, the reserved unsociable head of His Majesty's Government, would throw off his mantle of austerity and join in the rollicking games of the Stanhope boys and Hester, who was more at home in this free and easy household than when acting hostess at Downing Street.

Those were halcyon days for Hester. At Walmer she took over the management of the grounds which had been neglected by Pitt, and transformed a wilderness of weeds into a paradisiacal garden, bordered by yew trees and trim box hedges sprung from the chalky soil of Kent. Under the Castle's walls, guarded by guns pointed toward France, all kinds of flowers blossomed as if to defy the ever menacing threat of invasion from those shores, seen on clear days as a pearly transparence on the fringe of the sea.

But only at Walmer or along the coast to Dover was the threat of 'Boney' in the mouths of village folk. The delights of a summer season in London were not to be distracted by the thought or fear of a death struggle between the First Consul, Lord of the Land, and Nelson, First Lord of the Sea. Names, more often than either of these on every feminine lip when not discussing Hester Stanhope, were those of Lord Granville Leveson-Gower and his elderly inamorata, Lady Bessborough, sister of the Duchess of Devonshire.

It was her ladyship's boast in after years, at her confessed age of fifty-one, that she was 'followed, flattered, made love to, and for seventeen years had loved almost to idolatry the man who probably loved me least of all'. . . .

This was Lord Granville, son of the Marquis of Stafford, and a staunch supporter of Pitt despite the 'idolatry' of one of the greatest of Whig ladies.

He was considered beautiful by the women of his day who admired that effeminate curly-haired Adonis type, and it was he who held the adoring Lady Bessborough in the hollow of his hand.

On his return from the Grand Tour which all young men of fashion were considered *out* of fashion if they did not undertake it, he had been claimed by Henrietta Bessborough, 'devoured,' was the judgement of the cattery surrounding him who had not been successful in capturing the latest hero of the drawing rooms.

Having launched on a political career, and as a devotee of Pitt, he was more often seen at Downing Street than at the Bessborough House in Cavendish Square. It was soon brought to Henrietta that her idol's visits to Downing Street were rather more romantic than politically inclined.

Hester's infatuation for Camelford had died a natural death some time before his unnatural death, killed in a duel fought in a Kensington field on the strength of some malicious spite promoted by one of his discarded women.

With a score of suitors queueing up at Number Ten for 'the Stanhope's' favour, she, immersed in her social activities, shrugged away the thought of Camelford, mourned his passing for one lively week at most, and turned to more attractive game.

It was her first passionate emotional conquest if conquest it were, for while he came and saw he was not conquered. Leveson-Gower could have had his pick of women from the high world, the half world or the low world, and although not immune to Hester's sirenic allure that made fools of the men and foes of the women, if Granville's purpose were marriage, which in this case appeared to be Hester's, a dowerless wife was not his aim. Her prospects were less appealing than her physical attraction, her exquisite fair skin, those wonderfully blue eyes under the dark wings of hair, her tall boyish figure – bosoms were 'out' in that early nineteenth century. The unruly crop of curls, cut short, suited her more than it did the mature Henrietta, who wisely, after attempt to follow the fashion, renounced it and resorted to out-of-date powder, disguising her greying hair. It is likely, so submerged was Hester in her first serious attachment, that she might have yielded to Granville's possible desire for a liaison in a society where the chastity of women was regarded as a bourgeois sentiment; where marriage vows were made to be broken and where amorous relationships both in and out of the alcove were accepted with a tolerant indulgence. Now, as never before, was Hester Stanhope the topic of the day, her name linked with that of Lord Granville to her detriment: not his.

'She makes herself ridiculous,' wagged feline tongues, incited doubtless by Lady Bessborough who had taken upon herself, maternally, to warn her laggard lover against this latest feminine entanglement.

'She is a notorious flirt and will only hurt you if you lose your heart to her. Also consider your prospects with Pitt. He has a high opinion of you and I know he has in mind to offer you a promising future. Don't,' again she stressed it, 'don't, dearest boy, let your heart run away with reason.'

But it was Hester's heart, not his, that ran away with reason.

Rumour had it, to be swallowed with a grain of apochryphal salt by the older members of clubland and the dowagers of Mayfair who had never been stricken with either Stanhope or Granville fever, that Hester had demanded to know if his intentions were honourable – or not.

'Decidedly not!' cackled the blades of St James's whose 'honourable' intentions had been disdainfully ignored.

One may believe the incident that brought this *affaire* to its abrupt finale went something in this wise.

Granville calling on the Premier during a weekend at the Putney villa, was entertained by Hester in the garden.

'They are talking about us,' she reminded him while they walked in that village garden along a path lined with roses.

'And what,' he remarked with his engaging smile, 'do they say of us?'

'That your attentions to me,' she blurted after a moment's pause, 'should be decided one way or the other.'

'Meaning that I should offer myself to you with all my worldly wealth which is as much as will sit on a sixpence, or to convey to the Prime Minister, your guardian —'

'He is not my guardian,' she interposed, disliking his tone and his manner that at this moment she could have hated him as much as she believed she loved him. 'I am well of age and, unlikely though it might seem, because you must have heard my name bandied as loosely about Town as that of Caro Lamb* who served herself stark naked on a silver dish at one of her dinner parties, that I am still a virgin.'

'A state,' said he, stooping to pluck a rose and hold it to his lips, 'which can be easily remedied.'

* Lady Caroline Lamb: See *This for Caroline*.

43

His eyes narrowed in appraisement of her beauty; although not strictly beautiful, she emanated beauty as did the rose whose perfumed heart he sensuously inhaled.

'Not so easily,' she rejoined in a flash of the Stanhope temper. 'If you, who may have for me no more than a passing fancy, would take and rape me here and now, you would find me less amenable than any Sabine woman who, I take it, enjoyed to be raped! Do you,' she flared at him, 'want me or don't you? And not,' she emphasized, 'as you would want a – a whore, but as your helpmate, your comrade' – her voice dwindled, 'or – your wife?'

He was staggered. He knew her forthright, possessive, exacting, with just that streak of masculinity which he had found much more exciting than the feminine trivialities of the girls who fluttered round him; but this deliberate assumption of his, the male prerogative, was a dismaying stab to his pride. Not lent to self-analysis, he who had responded to the passion of a woman old enough to be his mother, resented this reversion of all he held as his right and not the right of any woman younger than himself and far in advance of any other, had he known it, of her time.

'My wife?' he echoed, his eyebrows, sun-gilded, shot up to the clustering curls. 'I would not dare to contemplate marriage with you who honour me above my worth.'

His exaggerated bow stroked her fury to a flame.

'So far above your worth am I,' she was well away now, 'that my suggestion, as you call it and to which I have demeaned myself, is worthy only of the honour of a – rabbit!'

It was all over clubland and retailed to Lady Bessborough for Granville to be comforted with caresses and dove-like cooes.

'You are well out of that unfortunate embroilment. She is utterly shameless, unmaidenly, if maiden she is since it seems she does profess too much her – virginity.' The lady tinkled a laugh.

For Hester it was more of a blow to her pride than her heart which she may have thought broken but was only bruised. Undeniably she suffered from the bitterness of her humiliation in her world that knew her for a jilt. Delightedly the women who had yearned for Leveson-Gower played with the news of it as a cat will play with a mangled mouse.

'Down on her knees and he left her there begging as a lap-dog for a tit-bit!' Went the talk at Almack's where the waltz was at its zenith and the *ton* met to mingle and whirl like dancing Dervishes.

Those who hoped to have gained the coveted prize where others had failed, came in for their share of the tongue-wagging. 'The lowdown sod,' was the disgruntled verdict of one who, in vain, had courted the Stanhope, 'to fling her back and lick the dust which many would gladly have licked from her shoes. . .!' 'And which,' chimed in another, 'shows that Granville's preference lies with his own sex rather than hers.' This from yet another who also had hoped for her favour, 'unless she be old enough to have borne him!'

'As for instance Oedipus?' suggested Mahon having, in his student days at Erlanger, studied the classics and read his Lemprière. He had recently married the daughter of Lord Haddington and been promoted by Pitt to the Lieutenant-Governorship of Dover Castle. All differences between him and Hester forgotten, he was ready to call Granville out on his sister's behalf. 'Were it not,' he told her loftily, 'that I only fight with gentlemen.'

Pitt, who had more to do than busy himself with the chit-chat of clubland and Almack's, was heartily sick of it all. He was also put out to see Hester put down. Injudiciously she told everyone including Lord Granville's elderly mistress, how she had been treated by the one man in her life she had ever loved.

Henrietta, masking triumph under cooing sympathy, rejoiced. Not so did Pitt, who was determined to be rid of Granville and his dangerous propinquity.

'A confounded nuisance,' his Foreign Minister was told. 'Give him the Embassy at Petersburg,' which Granville, with alacrity, accepted. He, too, was sick of it all and of Hester whose name, coupled with his as a jilt – none knew for certain who was the jilt and who the jilted – made off to Russia to find himself less *persona grata* at the Court of the Czar than at the Court of Hester Stanhope.

After his departure she too departed to nurse her grievances at Walmer, which gave the scavengers of garbage scandal enough to besmear her with the alleged birth of a child by Leveson-Gower.

'Not a hope!' chuckled clubland. 'He's about as potent as a jellyfish unless manipulated by the Bessborough!'

But soon the tongues that spat their venom at the pair of them were silenced by the thunder of guns announcing the victory of Trafalgar, followed by the death, killed in action, of the one-eyed, one-armed Admiral of the Fleet.

The whole country mourned him; the Prince at Carlton House wept maudlin tears into his drink, and Hester, back again in London beset with sorrow for Nelson, had now a greater grief to bear.

Pitt, who had been ailing before she went to Walmer, was in far worse case than before she went away. Yet he rallied, and Hester was thankful to see him cheered in the streets on his way to the Lord Mayor's banquet.

Loyal Tory citizens untied his horses and dragged his carriage through the shouting crowd to the Mansion House where he made his memorable and shortest speech.

I return you thanks for the honour you have done me, but Europe is not to be saved by any single man. England has saved herself by her exertions and will, I trust, save Europe by her example. . . .

It was the defeat at Austerlitz that broke him. No matter he had said, perhaps too confidently: 'Roll up the map of Europe, it will not be needed these ten years'. All he had worked for, hoped for, had crashed in bitter disillusionment.

At Austerlitz the Battle of the Three Emperors, Russia, Austria, and the recently self-crowned Emperor of France, Pitt's Russian and Austrian allies were routed and the 'Little Yellow Dwarf', with a giant's stride, soon bestrode the whole of Europe.

When the news of the battle and its tragic result came to Pitt, his face assumed what Wellington called its 'Austerlitz look'. His exhausted body, despite its spirit's strength, could not bear the weight of further burdens. Wracked by illness he made a last journey to Bath to fight his old enemy, the gout; but he was past the skill of his doctors.

Hester, agonized, saw him on his return mount the stairs at Putney clinging step by feeble step and aided by his servant. His personal physician, Sir Walter Farquhar, pronounced him in gravest danger.

Hester and James – Charles was with his regiment – watched at his bedside. Struggling to breathe he bade Hester:

'Keep an eye on James . . . Charles will do well . . . under General Moore but' . . . the weakened voice uttered his dying thought for those to whom he had been more than a father . . . 'but James . . .'

The young man kneeling by the bed took the wasted hand in his. Tears dropped on the head where the thinning hair receded from the pale dome-shaped forehead; while Hester stood in silence, stunned, and shed no tear.

'James,' the slow weak voice continued, 'might fall

47

into . . . wrong ways unless you, Hester, will . . . care for . . . him.'

'Yes,' her lips moved to say, 'I will. I promise.'

'Dear one, I know . . .' that voice gained strength to tell Sir Walter who had returned to the room, 'I know she will. She . . . loves me.'

More than any man of her past or maybe in her future did she love him, the lodestar of her life, its brilliance darkened by the shadow that fell upon him as, with his last breath, they heard him say:

'My country. . . . How I leave my country!'

He left her to a hashed up Ministry of All-the-Talents; to a half mad, half blind King who could still assume authority by virtue of his Crown; he left her to a decade of war against the bitterest enemy Britain had ever fought to conquer and whose conqueror, almost ten years later, when walking in a Brussels street with his gossip, Creevey, said, pointing his cane at a British soldier lounging at an opposite wall: 'If we had more of that article we could win.'

And although Wellington had no more of 'that article', three days later we did win.

*   *   *

With the death of her beloved uncle, Hester had ceased to give a thought to Granville. In this overwhelming grief that now obsessed her she could honestly assure herself that she had been the greatest remarkable fool to take *au grand serieux* the vapourings of one whom she now decried to James and Charles as: 'A Jemmy-Jessamy with eyelashes an inch long, a face like a girl's and the mind of a rabbit!' Her shame at having fallen for that girlish face and those inch long eyelashes was the only regret she nursed in any errant thought of him. As for those who had slandered her, *l'affaire* Stanhope-Granville had become stale in their mouths with the news of Trafalgar and Nelson's death. The whole country had been plunged in mourning to mourn again, a few months later, the passing of Pitt.

And with him passed the spoilt darling of Downing Street. Although the Government in honour of Pitt had granted a pension of £1,200 a year to Hester and £600 a year to each of her sisters, she, accustomed to the luxury of her uncle's establishment, found herself unable to cope with what seemed to her a pittance. She rented a house for herself and her brothers in Montagu Square where she entertained the friends and brother officers of Charles and James at her expense; not theirs. They had all to do on their small pay to meet their own debts and extravagances and looked to her, as they always did, to help them out. Hester who would deny them nothing was now faced with tradesmen clamouring for unpaid bills. And since she was no longer courted, fawned upon for possible preferments to be distributed by Pitt if she should but drop a hint, only a few who had rallied round her at Number Ten called at the house in Montagu Square.

But she who craved for and missed the adulation of a lover was soon again to be involved in what looked to be something more than an infatuation.

Sir John Moore, awarded the Order of the Bath for his outstanding service in Egypt and Italy, was brought to the house in Montagu Square by Charles: her 'dear Charles's General'. She had not been prepared for the singular beauty of his person combined with a modest simplicity and lack of all attempt to impress her with the cultivated patter of those that, with like exuberance embraced politics, poesy and passion to evaporate as mist before a dawn.

He captured her imagination from the first. He had none of the superficialities and affectations of a Granville or those others who, for a time, had enthralled her. And he, having roughed it in camps and led his army into fiercest fighting during a recent campaign in Sicily, had no experience of the world where Hester formerly held sway.

As much impressed as Hester with him, was he when confronted by her tall boyish figure and those wonderful eyes; and she gave him subtly to understand that her interest in him lay less in the fact that he was General Moore in command of the army – and Charles, than in John Moore, the man of her choice.

Again rumour scattered poison seeds about her.

'She is desperate for a bed-mate,' went the talk at Almack's, 'whether in the marriage-bed or not!' . . . And had she, at long last, captured one whose intention did mean marriage? Moore, if not in love, was indubitably attracted and she, exulting in her power over one seemingly invulnerable, although no word of marriage had been spoken by him, lived in hope he would declare himself. Yet, when she thought him about to respond to her summons, for, in the past had she chosen to call, others would willingly answer, fate, or accident, or prudence if you like, caused him to retreat.

Facing her in that London drawing-room overlooking the summer green of trees in Montagu Square, watching a sunbeam light her hair with its gleam of bronze in its darkness while her eyes, so vividly blue, met and melted in his, words may have trembled on his lips, unuttered.

She, in her determination, spoke for him.

'I am betrayed into loving you . . . as I could not have believed it in myself to love.'

It left him lost of breath; his face, under the tan of Latin suns, was paler than her own creamy pallor which now was flushed as she repeated, 'As I could never have believed or hoped . . . to love.'

He found voice then to stammer:

'Such honour is too . . .'

'Don't!' Her hand shot out as if to wrest from him those tardy words before they could escape. 'Don't say it! I've heard a parrot repetition of the "honour" . . .' the corners of her mouth were uplifted in a smile of contempt or irony, 'I have bestowed on others,' (or on one other, she silently parenthesized, with a pinprick of remembrance of Granville's mockery), 'by taking the initiative which is presumably man's right. In the past, because of my position, men may not have been so bold to declare themselves, but now that I have *no* position, the guest of charity – Government's charity' – again that curl of her desirable mouth, 'there is no reason why you should withhold that which you, that I – had thought —' her firm tone faltered. And the Lady Hester whom he had deemed so far above him with half the peerage and the late Prime Minister in her pocket, all men enslaved as was he, but dared not, even now, admit it, saw her suddenly, endearingly, young; shy, schoolgirlishly young. He had guessed her nearing thirty, but at that moment she might have been thirteen.

'I have,' her very voice had seemed to blush with the colour that flooded her cheeks, 'presumed too far. . . . I must apologize. Forgive me.' He could have sworn he saw tears stand in the blue loveliness of those eyes, 'And ... and forget.'

If he could have loved her when he thought her unattainable, now that she was offered for his taking he knew himself handfasted, and confessed.

'I shall never forget.' His voice rang strongly in a rush of words spoken at last. 'Nor shall I ever cease to wonder why I, so far beneath you, should deserve that you should honour me. Yes, I will repeat it – *honour* me and care enough to say what I have never dared to say!'

'Care enough!' She sat, her lips just parted, gazing wonder-charged at him who had risen to stand before her, not yet to touch but so close she could almost hear the hurry of his heart. 'If you could only know how I have longed to tell you that I care enough, too much ...' A small strangled laugh escaped her, 'because *you* seemed not to care.'

He knelt to her now. Her fingers caught at a silver button on his coat. 'Not to *care*,' again she said it on a laughing whisper, 'more than one of these.' So fiercely did she twist the button that, already loosened, it slipped its thread. 'I'd sew it on for you,' she said, 'if I could sew, but I can't.'

'I can.' He gathered her into his arms. 'I've sewn patches on the soles of my boots when my servant was killed beside me, and my feet were raw with marching. I am not fit for you, my charming, I'm rough, uncouth.'

'Be rough, uncouth, but . . . ready.'

Again that laughing whisper, smothered by his mouth on hers; and when his lips withdrew from that long, stormy kiss, he was white with the passion that consumed him.

A shiver of triumph swept through her.

'Are we to be married?' She felt as if all the blood had drained from her heart as she said it and waited for his answer. When it came she sat still as stone.

'So soon as I may know myself not needed where at present I must be.'

'Where?' It was no laughing whisper now but a peremptory demand. 'Where must you be needed more than here – with me?'

'Where I am most wanted.'

He had got upon his feet, was looking down at her, who flung at him hotly:

'Who can want you more than I?'

And he answered her with quiet:

'My country and my King.'

'A half mad, blind, deaf old King – Defender of the Faith! Is it for him you would sacrifice yourself and – me?'

'Hester,' he took her hand and held it close to tell her: 'I am first and last a soldier. Our country is at war. Our King, though blind, half mad and deaf, is the head of our

52

country. Would you have me desert him and my country for my love?'

'How can marriage if marriage is what you want of me, make you desert your country or your King? I'd follow you,' she too was on her feet, her face almost level with his. 'I'd be behind you to buckle your boots even if' – laughter dawned in her eyes again – 'I can't sew. But I'd make a well set-up uniformed fellow, and I'd learn if you'd teach me to shoot with a gun. *Why* can't we marry?'

She wound her arms round his neck; decisively he disengaged.

'One cannot serve two masters or – two mistresses.'

'Then let me be one of your two mistresses – if you will. What do hypocritical conventions mean to me? And you can take as the other, your country and serve her, so you will let me serve – you!'

She spoke lightly, jestingly, that he might not know he lashed her pride. Must it always be so? Must she for ever offer herself to be rejected? What was wrong with her, she achingly wondered, that men, and this man who more than any, she could swear, found her as much to be desired as she was desirous, retreated at the point of his surrender? Well! She would let the world know of their betrothal come what may, heroics, duty to his King, his country and war with Napoleon be damned! He was hers but . . . was he?

It had been she who spoke of marriage; no word from him of any bond between them. She had dragged admission out of him, had played *his* part to lose or win or – what?

'Kiss me!'

Her half open lips demandingly invited.

She had pierced his armour. For all his vaunted duty to his calling he was no man of steel. His hand strayed to her breast; through the thin muslin of her gown its tender stalk uprisen, hardened to his touch and lost him, for a

a

timeless second, his control. Fiercely he took her, but even as he felt her yield to him and knew he could have had her in that moment, he tore himself away. 'Not now . . . not yet,' he muttered below breath, and, 'I must leave you,' he made his voice firm to say: 'God! How am I to leave you?'

'Love me,' she murmured, more lost than he. 'Never leave me. You must stay.'

'I must go.'

Down the stairs, into the hall, past a servant who would have let him out, he went. The door slammed behind him.

At her window, a hand pressed to her mouth where it seemed his burning kiss still lingered, she saw him get into his carriage.

Nor did he look up to see her there.

THREE

Three months after the death of Pitt another great statesman was lost to Britain, and when Fox died the inefficient Ministry of All-the-Talents died with him, leaving fresh proof of power to the enfeebled Crown. Had Pitt lived he could have imposed his will upon the King who, vacillating between insanity and sense, had implicit faith in the 'Younger Pitt', as he had in his father before him.

Meanwhile Napoleon was sending forces to the Iberian Peninsula with intent to immediate invasion. General Moore, ordered out to fight Bonaparte's overwhelming forces of near upon a quarter of a million, had a bare thirty thousand against them.

On the eve of his departure he paid a brief visit to Hester. She received him in her scarlet riding habit, having returned from the Park where she rode every morning. More than any of her woman's clothes did that boyish kit become her, as well she knew, and had purposely not changed into a gown remembering he had called her his 'beautiful Amazon', when he first saw her in her habit.

But on that August morning still no word of marriage came from him, nor never since that memorable meeting when he had seemed on the point of declaration. She could excuse him for that as during the past year he had been involved in his military duties with only a few intermittent leaves. In command of an army in Sweden he had recently returned to be sent to the fighting front again. Hester, however, could find little comfort in the thought that he must, as always, put his duty and service to his country before her. Pride had restrained her from prompting him as previously she dared to do and risk rebuff, unless – the thought chilled her – he had ceased to care and would wish to stay for ever unpossessed.

'I should have been the man.' Her voice sounded loud to her ears as her eyes voyaged to rest upon the chair where he had just now sat. She had gestured him to sit beside her on the sofa, but he chose to be seated at a distance, thinking, she hoped, not to trust himself too near her. Why . . . why? She beat the knuckles of one hand into the palm of the other. Why is he so aloof? She could have sworn he wanted her. She had broken his defences once, she could break them again if he were not so damnably withdrawn. He had said, 'One cannot serve two mistresses', and she had offered to be his mistress if he would only let her serve him!

He had dropped a gauntlet by his chair and forgotten to pick it up. He had taken her hand in his, ungloved; his clasp was firm. He held that hand just a few seconds longer than mere courtesy, bent his head to brush it with his dry warm lips, and:

'When I come back,' he said, 'there will be much to say and to . . . tell. Goodbye, my dear . . .' And with those words unfinished he turned and went from her. . . . Only his glove remained, and this she lifted, smoothing its leather fingers stained with sweat, the left-handed gauntlet with which he held the reins. He had worn that glove to come to her hard-riding from – where? His camp would have been out of London. How little she knew of him either as man or soldier. . . . 'When I come back.' Yes, when or . . . if? Her heart narrowed. He, in command of his army, would be at the fighting front with his men and not as some others of officially high rank who were safely posted at headquarters behind the firing line.

Weeks passed; no news from him or from Charles who had gone with his General. James, too, had followed later, excitedly to tell her of his promotion before he embarked. He had left the Navy and was a fully fledged junior officer proudly to serve under General Moore and for the first time to be engaged in mortal combat.

At last, in October, she heard from Moore, who wrote from Lisbon:

> Charles's regiment was in the number of those named to remain in Portugal. . . . This was breaking his heart and so was it mine, but I have at last contrived to take the 50th with me and now all is well. The regiments are already marching. His (Charles's) will move in a few days. . . . I wish you were with us; we would give you riding enough in your red habit, à l'Amazone, you would do us all much good. . . .

Impersonal and tepid though it was that allusion to 'l'Amazone' caused her to read between the lines in hope that he thought of her more warmly than when he last had seen her. And a month later from Salamanca, he wrote to give her dreadful cause to fear for him and her beloved Charles, who:

> . . . is not yet arrived. His was one of the last regiments to leave Lisbon. . . . We are in a scrape but I hope we shall have the spirit to get out of it; you must, however, be prepared to hear very bad news. . . .

'Very bad news. . . .' O, God, she prayed, spare him and my loved ones. Keep them safe. How can I bear to lose them . . . and him? But a few lines further on she was heartened to read:

> Farewell, my dear Lady Hester. If I extricate myself from our present difficulties and if I can beat the French I shall return to you.

Was that a promise, a pledge? Did he intend to convey that he was hers, handfasted, sealed? She swung between doubt and hope.

More weeks of anxiety to torture her, as so many mothers, wives, sisters, lovers, were tortured throughout all Britain fearing to hear what they dreaded to hear, waiting day after day, night after night, for news that would lift them to heaven in God-given thankfulness or sink them to hopeless despair.

At length came the longed for news of Moore's daring advance with his small army to threaten Napoleon's giant force at Lisbon and Cadiz, and drive out the invading French. By Moore's retreat to Corunna through the mountains in bitterest winter weather, he had saved his main body from Napoleon's pursuit. It was a brilliantly successful victory, but . . . it killed Sir John Moore, and his young Aide-de-Camp, Charles Stanhope.

*   *   *

The account of Moore's death was, in due course, brought to Hester by Colonel Anderson, close friend and comrade of the General for more than twenty years. Seated there in the very chair where Moore had sat at their last meeting, the Colonel told how he walked beside the stretcher bearers who carried their wounded General to the rude lodging behind the lines. One of his officers had attempted to unbuckle the sword which was on the side where the bullet had shattered his arm as it pierced its deadly way to his lung. But: 'No,' he bade him, 'no! Leave it where it is. I had rather it went from the field with me. . . .' They buried that sword with him.

Listening to what Anderson had to tell her, Hester saw as if she were there in that hut – a shepherd's hut most likely – behind the firing line. Flickering candle light distorted shadows on the wooden walls and lent to the pallor of the dying face a gilded warmth. His servant and the younger officers, grouped around that truckle bed, heard the fainting voice that had so often cheered them on and strove still to cheer them with: ' 'Tis nothing . . .

58

All's well. . . .' He spoke of his wound while the surgeon, who knew there was no hope, could only strive to staunch the flow of his life's blood. 'He said,' Anderson cleared a rock in his throat to tell her who sat unstirring, 'he said . . . "I hope the people of England will be satisfied". . . . I just managed to hear him for his breath was shortening and he "hoped the country would do him justice". . . . As it will!' A mottled red suffused the hot colour in the Colonel's face as he set his jaw to say: 'I'll see to that.'

He did not tell her how Moore's command of the campaign had been unfavourably criticized in Parliament, although his main body of men, at the cost of his life and innumerable other lives, had succeeded in defeating Napoleon's hopeful capture of the British Army compelled by overwhelming numbers to re-embark. The return home of his forces, while successful in thwarting Napoleon's intent to grab the whole Peninsula, had caused a moral and political crisis. He could not tell her that. . . . Why harrow her further with Parliament's lack of acknowledgement of and ingratitude due to him who, by his daring advance, had threatened the enemy's flank and rear, saved Lisbon and Cadiz and possibly the whole campaign. 'What,' inly blazed the Colonel, 'can they who sit in judgement, safely housed in Westminster Hall, know of military tactics and the genius of him whose action fought to cover embarkation brought about a brilliant victory.' . . . And now hosannas were being sung in praise of Moore's successor, Sir Arthur Wellesley, soon to be raised to the peerage as Lord Wellington.

Anderson cleared his throat again and, taking his handkerchief, blew a trumpet blast through his nose to dispel a moisture in his eyes. Avoiding that stony unseeing look of hers: ' "I always wished," Moore said, "to die this way," meaning in battle, and asked us standing there – two or three times he asked us – "Did we beat 'em?" Meaning the French, not realizing that he had sent

59

Boney's army – his Grand Army,' the Colonel grinned awry, 'as he calls 'em, scuttling with their tails down. It was as great a triumph for him as any of Marlborough's vaunted victories. Think of it!' Anderson waxed hot. 'He beat the French – countless thousands of 'em with a force of less than ten thousand when the holocaust was reckoned up. And these damned old women in Westminster – all they can say is' – he checked himself at sight of those eyes turned on him in a blind questioning stare —

'Say what?' The words, so faintly spoken came from her almost closed lips.

'They say, of course,' blundered Anderson, 'that it was a – a splendid victory. And then he spoke of his mother and of us, his friends, and of his Will and what he wanted us to do with it – and then he spoke of you and of your brother – your younger brother —'

'James?' her white lips whispered.

'Yes, James. He told him, "Your sister . . . tell her I remember and . . . remember me to her." That is what we heard. His last words . . .' And now Anderson made no attempt to disguise a tear that rolled down his weatherbeaten cheek, 'his last thoughts and his last words were of you.'

He left her seated there sight-blinded and so still it was as if her heart had ceased to beat.

Before he went he handed her a tattered leather gauntlet. 'This,' he said, 'was his. I thought you would care to —'

She took it from him wordlessly. He found it hard to leave her there so lonely and so lost, but fearing to prolong his stay further to intrude on her soul-searing grief, he left her.

After he had gone she bestirred herself to lift to her lips that gauntlet stained with dried blood – his blood. She had the fellow to it or one similar that he had left lying on the very chair where sat his friend who brought his last thoughts, his last words . . . of her. And then a stricken cry broke from her through that silence: 'Dear Christ! Take me – take me too! I cannot live without him. . . .'

But live without him she must and did. There was one other who needed her care, as always she had cared for these sons of her father who had never cared for them. She must keep her promise to her uncle given on his death-bed. James . . . her 'little James'. Within a month of hearing of her bitter loss he had come immediately on his return from Corunna broken-heartedly to tell her that Charles too had fallen in that same battle and almost at the same moment which had bereft her of all, as she then believed, that had made life bearable.

In comforting James, who had been devoted to Charles – the two younger boys were nearer in age to each other than to their elder brother Mahon – Hester could forget herself and her own sorrow. James, highly emotional, and more sensitive than any of the Stanhopes, was completely shattered by his first experience of the horrors of war. He, on the verge of a breakdown, decided her to take him away out of London that to her had now become too full of anguished memories. It could never have occurred to her that had Moore lived she might have suffered a more humiliating and unendurable sorrow in that his love for her would have proved to be less ardent than hers for him. As she had given to the world they were engaged he could have been persuaded to marry her, but would such a marriage have brought her the happiness which her possessive soul demanded? Neither he nor any man, if she could have known it, would satisfy her. And although she so desperately wished for wifehood, marriage was not her ultimate goal.

Her infatuation for Granville had left no soreness, not a scar; nor when he returned Henrietta's 'idolatry' by marrying her niece, daughter of her sister Georgiana, did

Hester give one regretful thought to him. Granville, like Camelford, was just another amatory adventure to be cast aside, forgotten as a man forgets and casts aside a light o' love.

She took James to Bath. He refused to drink the waters which she, at her doctor's advice, as she was in worser case than James, attempted to take, loathed them and discontinued further treatment. She had lost her looks; grief had lent to her face haggard lines that had no right to be there at thirty. She was no beauty but her lovely skin and those extraordinary eyes, gave her beauty where strictly there was none. She had taken pains in the past with her face and careful cosmetics when all set to attract, but now she cared nothing for her appearance.

Bath was not as she had known it before the war; its habitués were mostly wealthy tradesmen and merchants, 'Riff-raff upstarts', she disdainfully described them. 'Wonder 'tis,' she told James, 'that Papa don't take lodgings here to be among the common herd that he favours and entertains at "Democracy Hall".'

She and James were now outcasts from their father's house. Lord Stanhope having washed his hands of both them and his two other daughters, had taken to himself a housekeeper who gratified his parsimony by supplying him with the scantiest ill-cooked food and pocketed the money he gave her for the staff.

Hester, who had never received one word from her father nor any monetary help since she and her brothers had left him, was in sore financial straits. She had let the house in Montagu Square and, although Charles in his will had left her ten thousand pounds which was extremely unlikely he had to leave, she, so far, had not been handed a penny of it by the attorney in charge of his affairs. James to whom, as with Charles, she could deny nothing was always borrowing money from her which she would never press him to repay. Her twelve hundred a year was not enough for either her or his expenses; both were extravagant and always in debt. She was thankful when James had sufficiently recovered from the loss of Charles to be sent on a mission to Spain.

Her uncle, Lord Chatham, offered her nothing but sympathy for her brother's death; and because of her position at Downing Street, royalty in the person of the Duke of York had deigned to favour her, yet if she looked for any material support from H.R.H. other than his insincere condolence, she was again disappointed.

She had no place now in society, no home, no man, and without a man in her life she was lost. She must get away from it and out of it all; but where to go? When at Bath and during her drives into the borderland of Wales, she had come across a farmhouse situated in a valley of the river Wye. Now James was off her hands she could bury herself in the depths of the country and lose the world and her memories.

In that out of the way hamlet among the Welsh folk whose outlandish tongue she could not understand nor they hers, she was content to live the rusticated life of a lady of the manor; the 'manor' being Glan Irfon, a primitive farmhouse with a parlour, 'not,' she tell us, 'a dozen feet square'; a bedroom even smaller, and a cow named Prettyface.

We find her skimming milk, churning cream, making butter and generally acting as dairymaid. She would have tended turkeys if they had any, or geese which they had not. She regained her health, enjoyed her rides in the mountains to the wonder of the villagers to see her breeked, her red riding skirt discarded and her dark hair tumbled from beneath her three-cornered hat. But this rural simplicity soon began to pall; she could no longer endure the monotony and solitude of a pastoral existence, and when James returned from his mission accompanied by a friend, a Mr Sutton with the singular Christian name of Nassau, she went back to London and exerted herself to attract him, was dismayed to find him insufficiently

63

responsive and dismissed him as neither worth her while nor her wiles.

She must now face the fact that she was no longer the much admired, desired Lady Hester, but a spinster in her thirties who had lost touch with a world where once she had queened it. In London there was none of her erstwhile friends to welcome her, nor none whom she would care to welcome. The wanderlust was upon her that, although she knew it not, would lead her to unimaginable countries and adventures undreamed of.

James had been ordered to join his regiment in Spain and would shortly embark in His Majesty's frigate *Jason*. She at once decided to go with him.

It needed some strategy, but by persuading her doctor that a sea voyage would benefit her health and having reported to him various imaginary symptoms, she managed to secure a passage in *Jason* for herself, her maid Williams, and Nassau. He, as result of her ultimate indifference to his lukewarm response to her overtures, had latterly renewed his attentions to receive high-handed rebuff. He had a pretty conceit of himself and being endowed with a considerable fortune, was unused to a rejection of his advances. Consequently he became her willing slave as others before him, partly because she, having regained her health in the simple life she had led in Wales, had also regained her physical attraction that so many had found irresistible. Her skin with its golden sheen from exposure to the sun and all weathers was, as ever, lovely; the red-lipped provocative mouth tantalized while it repelled any man who did not come to her call.

Jason, commanded by Captain King had, under convoy, a small fleet of transport and merchantmen bound for Gibraltar. Hester thinking she might need medical attention while abroad and having little faith in foreign doctors, had been recommended to a Doctor Meryon, recently qualified. Little did she guess that this insignificant young man was destined to give to the world and to

64

posterity, the memoirs and incredible adventures of the first Englishwoman explorer of her time and for all time to come.

With James, Nassau, Williams, Dr Meryon, and her dog which she had found astray on a Welsh mountain, she embarked from Portsmouth on a spring-like day in March. As they sailed out of harbour Hester watched the coast recede into a hazy blur on the horizon of a land that, had she but known it, she would never see again. Her future was a palimpsest to be recorded, unerased.

The voyage which began with a calm soon ran into heavy gales. While Williams, Nassau and Meryon were prostrate below, Hester was completely unaffected by the plunging of the ship through troughs of mountainous waves. With James, who as a midshipman before he was gazetted to the army and had long found his sea-legs, she joyed to defy the winds that tore at her loosened hair as she staggered along the deck to the admiration of the tars and Captain King. Clinging to the rail of the ship that plunged like a startled stallion at the unexpected blast, her gear and rigging groaning, creaking, rattling above the yell of the winds, Hester looked down at the white circles of foam breaking in fountains of silvery spray, and laughed at the drenching of her tossed hair and her cloak that spread behind her like the sails of the ship, now furled against the storm.

She learned the names of the stars on moonlight nights when the gales dropped and the ship, proud as a swan, sped through waters smooth and gentle as a lake. But off Trafalgar the vessel got into trouble again and almost ran upon the rocks in a sudden squall that swept down upon the gallant little frigate and savaged her from bow to stern. Bravely she weathered the worst of it until, with the waning of the moon in a month from the day *Jason* sailed out of Portsmouth, a steady wind brought her in sight of the Rock.

As they neared land Hester rose at dawn to see the sky a steely grey and stars fading behind night's lifted curtain; then as she watched, pennons of clouds, amber-stained and reddening, parted to reveal the risen sun set fire to sky and sea enriched with that splendid conflagration.

Stretching out her arms as if to greet the wakened day: 'My day!' she cried aloud above the screech of the wheeling gulls. . . .

Her day, and the dawn of her Great Adventure.

PART TWO
Love in the Wilderness

ONE

'Here, then, we are,' wrote Doctor Meryon, 'and receiving the politest civilities from the chief people of the place.'

The doctor, quite something of a snob, was overwhelmed with the 'politest civilities' offered him as medical attendant on her ladyship, especially when invited to dine at the Governor's house, oddly named the Convent, and to sit at the Governor's table with 'all the best company.'

If 'all the best company' delighted the doctor it did not delight Lady Hester. After a week or two in Gibraltar, she was thoroughly bored with the company, the town, swarming with soldiers and officers stationed at the garrison, and with their wives, whom she called a 'lot of packhorses'.

Forced to attend functions arranged in her honour, dinners, dances, and afternoon tea parties held by the 'packhorses', each trying to outvie the other for the patronage of the famous Lady Hester unaware, since they were ten years behind the times, that she was no longer famous and now forgotten by a world which they had never known, she decided to move on.

'I must get away from here,' she told James, who would, in any case, shortly be got away from there since he was to join his regiment of Guards at Cadiz. 'I'm sick to death of this Rock full of monkeys and men and one cannot tell t'other from which.'

Given a suite in the Governor's house she raked up a graciously mendacious excuse to depart. . . . 'My doctor advises me to leave Gibraltar. It will be too warm for me, he says, during the summer months, and is also too warm for my dog.' A genuine reason for leaving. He was already feeling the heat too much for him and his thick coat, part sheep dog, part hound, with a touch of the spaniel. He had been scarcely weaned – 'thrown out of the litter as a runt,' she supposed, when she found him lost on a Welsh mountain, brought him back to the farm and reared him. So now she had another young creature to care for, as she cared for her young brothers and sisters more than she ever had cared for herself.

Nassau also was thoroughly bored with Gibraltar chiefly because Hester had cooled to him as he waxed hot for her. He told her he would shortly be leaving for Minorca in the hope she would suggest she go with him. No such suggestion came. She found him a poor substitute for any of his predecessors in her predatory pursuit of them. If he wished to go, she made it unkindly plain that he could go, but not with her.

While Moore would for ever live in memory, she had long since wiped Granville off the list of those for whom she had no further use; and if once she had believed herself inconsolable, she was now prepared to be consoled; but not with Nassau.

Seated on the balcony of the Governor's house she idly watched the red and white sailed ships and fishing boats in the harbour below. It was a blue and golden day and hot as hottest midsummer in England. The sun-bewitched water shone with a million diamond sparks on the gentle ripples of waves where a luxury yacht lay near at anchor. She was creamy white and gleaming in the sun's sharp rays from every porthole and all her polished brass.

Shading her eyes from the fierce glare of sea and sky Hester saw the figure of a man appear upon the deck. She could see him clearly as tall, well shaped, fair haired, as he turned to say something to a second man who had joined him. Both were bare-headed and both, she judged, young, almost identically dressed in white trews and dark blue yachting suits.

It was unusual for a private yacht to be cruising in the Mediterranean when the British Navy was scouring the seas in chase of the French, and blockading Napoleon's convoys that threatened us in a war of mutual starvation.

'Whose yacht is that?' she asked a footman whom she had ordered to bring a bowl of water for her dog that lay panting at her feet.

His lordship the Marquis of Sligo's yacht, her ladyship was informed.

Hester pricked her ears. Peter Browne Sligo! She had met him in her former life, so far distant from this narrow life on a rock 'full of monkeys and men' that it might have been upon another planet. She had known him for a debonair extravagant, immensely wealthy and irresponsible young rake, with a retinue of equally rakish and irresponsible young men.

That evening Sligo dined at the Governor's house and brought with him his guest on the yacht, Michael Bruce, whom Hester at once found more to her taste than Nassau Sutton. He, having delayed his departure for a few days before the arrival of Sligo and his yacht, left in somewhat precipitate haste when he knew himself entirely – and hopelessly – supplanted by Michael Bruce whom that indefatigable scribe Dr Meryon records as: '. . . . A most pleasing and clever young man and handsome enough to move any lady's heart. . . . I don't like Mr Bruce.'

And Mr Bruce didn't like him, nor any man, including Mr Sutton, who seemed to 'like' Hester too much.

It was a case of mutual attraction compulsive as the mating of amoebae in a pond. Michael, after that first meeting: 'She's bowled me over, absolutely,' he confided to Sligo when, having dined at the Governor's house, they returned to the yacht and were on deck for a last drink. The moon had spread a cloth of silver across the waters of the harbour where a few little boats – most of them had gone out fishing – still rocked slightly in the breeze. 'I'd marry her,' said Bruce staring up at the reflection of moonlight in a window of the Convent that he fondly thought was hers but was that of her maid, Williams. 'Yes, I'd marry her if she'd have me.'

'Marry your mother!' scoffed Sligo, 'which she's old enough to be if she were a Hindu. 'Sides,' he drained his glass and poured another for himself and Michael, both having liberally wined at the Governor's hospitable board. 'She'll have your guts. She's a man-eater. For me – hic – (he belched discreetly) – 'I don't care for those breastless hipless lanky women an' so tall I'd a'soon bed with a giraffe.'

'You disgust me,' said Michael coldly, getting up. 'She's a won'erful woman an' has more intel'gence,' he too had liberally wined, 'an' more wit of her parts —'

'Have you seen 'em – already?' chortled Sligo.

'— than you have in your whole libr'y of arc-ee-ol'gy,' pronounced Michael with dignified disfavour. Sligo was something of, or prided himself in being, an authority on archeology. 'And I'm going to ride with her tomorrow,' Michael gave another fatuous glance to Williams' window. 'Goo'night.'

So that was how it all began; but neither could have told how it would end.

*   *   *

She who believed her life was broken on the day that brought her news of John Moore's death, had found in Michael Bruce revivication. His undisguised and fervent interest in herself rekindled that which she had thought to be the passing of her youth. Had she but known it her youth had never passed; it stayed arrested in its flight between the bud and blossom. And now, in her thirties, she had flowered with the knowledge that she, no longer the pursuer, was pursued.

In the sunfilled gardens of the Convent their intimacy ripened, each to discover in the other a quickened sense of new impressions. She may have realized that what he sought in her were the fruits of her experience, unaware that her experience in the consummation of her womanhood had been solely cerebral. Since Bruce was in the nursery Hester Stanhope had been branded as much of a society courtesan as any of Prinny's entourage or the ladies of Devonshire House. He could not know, such was the natural conclusion to be drawn to see the many who had sought her favour in the past, that none had been granted more than half promises or the best, or worst, frustrated exploration of a demi-vierge. 'Thus far and no farther,' may have been her limited allowance to those who looked for and expected all. The impassioned Bruce might well have been surprised, to inflame his ardour more, had he guessed her still a virgin.

James, who had thought to be indefinitely stationed at Gibraltar, was now gone to Cadiz. Sligo also decided to leave the garrison owing to warlike conditions prevalent on the Rock and of the ever watchful British Navy in the Mediterranean. He therefore set sail for the neutral waters of the Ottoman. Bruce, invited to go with him and by this time enslaved by Hester, stayed behind awaiting her command to follow wherever the spirit moved her. It was not long in moving her to Malta. Bereft of James she was glad of Michael's company to this, her next port of call.

They embarked from the Rock in early April, with Bruce, the ubiquitous Meryon, her maid Williams, and her dog. So to Malta they went. Meryon, after the 'splendours' of the Governor's table at Gibraltar, had been loth to leave the 'best company' with whom he had associated, but was agreeably surprised to find, as he records it, that he sat at the table of the Governor of

Malta, General Oakes, 'with a string of Lords, Ladies, Counts and Countesses.' Not so agreeably surprised was he with the apartment accorded to him, not at the palace of the Governor whose invitation Hester politely declined, but in 'a lump of a building with a beggarly exterior,' was the doctor's opinion of the house of the Commissary General, Fernandez and his wife.

Half London, or the London Hester had known in her Downing Street days, flocked to Valetta; and because of the presence of the adhesive Bruce and to avoid inevitable gossip on the assumption of a relationship that was rapidly advancing beyond the, presumably, platonic stage, she chose to be the guest of Mr and Mrs Fernandez. One may believe the Commissary General of Malta had married below his station in life for his wife was the sister of Hester's personal maid, Elizabeth Williams. Hester, however, much preferred the unpretentious household of Sant' Antonio, 'that lump of a building,' to the palatial residence of the Governor which had so delighted and impressed Dr Meryon. But with the gardens of Sant' Antonio the doctor has no complaint.

'*O Dio, quanto bello!*' he rhapsodizes, 'where the vines twine in such luxuriance to excite wonder in the mind of an Englishman.' And where Michael may have first declared himself to excite wonder, if not entirely unexpected, in the mind of an Englishwoman.

Fired with a responsive fever to grasp at youth and warmth, she endowed him with qualities more of hers than his. While she knew him weak, unstable, yet she found this his chief attraction, the very complement of her arrogant possessiveness.

That he loved her in so far as the spoilt son of an indulgent and immensely wealthy father could love any other than Michael Bruce, she did not doubt; and heard his stammering avowal in the garden which had so excited the mind of Dr Meryon, with something between tears and laughter. He was so terribly in earnest. Having

74

begun in the stilted fashion of a pompous middle-aged bachelor making a proposal of marriage to an equally middle-aged spinster as they walked between the 'luxurious vines' along paths lined with orange trees and a wealth of sub-tropical flowers sending forth their fragrance on the heavy air in the cool of the evening, he dropped his speechifying and could only tell in broken phrases that he loved her. . . . He would love no other while he lived and, when he died. . . . He had never loved before (how he harped upon that word she had so often heard but never surely with such eager warm sincerity). Could she not give him hope? Did she care for him no more than just a . . . another . . . one of the many who had loved her? . . . Why did she laugh? Was she laughing at him?

His fair young face was pale in the shade of the palms that spread their shadowed shapes before them on the grass. A young crescent moon, just risen, lay on her back cradled in the branches of a cypress.

'I am not laughing,' she told him with a catch in her throat, 'or if I laugh it is not at you but at myself.'

'Why at yourself?' he snatched her fiercely to him, his eyes sought hers angrily. 'Or do you laugh because you make of me your fool? You have let me think you care for me. You like – you like to have me with you. When James went you were glad to have me with you.'

'Yes, and always I'll be glad to have you with me.' She spoke composedly against the throbbing of her heart, so youthfully impetuous was his avowal.

'Does that mean,' his hands hurtfully clutched her bare shoulders level with his own. She was wearing a thin muslin gown, a concession to the dinner hour of the Fernandez household. His wife adhered to the fashion of dinner with several courses as in the Governor's residence. 'Do you mean that I may hope? That you are not in – indifferent to me? That I do not presume – dare to ask that you and I – that you will honour me in – in marriage?'

'Oh, my dear!' She took his hands from her shoulders gleaming white in the early moonshine, so swiftly in those parts does night fall to spread a bridge of dusk between dark and the ending day. 'Do not think that you presume. There is a part of me which has longed to hear' – again that smallest laugh – 'what you so delicately tell me.'

'Delicately!' he burst forth with. 'Is it delicate – or would you say,' the young voice cracked, '*in*delicate to tell you that my whole strength and manhood cries out for you – wants you? I *want* you, Hester,' he said with sudden forcible determination, 'not only as a man may want his woman but as a man must want his wife. *My* wife!'

'Your wife,' she echoed, pondering the words, turning them over to examine them, so it cruelly struck him, as if she were microscopically examining the carcase of the butterfly that had died its short day's spell of life. Only yesterday she had lifted the dead lovely thing, and in this very walk under the palm trees when the sun had baked the earth and all earth's tiny creatures.

She shook her head, releasing her under lip caught beneath a tooth. 'No, my darling, no.'

Her darling! He made again as if to take her to him at that word, the sweetest of all words to lovers' ears.

'Your wife?' she repeated it, her eyelids lowered. 'Do you not know I am twelve years older than you?'

'What of it!' he cried loudly. 'As if age mattered. God alone knows what is age, for in His sight – you remember – it says a thousand years are but – I forget – yesterday or another thousand years? What are years or age in time-lessness?'

'When you are fifty,' she brought herself to say, 'I will be sixty-two.'

'What would I care if you were *eighty*-two even now

and in this minute! I love you – *love* you – do you not understand? Hester!'

He engulfed her in his arms, his seeking mouth on hers. . . . She was not proof against this feverish enchantment and the promise that it held, too long delayed. Too late? No! Not too late to know herself at last to be fulfilled. Yes! What was age to him, to her, to love? She was yet young in body, reborn to give all that he demanded, never given, never known to any man until and now – to him!

The days following this surrender of herself to Bruce were narrowed to their nights when they would lose themselves in mutual and complete abandon. To Hester their relationship was an ever increasing source of life and living; a completeness that filled her with a triumphant sense of power. He was hers! . . . Hers to protect, to care for and guard as she had cared for and guarded her brothers and, dearest of the three, her Charles, gone from her now for ever, and in his stead this young ardent lover for her comfort.

It was characteristic of Hester that she made no attempt at subterfuge; this new found joy which had come to reawaken her dormant youth must be no contraband adventure, no backstair intrigue, no secret visits to the alcove. The whole world must know of her transfiguration.

If not shouted from the roof of Sant' Antonio, she announced it to that household and to the Governor, General Oakes with whom she had endeared herself in a friendship that would last to the end of her days, with the same, if not so modest a pride, as a young girl will announce her betrothal.

The ladies of Malta raised eyes and hands to heaven. 'For shame! She is *shame*less. In another walk of life she would be earning her living at it. . . .' 'At what?' Hester might have scornfully asked. 'At a soul-uplifting spiritual and physical expansion?' Further emphasized in one of her long-winded letters to Michael's father to whom she unreservedly wrote of this relationship.

To Crauford Bruce who must have been exceedingly put out to learn that. . . . 'While loving Michael to distraction she looked forward to the period when like some dethroned Empress, she must resign him to some thrice happy woman really worthy of him. . . .' She adjured the scandalized Crauford 'not to imagine his son had fallen into the hands of an artful woman . . .' Which did nothing to alter the father's fear that his son had fallen into the hands of a whore. Nor did her self-denigration as a 'dethroned Empress' in the event of Michael transferring his affection to 'one really worthy of him' sugar the pill she was forcing Crauford to swallow, while assuring him that this son of his was endowed with an 'elevated and statesmanlike mind, brilliant talents' (as yet to be discovered) 'and a beautiful person.' None of which can have had the desired effect of persuading Crauford Bruce to accept his son's avowed mistress as if she were his wife.

Hard on that letter from Hester came one from Michael to Crauford written and possibly edited if not dictated by Hester since the style of both is distinctly similar. His letter is as lavish with superlatives in praise of his lady as hers in praise of him. She is 'so highly born, so splendidly connected,' which the Bruces were not, more than that Crauford was a banker of considerable wealth and importance in the city of London and a not very conspicuous Member of Parliament. He goes on to assure his father that 'far from being ashamed he is proud to confess that he loves and admires Lady H. Stanhope, whose conduct has been the most open, most ingenuous, and most honourable. . . .'

One may wonder how this assurance of his lady's conduct as most 'open, honourable', etc. was received by the father of a son who confesses pride at involving himself

78

with a mistress many years older than he and whom, it appears, he generously supported on his father's money. Certainly Hester's inadequate allowance as 'the guest of charity', so did she consider herself as the recipient of a Government grant, would not have covered the expenses of her present circumstances nor would her means have been sufficient when again the spirit moved her to leave Malta for Turkey.

The heat had become insufferable in those summer months, and as her maid Williams had arranged to stay at Sant' Antonio with her sister, Mrs Fernandez, another maid, one Ann Fry, a timid little creature, who it is doubtful had she known what she would be let in for as attendant to her adventuresome lady that she would have accepted the post.

As to Dr Meryon's reaction to his patient's 'open, ingenuous and honourable' intimacy with Michael Bruce, we find, despite invitations to the Governor's parties where he tells us he 'meets with persons of high rank' so much above him that he considers it a 'great condescension he is permitted to mingle with them at all', that the doctor is not unwilling to leave Malta. His initial dislike of Bruce was much increased since Michael had 'effected his purpose' so Meryon's busy pen, spluttering indignation believes, 'of excluding him from the General's table.'

His lady's decision to leave Malta was therefore welcomed by the doctor in the hope – a hope to be indefinitely deferred – that the deplorable relationship between herself and Bruce might end with their departure for Turkey.

They left Malta in the frigate *Belle Poule* bound for Zante. Hester so far had been lucky in her transport in His Majesty's ships, for at Zante another passage for her and her suite was secured in Government transport to Patras.

Hester was delighted to find Sligo at Patras, ready to join her expedition to Turkey via Greece.

Sligo's arrival had caused intense excitement in the harbour and among the natives of Patras. He had collected on his cruise in Ottoman waters and the various ports where he landed, an extraordinary retinue that consisted of two Albanian servants, a Turkish cook, a dragoman and three English liveried footmen all armed to the teeth with sabres, blunderbusses and pistols greatly to the alarm of Ann Fry, Hester's maid. Not so her ladyship who would have taken arms herself against attack if called upon to do so.

Sligo sent his yacht back to Malta, and the only passage now available for Hester was a primitive open boat, a *felucca*, very different from the men-o'-war where she was received with every courtesy and consideration by the captains of the Royal Navy.

With Sligo's servants and her own which included her Persian cook, two menservants, the doctor, Bruce, and their valets, there was scarcely sufficient accommodation for herself, Ann Fry and her dog in the dark and evil smelling and none too clean quarters allotted for her personal use below. She preferred to sleep on deck under an awning while the rest of the party sprawled on mattresses, the servants, footmen, cooks and all of them segregated from their masters at a convenient distance or else sharing vermin-ridden bunks with the crew.

The heat was intolerable and Hester scarcely slept at night, while during the day Ann fanned her with palm leaves, and the greasy Greek mate brought her lukewarm citron juice for her, doubtful, refreshment.

At Corinth they crossed the isthmus with Sligo's still more bizarre cavalcade augmented by couriers, interpreters, twenty-four riders in all, and the two superbly arrayed Albanians with their silver mounted pistols. Hester led the procession riding cross-saddle and breeked on a milk white stallion so that wondering villagers took her for a beardless boy while the long-suffering Ann went bumping along behind her on a donkey.

At the small harbour of Keuriki they again embarked in a still more awful boat that was to take them to Athens, and as they entered the Piræus Hester saw a stark naked young man, his auburn curls glinting in the sun as he dived from the breakwater into the sea.

'Good Lord!' exclaimed Sligo. 'That's Byron. What's he doing here?'

What Byron was doing there was his research in Grecian waters for *Childe Harold*, still in embryo.

'Byron?'

The name, vaguely familiar to Hester would, eighteen months later, resound throughout the world. Sligo, with whom Byron was an old Harrovian schoolmate, cupping his hands, hailed him: 'Hey! Byron. Here's Sligo. Hurry and dress, and then come and join us. We are about to land.'

Neither Hester nor he were impressed with the other so soon to be the darling of society and Lady Caroline Lamb.

Hester tells us: 'He had a great deal of vice in his looks, his eyes set close together. . . . A strange character. One time mopish, and nobody was to speak to him, another he was for being jocular with everybody. . . .' Not particularly with her of whom he wrote to one of his friends: 'I do not admire that dangerous thing, a female wit . . . She evinced a disposition to *argufy* with me which I avoided either by laughing or yielding. I despise the sex too much to squabble with them. . . . She is going to Constantinople.'

She took a villa at Therapia some few miles from the city. In the glowing oriental spring it was climatically delightful, but not in the winter. The stone floors, high vaulted rooms, and the icy winds sweeping down from the Bosphorus flew to her lungs and laid her low for some weeks.

Bruce, with typical thoughtlessness and notwithstanding his avowed devotion to his mistress, left with Sligo

81

for Smyrna. He promised to return so soon as Sligo had completed his research for certain archeological remains in which Bruce also expressed an interest. Hester made no attempt to dissuade Michael from going. She was not and never would be exacting toward her young lover. She indulged him as she had always indulged her brothers. As for him he was genuinely in love with her. She had given him in this, his first experience of a passionate and all absorbing relationship, a new horizon that opened out a quickened sense of life, an irresistible real and attractive intellectual excitement that was not wholly physical.

Of his intent to marry her, as he persistently impressed upon his father in his letters, there is no doubt. It was only Hester's equal determination not to enter into any legal and binding contract that deterred him from urging her to take the final step. Also, regarding him with the same half-maternal love she had bestowed upon her brothers, putting their interests, their well-being and welfare before her own, she knew that marriage with this boy of twenty-three could only end in disillusionment for him. Sooner or later he would resent her dominance for, as well she realized, she was born to dominate. At the back of her mind she would often recall the fashionable fortune teller, 'Brothers', who had told her she would reign as Queen of the Jews and leader of men in far-off lands. . . . She had never quite forgotten this, although she would ridicule the thought of it, while in part believing.

She was reminded of it again when riding alone as usual to the consternation of Ann Fry, who did not dare more than to advise her ladyship against venturing unaccompanied among 'them heathen Turks.'

'Nonsense!' Hester rammed on a riding hat hiding her hair, which she now had grown long. 'I'd be taken for a man among any of these idiotically bedizened Turks.' And away she went into the heart of the city.

Halting on the fringe of the crowd that had come to

watch the Sultan pass on his way to the mosque, she must have seen the same procession with all its pomp and circumstance, its glory and its glitter as that which Lady Mary Wortley Montagu had seen and recorded in her incomparable letters. And now almost a hundred years later, Hester watched another Sultan, Mahmoud, pass, splendidly arrayed, sparkling with jewels mounted on his beautiful white stallion with its gold embroidered trappings. Preceded by his bodyguard, the janissaries, their scimitars blazing steely fire in the sun's fierce rays, were followed by the royal gardeners in so rich a variety of colour that they looked, so Lady Mary tells, us,* 'like a parterre of tulips.' After them rode the Aga of the janissaries, an equally resplendent figure, sprouting enormous white feathers from his turban; and not the least in this imposing extravaganza, was the Kylza Aga, chief black eunuch, a swollen gross and over fattened monstrosity in a gold embossed pelisse and jewelled turban waddling before his other dozen eunuchs.

Those who were not bowed in devout prayer before the All Highest, may have wondered to see the white-skinned young man, never an unveiled woman surely, riding breeked, cross saddled, and staring, all eyes, at His Sublimity. The clink of steel, the tramp of hundreds of feet and the sound of horses' hooves on the hard sunburnt road where myriad flies settled on the fallen manure and refuse unswept in the gutters, mingled with the sing-song chant of prayers from the devotees who hailed their Sultan with ecstatic cries and entreaties to Allah and Mahomet to protect their All Highest, descendant of the Prophet.

'Prophet,' muttered Hester. 'As much as that wizard, charlatan, warlock "Brothers" who should be put in the stocks for telling me – a gullible fool – that I too am destined to be a leader of men. Yes! And that I'd be a queen of the Jews.' Did he mean a sort of female Christ –

* See *A Toast to Lady Mary*.

she dared to wonder – *and* a prophetess, if not in my own country in countries far away? A lot of nonsense! Was it? . . . Or could it mean she had been guided on this odyssey to lands yet to be explored by her in the fulfilment of her destiny?

She turned her horse's head toward Pera and found Ann, much relieved to see her mistress safe and sound and not abducted, raped, or murdered by 'them heathen Turks.'

'You are right,' Ann was told as she removed her lady's dusty riding boots. ' 'Tis a heathen city. I am away, out of it all. We're off to Athens and civilization. Pack my bags.'

But before she left Constantinople she had altered her plans again. Instead of immediately departing for Athens and finding that 'heathen city' unbearable with winter approaching, she decided to take a villa on the banks of the Bosphorus; an unwise choice having already experienced the effects of the sea-cold winds. She was also impatiently waiting Bruce's return from Smyrna, having received from James – James of all people! – a letter expressing his disapproval of her liaison with Bruce of which she had made no secret to all and everyone, including Sligo, who may have imparted the news of it in his letters home, that the famous, and infamous, 'Lady H' was living in sin with a boy almost young enough to be her son. Not that Sligo would have cared whether Hester did or did not 'live in sin' with Bruce or with anyone else; but for her, that James, her 'little James' whom she had promised her dying uncle to protect 'from falling into bad ways', should dare to upraid her for an 'illicit association' with Bruce to set all London talking, as if she had not offended the proprieties enough. . . . And so on, resulted in an indignant letter from her to General Oakes.

'Thank God, he' (James) 'has not my death to reproach

himself with nor would I wish him ever to know not only all the misery and suffering his imprudence has caused me.' (Imprudence? the General may have asked. Imprudence, if any, was on her side, not that of her young brother acting as if in elder-brotherly capacity on behalf of his sister's good name which, the General might have admitted, she had so blatantly disgraced.) 'If he chooses to act as a brother towards me in private,' she continues, 'all very well, if not I shall never cease to pray for his welfare but will never see him again nor will I allow him to torment me by letter. . . .'

However, she does not scruple to 'torment by letter' General Oakes in page after page of her grievances against James until Bruce and Sligo came back from their expedition to Smyrna. Now, her quarrel with James forgotten, she was preparing to enjoy a honeymoon with Michael and sent Dr Meryon to negotiate for the renting of a villa at Brusa. Nothing of a villa was this, but three cottages one of which was given to the doctor, one to the servants and the third to Hester and Michael.

Much to Meryon's disgust did he find himself segregated as if he, too, were a servant. He attributed this slight to Bruce's influence and was flattered to think that Bruce was jealous of him.

Sligo, who had again been treated to a rhapsodic account of her love affair with Bruce and her full admission of their relationship, had gone to Malta, bored with these intimate incessant revelations. And while those two were blissfully engrossed in their flagrant delight, the doctor in his isolated cottage, or on his solitary rides through the 'beautiful country' about which Hester raves in letters to various correspondents, Meryon sulked.

Brusa!

To the young Minister Plenipotentiary at Constantinople, Stratford Canning, with whom Hester had been on friendliest terms, later to involve herself in a violent disagreement as result of some diplomatic interference on her part to do with the French *Chargé d'affaires*, she writes, while still in Canning's good graces:

> How I wish you were here to enjoy this delicious climate. . . . The town of Brusa is situated at the foot of Mount Olympus. The view is quite delightful over an immense plain more rich and beautiful than anything I ever beheld covered with trees, shrubs and flowers. As for the women . . .

Notwithstanding her professed dislike of her own sex she is ecstatic about them. Once when out riding alone and dressed in the Turkish costume she had now adopted with its baggy breeches, embroidered tunic, fez and top boots, very much as a page would wear in the seraglio, she came upon a group of women bathing, nude. Sighting her they scrambled out with screams, and fled to be wrapped and veiled by their maids believing they were watched by a handsome blue-eyed youth with shocking intent upon their virtue. Hester was vastly amused and determined always to adopt male dress not only because it was more convenient for riding but so that she could venture, disguised as man or boy, where women except in the seraglio were not permitted.

She had no fear of interference from the high-up Pashas and Beys whose homosexual predilections might have caused her much embarrassment had not the fame of Lady Hester and her eccentricities spread throughout Pera and Constantinople. Moreover, as niece of the late Prime Minister of England, she could do no wrong. After two months in paradisiacal bliss with Michael at Brusa she, always on the move, rented a temporary residence at Bebec on the Bosphorus a few miles from Constantinople. There she contrived to meet and to be lavishly entertained by all the most distinguished persons at the Porte to the extent that the Pasha, at her request, allowed her to inspect one of the ships conducted by the Captain of the Fleet – on one condition: That she must not appear in women's dress. She was thankful to have become accustomed to male attire and quite understood, as she assured the Captain, who had little sense of humour but much pleasure in pleasuring women, that she could not very well come aboard his ship among his officers and men in a thin muslin gown half naked and damped to make it cling and, as dictated by the prevalent Western fashion for ladies' wear, to reveal the outline of their legs as far as might with decency be seen.

So she managed to obtain, she doesn't say how, probably from some old clo' Jew in the bazaar, the cast-off uniform of an officer in the service of his Britannic Majesty, and clambered on to the deck swaggering about in a military great coat, cocked hat, epaulettes and the inevitable top boots. This caused considerable shock to His Majesty's Minister, Canning, when he heard of it.

She was to shock him still more very soon.

It is likely that Michael did not entirely share Hester's enjoyment in these naval manœuvres although he was invited to accompany her in her inspection of the Turkish Fleet. In a letter to his father with whom Hester's correspondence indicates she is now on best of terms – Crauford Bruce has become resigned to the relationship since the great Pitt's niece has placed his son on a pinnacle 'as near perfection as human nature is allowed' – she tells how the Captain of the Fleet, at the Pasha's command, showed her over his ship. The Pasha said he would have had that honour himself had not his wife, or one of them, died that very morning. The bereaved widower mourned her for almost twenty-four hours and when the obsequies were over the next day, Hester and Michael were invited to dine with the Pasha the same evening. He appeared to be in cheerfullest mood; laughed, cracked jokes in approximate English-French and was delighted with Hester's uniform worn for his benefit at dinner. Bruce pressed by Hester, reluctantly agreed that he found the Pasha 'handsome and agreeable'.

Certainly Hester finds him so even if he did casually announce when receiving her alone – we wonder how Bruce liked that – how he had cut off a head a few hours earlier.

We are not told how often, or if on only one occasion, Hester is entertained alone by the recently widowed Pasha, but that she greatly attracted him is certain, for Michael writing to his father tells him he will be 'not a little amused' to learn that the Pasha has serious thoughts of proposing marriage to Hester 'and had imparted his intentions to her doctor'.

One may wonder how the doctor liked *that*.

All this might have brought about an eruption in the comparatively blissful household at Bebec had not a matter of more moment engaged the attention of all three, and reduced Hester to a state of hysteria that caused her to write round to everyone, including Lord Wellesley* full and febrile accounts of it.

'And all because,' she complained for the fiftieth time to that patient Griselda, Ann Fry, 'I wanted to spend the winter in the South of France. You know how this abominable Bosphorus air affects my chest. All very well in spring and summer but the winters here are dreadful.'

To which Ann could not but agree that the air of the Bosphorus was very chill indeed, even when the sun was shining and her ladyship must surely not risk any such danger as might result from . . .

'Don't burble at me!' was all Ann got from her ladyship for that. 'If I can't go to France, I'll go to – Jericho!'

Nor did she know that what she spoke at heated random would actually be very near the truth.

---

* Marquis of Wellesley, Secretary for Foreign Affairs, elder brother of Lord Wellington.

TWO

'But all I wanted was a *pass*port from the Frenchman,' was Hester's reiterated plaint to Michael when the stir her request had created assumed the proportions of a diplomatic crisis. 'From the fuss and bother that pompous little ass, Canning, has made about so trivial a thing to believe I am working as an enemy agent against *us* is ludicrous. And only because' – she was pacing the patio with panther-like strides while Michael sat slumped on the end of the *chaise longue* she had vacated – 'because,' a rising crescendo gave emphasis to repetition, 'I asked him to help me obtain a passport for the South of France!'

'After all,' ventured Michael in attempt to stem the tide, 'de Maubourg is *chargé d'affaires* for France, and —'

'Of course he is! That's why I asked him to see me and discuss it. There was no secrecy about it – all open and above board, at least —' a momentary pause, supplemented by Michael:

'Not quite above board, dearest, as it might perhaps have been interpreted by Canning – I mean that you met de Maubourg on the shore and at evening alone, and so —'

'And so what?' Hester ragefully demanded, 'what harm is there in that? I didn't want the whole of the French Embassy listening at keyholes if I saw him in his office.'

'Quite.' Bruce nodded placable agreement. When his love was in her tantrums, as he would have mildly described the Stanhope temper paramount in Hester now, it were best to let her have her head, or voice. 'You

89

had – I see that – to execute tact in dealing with, er, with one of Napoleon's emissaries, as it were, and, after all —'

'Oh, for goodness sake!' Hester clenched a fist in the air as if in ready descent on the inoffensive Michael. 'You and Ann – you burble, the pair of you, and offer no advice more than to rile me! I don't expect a simpleton like Fry to understand or to advise me how to get it into Canning's pig-head that I acted in all innocence. The mere fact I asked de Maubourg to meet me on the shore in full view of anyone who happened to be passing – I saw some of Canning's staff bathing and the Frenchman's lot too – and all talking and laughing on best of terms together. I was doing nothing that could with any sense have been interpreted as working for Bonaparte against US!' capitalized in burning indignation. 'As if *I*,' she thumped her chest, 'who have entertained our European allies and our own royalty on intimate terms as hostess at Downing Street, would be acting against the interests of my country when all I wanted was a passport to enable me to enjoy a winter on the Mediterranean and not at the mercy of this vile winter climate. You know what *last* winter did to me here on the Bosphorus. All very lovely in spring and summer-time, no doubt, but I'm not going to die of pleurisy just because Britain happens to be at war with France.'

'No, no! I mean, yes.' Michael essayed in a fluster to soothe, while the awful thought came to him that the fact she had been seen in close and seemingly accord with the French *chargé d'affaires* might well be misconstrued unless – the awful thought gained jealous impetus – unless his dearest love had made an assignation *not* for the plausible reason to obtain a passport for France, but for some other, more personal . . . No! Surely not! Caesar's wife and his, as near his wife as in God's sight she was . . . oh, no, no! Not that! Suspicion ran away with him to utter the unutterable.

'Not with that pimply faced gibbering ape! You and he...'

'What the devil,' his dearest love raged round on him, 'are you muttering about now?'

'Nothing, love, only that you should not walk – should be careful not to walk alone nor have to do with ... I mean, after all, we *are* at war with France, and none of them, especially their diplomatic service, apart that they're an enemy, is to be trusted and, after all, you know how they ... how people particularly ours always on the watch as Canning has to be ... and how they talk,' was the finale to this comprehensive speech.

'I know how *you* talk!' snapped Hester, 'to no purpose. Let me think now.... I'll write to Wellesley. Yes! I will. I'll tell him all. And I hope he'll have that priggish pig deported for having put the worst possible construction on a perfectly justifiable and friendly request.'

'Not the *worst* possible construction,' Michael gaining courage dared to say. 'After all to a man of limited capacity beyond his own – um – official calling, he might have believed de Maubourg had some other and more nefarious intent in this, er, friendly request.'

'If you insinuate that it might be thought I chose an evening by the sea to meet and be tumbled on the shore of the Bosphorus by that tape-worm de Maubourg, then,' again Hester raised a threatening fist while Michael ducked, 'you're a greater fool than Canning! Let me be now,' as, contrite, he strove to speak. 'Go indoors. And take the dog with you. He's too hot and so am I. I'll be sorry for what I've said if I say more, and so will you!'

'Poor precious,' murmured Hester referring not to Michael but to her dog. 'You want to get away from here too.'

Yet she must admit to the beauty of this land of which Lady Mary Wortley Montagu wrote: 'Here summer reigns with one eternal smile.' And while Hester composed her letter to Lord Wellesley her eyes wandered to embrace the glistening circle of Saracenic temples like clusters of carven pearl seen in the fervent sun at the feet of the cypress girdled mountains shouldering the sky to Asia; and above that lilac-tinted range a snow-capped peak, touched with fire, was raised to heaven . . . Mount Olympus.

The fragrance of the myriad roses breathed their perfume on the heavy air, and as she watched the Sultan's ships afloat on the dazzling waters of the Golden Horn amid the brown and red sails of merchantmen disgorging their cargoes of fruit, oil, spices, wine, her fugitive thoughts were captured to form words that would impress Lord Wellesley of her innocence in her association with de Maubourg.... *Because I despise the idea of war with an individual and cannot but lament a fault too common in our public men* . . . (I mustn't let him think I include him in this opinion. . . .) Let me see. Yes, I can let him know that *sooner or later over zealous nincompoops like Canning* (no, not nincompoops, diplomats), *must destroy the confidence our Government has placed in him.* . . .

Yes, I'll let him know that one of Canning's spies hobnobbing with those chattering Frenchmen had seen de Maubourg and me walking together on the shore. From the fuss all this has caused you'd think I'd been seen walking stark naked with him! Yes, and I'll tell his lordship to take no heed of a sneaking political Methodist's doubt of my loyalty to my country and who will next be teaching me my duty to my God. Aha! Yes, and I'll send it with a requeest to Wellesley. *The best reward for Canning's service here would be to appoint him as Ambassador Extraordinary abroad to various societies for the suppression of vice.* . . . That should do it!

The letter duly written and despatched and, when completed, covered several pages, is now in the British Museum; but it is doubtful if Wellesley ever received it for no answer is recorded. A copy was sent to Mr Canning who must have been in a rare state concerning his future due to that 'woman's malicious attack'. He conceived a horrific vision of her letter going the round of the Cabinet in a red despatch box, and himself a target of ridicule from uprising members who might have wished to step into his shoes as 'Ambassador Extraordinary for the suppression of vice', especially in Turkey. But nothing came of it more than to hasten Hester's departure from that village on the Bosphorus.

After the row with Canning and the racket in the French and English Embassies, for Hester had sent each a copy of her letter to Wellesley, Michael suggested it were better not to stand upon their going but to go.

'I always used to think,' Hester said with her wide boyish grin, 'that Turks and turkeys were one and the same when I was minding them at Chevening. Yes, I agree we must get out of here. It is getting too cold for me if not for my dog.' She stroked his head. He wagged a shaggy tail in response. 'The winters here could devastate me with those icy winds sweeping down from Olympus as well as from the sea. If we can't go to France we'll go to Egypt. You would like to dig around the Pyramids and excavate a mummified Pharaoh.'

'And get myself cursed for my pains!' Michael answered her grin, much relieved that he would not be drawn into argument to leave the scene of her battle with Canning from which neither had, as yet, emerged the victor, although first blood had been drawn by Hester's attack. 'But you won't,' Michael told her, 'be rid of the Turks so easily. The Ottoman Empire reaches farther afield than Athens and Asia Minor. You'll find Turkey in Africa, Syria, Baghdad, Damascus, Jerusalem and —'

'Then we'll follow the way of that road led by the Star of Bethlehem to visit the stable where the Child was born. . . . I can't wait!' Hester sprang up from where she reclined under an enormous striped cotton umbrella. 'Tell your man to pack your things, and I'll hurry the doctor with his. We'll start tomorrow!'

She had given up all hope of France.

Tomorrow and a series of tomorrows passed before all was ready for departure. A Greek vessel had been commandeered by Hester. The party consisting of Bruce and a young Cambridge friend of his, Henry Pearce, their several servants, the doctor and Ann Fry, sailed from the Golden Horn on a fine October day. Hester was allotted a cabin, none too clean, for herself and Ann, who slept on the floor along with the dog, while the doctor shared a cabin with Michael and Pearce.

As the dirty ill-equipped little ship left the harbour Hester stood on deck to see the lovely coastline gradually recede, and the snowy spur of Olympus draped in a mantle of diamond-pointed light.

'How glorious it is!' she cried to her attendant swains. Pearce, whom Hester dismissed as 'an ugly little quizz' and who had conceived the usual passion excited by her in any new male attachment, found her too entirely absorbed with Michael to make much use of him, and retired to adore at a distance.

'I always intended to climb Olympus,' Hester said, 'if you,' she turned to Michael, 'had not rushed me away in such haste.'

He forbore to remind her that the haste was hers, not his, and joined in her rapture of 'the Mountain of the gods and goddesses', as he was fatuously pleased to call it.

'Or should Lady Hester have ascended Olympus,' Pearce with equal fatuity enlarged, 'there would have been one more goddess to enrich the constellation of deities on high.'

'I think,' said Hester with a shiver and a sneeze, ignoring him and this nonsense, 'that the wind is rising and I need a warmer wrap. Ann! My shawl.'

The shawl was brought by a pale Ann who also had observed the rising wind with squeamish qualms. How to endure another dreadful sea voyage, she miserably wondered. God send, she prayed, that we shall arrive with safety where we are bound – and with our lives.

She did not pray in vain, for by a miracle they did arrive with their lives if not in safety and not where they were bound, but on a rock in the middle of the Aegean Sea.

The wind had risen to gale force and, as Hester's voyages seemed always to be attended by the caprice of the weather, they were twice driven off their course. When at length the island of Scio was reached they were delayed there for ten days waiting until fairer winds prevailed and they sailed through calmer waters until they landed at Rhodes where they stopped for a few hours to provision the ship. Little did they guess how soon they would return to that island. For two days they ran under sail and were half-way to Alexandria when a terrific southerly gale caught the vessel, tossed and buffeted by the violence of the storm that threatened every moment to capsize her.

Hester, below, striving to soothe the terrified Ann, heard a shout from the Greek captain to his crew, which she translated as: 'All hands to the pumps!'

The ship had sprung a leak.

But the pumps were out of order and quite useless. Despite the frantic efforts of the crew and passengers, the water flooded the deck and seeped through into the hold. The howl of the winds, the pitching and tossing of the frail craft as she struggled to combat the tumultuous waves that threatened every moment to sink her, was too much for the petrified Greek seamen. Three or four of them ran berserk and, lost of all control, flung themselves on their knees screaming to the Holy Mother to preserve them.

Hester, realizing the danger, bade Ann, no less frantic

than the crew, to pack whatever bare necessities might be needed, 'For we may have to take to the boat.'

'Oh, my lady, my lady!' wailed Ann. 'Is there a wreck?'

'Get on with the packing.' Hester had little patience for poor Ann's fright and plight. The maid had almost recovered her sea-legs during this voyage, but terror and the convulsions of the ship, that seemed to be standing on her bows one minute and performing acrobatics in the stern the next, was too much for her. Between bouts of sea-sickness she managed to collect a few clothes.

Then having attended to Ann and the excited dog, she went on deck to help Bruce, Pearce, and the doctor, all three assisting those of the crew who in the midst of the noise and confusion were not prostrate in prayer and fear.

Nor was the captain in much better case as he knew the ship was sinking and could do nothing to save her. Steering a perilous course for Rhodes he took heart when he sighted through the plunging sea what he thought to be the island. The one boat, a long-boat, was lowered and, helter-skelter, the sailors scrambled in, regardless of the captain's orders: 'The women first!'

The doctor had enough foresight to provide himself with a bag of dollars and a brace of pistols, but there was no time to salvage anything else. All their possessions, Meryon's treasured medicine chest, Hester's personal belongings, her jewels and gifts she had bought for friends, were lost as was also her dog.

Taking upon himself the duty of the captain to be the last to leave the ship, and for all Hester's coaxing, and despite her every effort to drag him from the sloping deck more than half submerged, he refused to budge, was swept overboard and lost in the stormy sea.

Hester, heart-broken, wept but still retained enough presence of mind to take the command which should have been the captain's, issuing orders until, after fruitless attempts to drag her dog to safety, she had to be hoisted into the boat.

But that which the captain had seen through the mountainous waves and the seething mists of spray was no island; only a barren rock. In all that nightmare of horror this, their one refuge, they eventually reached. None of the crew was lost although it is doubtful that the overcrowded, overweighted boat could have survived more than half an hour in such a sea.

On the leeward side of the rock when at last they were grounded on a strip of sand they found a narrow creek just large enough to land the boat; and nearby a cavity, scarcely a cave, but it gave some shelter for Hester and Ann from the onrush of the waves.

And there on that lonely rock, drenched to the skin, without food or drink, too utterly exhausted to care whether they lived or died, they laid themselves down wherever they could find a place to rest and intermittently to sleep through the deafening roar of waves and surf.

It was evening when they landed and at midnight the gale having somewhat lessened, the captain decided to get the boat across to Rhodes and bring back provisions. He would only take a few of his men rather than risk an overloading for with all the passengers and crew, the small craft, if too heavily laden, might capsize in those tumultuous seas. He promised to light a fire as signal that he had arrived on the island.

So off he went; and for thirty hours those huddled on the rock watched for the signal. None came. When at last all hope had gone, fearing the captain and his crew had perished with the boat, it was seen approaching. A feeble cheer went up, only to fade away when the boat riding the surf was beached on that strip of sand. Then it became apparent that the captain was not with the few who had returned, and they who brought provisions had already had their fill of food and drink and were riotously drunk on arrack, the native wine.

It was either a case of trusting themselves to these drunks of the captain's crew, for the remainder were too frightened to take command of the long-boat, or else to stay on the rock until daybreak in danger, if the storm increased, of being submerged in the torrent. They chose the first alternative: to depart there and then. And after several more hours of misery, for the rain was now falling in sheets from the lowering clouds to soak their half dry garments to the skin, they managed to make the island. But the boat was tossing like a nutshell in a whirlpool, and, as she touched the beach, a gigantic wave struck the boat. It was swamped and sank while they waded through the surf as best they could.

Hester, whose courage throughout these dreadful nights had never failed her, was now on the verge of collapse and unable to walk as she staggered up to the beach which proved to be marshland at the southern deserted part of the island. Bruce and Pearce, who had done more than their share of the work aboard the stricken ship that the seamen had refused to do, carried her, sinking up to their knees in slush, and finally came to a windmill and were received by the miller who seemed to be the only inhabitant of that isolated marsh.

They induced the miller to light a fire outside the mill on comparatively dry soil. Round this the men collected and slept the sleep of the bone-weary. Hester, on heaps of straw in the miller's granary, was thankful for any sort of couch and, regardless of pinpoints of red eyes glaring at her out of the dark or of an ominous scuttling and scratching, she slept, nor did she wake even when scampering bodies ran over her to scrabble where she lay. But Ann, overwrought and still in abject terror, fell into hysterics and screamed to the somnolent Hester: 'Rats, my lady! There are rats here! Hundreds of *rats* . . . Oh, oh! My lady! I can't – I *can't* stay here with *rats*!'

She was eventually quietened, a resting place found for her within sight and sound of Dr Meryon who kept watch over her while Bruce guarded his love. She slept again, and did not wake until daybreak. Then the miller was despatched to a nearby village to fetch a conveyance that would take them to a more habitable lodging.

The morning after the storm, in one of those freaks of nature, was a clear, bright, sun-warmed day. The exhausted travellers awaited the return of the miller. Would he, too, as did the captain of the sunken vessel, desert them?

Hester had lost everything with exception of a treasured miniature of General Moore and the blood-stained gauntlet Anderson brought to her that John had worn at Corunna. These, concealed on her person, had not been swept away with all the rest of her belongings. But instead of lamenting their loss she grieved only for the loss of her dog between intervals of comforting Ann and ordering the cowardly crew and the servants to bestir themselves and collect what rags of clothes were left to the party.

The miller at length came back with a heterogeneous procession of mules, asses and villagers. Meryon had mastered sufficient Greek to make the miller understand that he and his auxiliaries would be well rewarded for their services. Having saved his bag of dollars and produced coins enough to bribe them, the doctor saw his party mounted on mules and donkeys and went off on a mule in search of an inn or a roof to shelter them.

Meanwhile, Hester and Ann on the donkeys, the men on mules, and most of the crew lagging behind on foot endlessly bewailing and cursing the fates, the English, the 'Woman who rode as a man and was a witch, a demon or the devil who had brought disaster to the ship and them', they came to the one available shelter within miles. This was reached after more than eight hours of jogging and bumping over rocky mountain passes along a path so narrow and bordering a precipice that one false step from their mules or asses would have hurled them to destruction. Ann, now resigned to any sudden death and had made her peace with God, the party arrived at a first halting place that could offer them a roof.

Scarcely more inviting than the mill, it was a flea-infested stable yet preferable to any hovel in the village, even more vermin-ridden and unspeakably filthy.

There they spent the night.

Meryon, hoping to secure some bare necessities and money from the British agent at Rhodes, having got rid of almost all his bag of dollars among the remainder of the crew who were of no help whatsoever from the after effects of arrack, had now gone by boat to Smyrna where he might find better equipment and clothes for his destitute party.

Hester, whose courage had not failed under circumstances that would have daunted the strongest of men, finally gave up and fell into a high fever. But there was still a long way to go over trackless mountains and rocky crags until they came to Lindo that still bore relics of ancient Greece and the ruins of Crusaders' strongholds when they had vanquished the Saracen. These would have engaged Michael's interest had not Hester, now in sorry case, called another halt.

She shivered and was hot, burned and was cold, and saddle sore from jolting all those weary miles, while with her ragged clothes that barely covered her and her hair hanging in lanky wisps about her shoulders, she presented a pitiable sight. As also did Michael and Pearce. Unshaven, a stubble of beard on their chins, bare-legged, shirtless, they and the rest of them might well have been mistaken for a caravan of wandering Jews or gipsies, to rouse hostility from the villagers had not the news of the shipwreck resounded through the island.

An exiled Greek who had come to cross purposes with his masters, the Turks, having heard of their arrival, offered Hester the hospitality of his house. It was noised among the island that an English princess had been one of the victims of the wreck and they all turned out to see the Great Lady. What was their astonishment when they saw the 'Great Lady' naked to the waist, the rags of what had been her gown clutched across her breasts with one hand, the other hanging on to the bridle rein of her donkey, and herself all but falling off the strip of webbing that served as a saddle, while Ann behind her was even more scantily covered, to her everlasting shame. What mortal sin, she may have asked her God, had she committed to be so cruelly served while attending her mistress to the best of her well-trained service as lady's maid? Not only to be cast adrift in an open boat on a roaring sea, wrecked on a rock and every minute expecting to be drowned, but to be thrown here among a lot of savages, so to Ann the gesticulating peasants must have appeared, and to be only half clad and indecently at that! And as for her ladyship . . . Oh, for a comb, a brush for her lady's hair and a needle and thread, mourned the perfect abigail, that she might set to some sort of rights her ladyship's garments, if garments they could be called.

However she was somewhat comforted by the reception accorded them by the kindly Greek, a Mr Philipaki, who instantly became Mr Philip Parker to Ann and from whom she was handed over to a serving maid with instructions from 'Mr Philip Parker' who could speak and understand a little English, to supply Ann with all she required for her lady's toilet.

Hester's recuperative powers, notwithstanding that her health had never been robust, now aided her recovery so that she was able to resume her journey after two or three days' rest.

Bidding a grateful farewell to that good Samaritan, her host, who had been equally attentive to Bruce and Pearce, the party proceeded on their way.

As they went jolting along the rough track to the town

of Rhodes, interspersed with villages at intervals, they came upon a *fiesta* in a clearing. It must have been a saint's day in the Greek Orthodox Church and even though, as Hester put it, 'Turks abound here', they could still practise their own religion in these isolated hamlets. The peasants in their picturesque native dress were partaking with the wildest hilarity in their dances in which Hester joined, nothing the worse for having been wrecked on a rock in the midst of a storm-tossed sea.

Whether Bruce, always something of a prude, approved to see his 'more than wife in the sight of God' as he regarded their relationship, prancing, whirling, shrieking with the best of them and, clasped to bearded rustics, performing orgiastic convolutions, is questionable. Then, as evening fell and bonfires were lighted, the leaping flames lent a lurid, fantastic glare to the scene that to Bruce, was a shocking display of barbarism.

Not so to Hester, excited as a schoolgirl with the fun of the fair. One of her most endearing qualities was this chameleon-like adaptability that could change her in a trice from the 'Great Lady' who commanded and demanded respect, could order a ship's mutinous crew in the face of incredible danger, and yet could revert to a youthful spontaneous enjoyment of a frolic that defied all conventional propriety.

It may have been just this, to Bruce, her spontaneous descent from the sublime to the ridiculous that caused in him the first, if subconscious, criticism of her whom he had placed upon a pedestal and looked up to with an almost deific worship. Perhaps, too, this was the reason why all men who fell at her feet, professed undying love, and, as was her boast, she 'could have married fifty times' and never did, had failed her when it came to the point of cementing a possible union.

And now, as she remounted her ass, Bruce was constrained hesitatingly to reprimand his love.

'Forgive me, dearest, but don't you think that it is

rather indiscreet to, er, have joined in that – um – I mean to have danced with those peasants. After all they are under Turkish rule and we, as Britons, should not – do you think – encourage what the Turks forbid – that's to say – after all they are serfs and must not follow their own religion only what the Turks command. And it is a kind of religious festival, is it not? After all, we have already committed a breach of etiquette in accepting hospitality from a Greek and he being exiled it might be a case of international law – I mean from the legal or political —'

'What the devil are you gabbling about?' demanded Hester, the flush of her exertions deepening to a flaming red as her temper rose. 'Do you think I care a damn' – Michael flinched at that – 'Yes, a damn!' she reiterated loudly, 'for these lousy Turks and their tyrannical dominance of Greece which they have conquered? The Greeks were civilized aeons before the Turks had emerged from savagery. They aren't much better now – a lot of heathens. Only the Jews and the Greeks are civilized in Turkey. These peasants here,' with the stick she used to urge her ass, she pointed to the whirling shouting chanting crowd of dancers, flower-crowned, 'they are simple Christian folk. They have but one wife each and the priest marries them in Holy Church. They are as they are and I am as *I* am and if you don't like me as I am then you know what you can do!'

It was not the first rift in their harmonious lute. Michael took fright. His love, he excused her while excusing himself, had been through too much, far too much. Her nerves were shaken and so were his or he wouldn't have been so tactless. She was right as always. The Turks were not to be compared to the Greeks in the decencies of human life and living, even as with these simple village folk. . . . He may have forgotten the scurvy trick played on them by the Greek captain of the wrecked ship and the cowardly behaviour of the sailors. He had no right to reproach her for what, after all – (this repetitive turn of phrase often occurred in his conversation with her and as often did rile his 'love') – was, after all, but innocent fun and a reverent joyous gesture to the Saint of their God. 'Who,' Bruce said aloud, 'is our God and has taught us to love our neighbour as —'

'Stop muttering,' Hester flung at him. 'I've had quite enough from you. I've noticed of late that you are becoming as priggish as Canning. . . . Let's on our way. We shan't be in Rhodes until midnight at this rate.'

She hastened her head-drooping donkey with a touch of her heel. Ann, who, on her ass, sat in bone-aching misery, gave thanks to her Maker that her mistress was about to leave these disgraceful performances, while Hester called over her shoulder at the much subdued Bruce:

'God send Meryon back from Smyrna with money enough to buy us new clothes. I'm covered in flea-bites and have scratched myself sore, and picked up a dozen of other sorts too, from my partners in the dance.'

What a woman! What an angel; What a – what the deuce, groaned Bruce within himself, am I to do with her?

What to do with her, as he wrote to his father in an account of the shipwreck was that: 'We are as yet quite in the dark as to our future plans. . . . Lady Hester intends to put on Turkish dress.'

*   *   *

The elaborate dress of a Turkish Bey she had adopted and in which Michael declared she looked enchanting, delighted her. She also dressed Ann as her page after the style of the boys she had seen walking behind their seigneurs. 'It is for your protection,' she told Ann, who made mild demur at having to don a pair of baggy pantaloons, embroidered shirt and a fez. 'It will ensure that

104

you and I can walk in male dress unmolested by the Turks because no Turkish women may be received or talk to a man, so you and I' – she stood admiring herself in a mirror – 'will be quite safe from interference.'

She spared no expense on her various costumes much to Meryon's concern. Having borrowed or been subsidized by the British Consul at Smyrna with sufficient means for their immediate needs, the doctor saw his ready cash fast diminishing. Bruce and Pearce were so taken with Hester's get-up that they also rigged themselves out as Turks since it would have been difficult to obtain English tailored suits. As both Hester and Bruce were recklessly extravagant they gave not a thought to ways and means while Michael could sponge on his father more than his allotted allowance of two thousand five hundred a year.

So vastly did her Turkish disguise become her that Michael said jokingly, if a trifle apprehensively:

'You'll have all the Pashas and Sheiks on their knees to you now. You know their predilection for boys.'

Which furthered her delight in herself and the clothes she elected to wear. The most favoured of these consisted of a silken shirt, a striped waistcoat, a baggy pair of pantaloons, lavishly embroidered, and a turban with a cluster of flowers at the side. But what pleased her most of all was her sword, a trifling dagger of a thing, stuck in a belt round her waist that also held a brace of pistols.

After a series of misfortunes her luck seemed to have turned when yet another passage was offered her by Captain Hope of His Majesty's frigate *Salsette* bound for Alexandria. The Captain, having heard of the disastrous voyage to Rhodes, at once came to Hester's assistance, and found her, as did Michael, irresistible in her Turkish dress.

But luck did not attend her on this voyage although less calamitous than formerly, for so soon as they sailed from Rhodes they ran into another terrific storm. While poor suffering Ann lay in her bunk, Hester, impervious to the tossings and rollings and plungings of the frigate and the shriek of the winds, roamed the deck with the Captain when he was not on the bridge.

Bruce, from afar, jealously watched the Captain's attentions and was thankful when passing the sea of Marmara, *Salsette* came into harbour at Rosetta; thence when the storm had abated and the sea was a lazy blue, the winds fair and the ship yielding herself gently to the tranquil waves they sailed into Alexandria.

Here Hester was received by the British Resident with the usual deference due to her as the niece of 'the revered, alas, late Prime Minister' whom he had only met once, if ever, very briefly. He placed a house at her disposal, and Bruce with Pearce and the doctor were lodged in an inn, but:

'I *hate* Alexandria,' Hester complained to Bruce. 'It stinks! It is hideous – I can't and won't stay here.' With which both Bruce and Meryon heartily agreed.

'Alexandria is more dusty than Black Friar's Bridge on a windy day,' was the doctor's opinion, 'and more crowded with blind than a hospital for ophthalmia. . . .'

And so to Cairo.

Cairo. . . . Hester's arrival created the usual stir, especially as few, if any, Englishwomen had ever before been seen in that city, and wearing, of all things, the dress of a Turkish nobleman which brought crowds of excited Egyptians to watch her and her retinue pass, while speculation ran high as to her sex. The daughter of an English royal prince or – the son of one?

The Pasha, learning the advent of her whom he had heard to be the daughter, niece, or close relative if not the widow – he was in rather a fix as to the exact relationship to royalty of the famous Lady who chose to explore the Orient and Egypt with a suite of noblemen and her 'Court physician' – received her with reverential pomp.

Meryon, whose own exploitation of his service to the 'royal' lady, had penetrated far and wide, was welcomed with similar respect, as also were Michael and Pearce.

A house had been found for Hester close by the Usbekieh Palace of the Pasha. Not large enough to take all her party, Pearce and Meryon had to find their own lodgings, and Bruce, of course, shared Hester's. She, prepared for some flamboyant reception from the Pasha, had rioted in an orgy of costume bought for herself and Michael. She chose the sumptuous dress of a Tunisian Bey with pantaloons of purple and gold. Her turban and girdle were of Kashmir shawls. Meryon shuddered at the expense. He made a list of all she had spent, the whole of it totalling, with the extravagant equipment she ordered for Bruce and Pearce, something near to three hundred guineas. The doctor was more modestly attired in the costume of a Turkish *effendi*, but only the dress of a Pasha or prince would satisfy Hester.

After four or five days she was ready to be received by the Pasha, Mehemet Ali, Viceroy of Egypt. He sent a procession to escort her with horses richly caparisoned, to mount her and her entourage, preceded by at least a dozen officials carrying silver sticks that the spectators might judge the importance of the visitors. And thus through the narrow dirty streets she and her cortège arrived at the entrance to the Palace.

The Pasha, at Hester's first sight of him, was disappointing: an ugly little man with a long beard and grey as cinders. Born not of the Pharaohs as she had supposed, but of humble origin, he had been a corporal, or its equivalent, in the Turkish Army even as was the great self-styled Emperor, whose dwarfish shadow, magnified to gigantic proportions, held Europe in the hollow of his hand.

Hester was welcomed by the Pasha in a garden pavilion adjoining the harem, elaborately painted and gilded. The doctor, Michael and Pearce filed behind and were gestured to be seated on stools while the Pasha, bowing nose to knees, conducted Hester to a red velvet divan magnificently embroidered in gold, and took his seat beside her.

It is likely he may have been embarrassed as how to address one so evidently of indeterminate sex, as even were the crowds in the streets who had hailed her as Princess, Prince, Lady, Lord, in their varied vernacular of which she understood no word.

Sherbet was offered in crystal glasses, coffee in delicate porcelain cups and, to be on the safe side in case his visitor was not a great Lady but a beardless youth, son of some English noble, she was ceremoniously offered the *narghileh*, the hookah. This with a withering glance at the grinning Bruce, she politely refused saying she did not smoke. Nor did the doctor accept the offer knowing the effect it would have had upon him; but the other two did, 'out of bravado', Hester told them later, 'silly fools!' . . . And watched them turn a sickly yellow after several puffs, and excuse themselves to their host saying if it pleased him to allow them to walk in the garden – and were hustled away by the doctor before they were disgraced.

So soon as they retired an interpreter appeared, for Mehemet Ali spoke no English and very little French in which Hester had attempted to converse.

From behind the lattices of the harem windows, where roses, flowering shrubs and creepers climbed in colourful profusion, veiled eyes peeped between the slats at the handsome young man of noble birth, as his rich dress of a Tunisian Bey proclaimed him.

With the aid of the interpreter, the Pasha's private secretary, who spoke fluent French and some English, Hester learned how Mehemet Ali had reorganized the country he now ruled and which had been victimized by tyrannical governance for centuries.

In spite of his unprepossessing appearance she could

not but admire this man of insignificant birth who had risen to power over a race whom he called – 'Semi-barbarians crushed under the heel of rulers who had not progressed since the days of the Pharaohs'. 'Granted,' he warmed to his subject, 'that my predecessors, aeons before Christ, your Lord, were masters of culture and of medicine to rival Hippocrates, and of the arts unsurpassed since the days of ancient Greece. See the glorious temples now in ruins. Look at the Pyramids. And what of those inspired slaves who built them before the beginning of time?'

Yet it was by the massacre of innocent Mamelukes that this puny little man whose tremendous inner force transcended his outward physical deficiencies, had brought the country he had conquered through a bloody holocaust to a better understanding of life and living. . . . 'Not as worms,' as if he took that thought from her, 'to be crushed under foot by the Lords of Creation as they believed them to be, but as human beings with the right to live as such!'

But, she wondered, could the shedding of blood and the extinction of thousands of bondmen, or the exodus of hundreds as in the time of Moses, bring about a more civilized and humane discipline among the overseers of these, his subjects, those poor wretches she had seen lining the streets where she had passed? Beggars exposing awful sores; children whose eyelids were black with flies; and women whose starved breasts suckled dying babies, and who raised feeble cheers of welcome to her in chorus with their skeletal men who hailed her as Princess – or Prince – from another world, a heaven as theirs was hell?

That first visit to Mehemet Ali was followed by several more. Their short acquaintance developed into a friendship based on mutual admiration. If on Hester's side it were respect for a cultured intelligence she had not expected to find among those whom Michael looked upon as inferiors in breeding, birth and caste, the Pasha regarded her with something warmer than respect. If he could have conquered a country to establish a governance on the lines of that great Englishman, the Lady's uncle – there was no doubt now as to her sex – it may be he aspired to conquer her. What though he were lowly born, was not that world famous conqueror, a Corsican peasant, of lesser birth than he? Was he not respected, not only by this Lady but by the leading diplomats of Britain for having brought order and discipline to a race of people who, but for him, might have deteriorated into savages? . . . So he may have reasoned while overwhelming his august visitor with favours.

She was presented by the Pasha with two magnificent Arab chargers. Michael received a handsome Kashmir shawl and a jewelled hilted sword as token of his relationship with the Lady of which Mehemet Ali soon became aware and did not at all resent. He knew enough of English modes and morals to realize that the pursuit of love was not necessarily bound by the sacrament of Christian marriage in London's High Society. He had learned, by his own deduction and from hearsay, that in the ruling European classes especially of England and France, there were as many seraglios as here in his domain; the difference being that while concubinage was accepted in the East, in Egypt and Asiatic Turkey as man's natural prerogative, the English practised their polygamy *sub rosa*.

Under these circumstances Michael must have found his position intolerable. To see her – his 'more than wife', as he constantly assured himself – honoured above all women in the land, above all the wives of the Pasha, and to be homaged by Mehemet Ali and his Court as if she were royalty and he, Michael, no more than an appendage, was gall to him.

He let her know it.

'Is it not time,' in the fastness of their privacy – the villa hard by the Pasha's palace – 'that you abandon this fancy dress of a male impersonator and conduct yourself as befitting,' he was always inclined to pomposity when in disagreement with her if he ever dared to be, 'as befitting the social rank and heritage to which you belong?'

'And where do I belong?'

Seated cross-legged on a divan, wearing a full sleeved white shirt, embroidered waistcoat and crimson velvet trousers, her head turbanless, her long dark hair falling straight as rain about her shoulders, she glanced up at him glowering above her. She spread her charming hands. 'And where or what is my heritage? Cast off, ignored by my father, my family? Those who bowed to me, even as do these out here' – she nodded toward the gardens seen between the jalousies of her windows that overlooked the grounds of the Palace where a few of the courtiers strolled – 'do bow to me as when I was *persona grata* at Downing Street, niece of the greatest Prime Minister our country has ever known or will know unless another, a century hence, should take his place.' (Will she never forget who she *was*? It is becoming an obsession with her, groaned Michael's inner man.) 'If I should choose to explore lands unfamiliar to us in England, or to any woman of England, is that unfitting to the niece of Pitt?' (Say it again, inly muttered Michael.)

She said it again. 'And as the niece, beloved of our greatest man of politics if, in these "barbaric" countries as you call them who are more civilized here in Cairo than in many of our European capitals – if I wish to exploit the advanced views and ideology of the great Pitt —'

'It is not Pitt,' he came out with hotly, 'whom you exploit, it's yourself.'

She was appalled. His criticism stung her to the quick. Who would have believed that this delightful young lover whom she had taken to share her life would reveal so totally unexpected a facet? She had given him absolute freedom to sever their connection despite his earnest demand that they should be lawfully husband and wife. That he, as it seemed, was incapable of sympathizing with her motive in pursuing her explorations into these countries in order to obtain a more complete understanding of the customs and character of their people that were only just emerging from the oppression of antediluvian tyranny, mortified her while at the same time she longed for his approval. . . . Did he tire of her? Was their idyllic love, their absorption in each other, only an ephemera?

She showed nothing of these fears in the face upturned to his. True, she had paled slightly, but if he noticed it he may have thought it the reflection from the green slats of the jalousies at the window to shield the sun from the noonday heat.

She took a sweetmeat from a gold bonbonnière, another of the Pasha's gifts, meditatively crunched it, and:

'Are you tiring of me?' she asked him calmly, the question somewhat marred by the bulge of a sugared almond in her cheek. 'Do you want to go back to your father and all that England holds for you? As you knew from the first you are free to go whenever you will. I have written this to your father in my letters to him. I would wish,' her voice a little faltered, 'to see you married to – to one of your own age more worthy of you than am I.'

'No, no!' He was beside her on the divan, the breath of his words on her lips. 'My love, my dearest love! Forgive me. It is I who am not worthy of you! How could another – a chit of a girl – usurp you and all that you are to me – all I want of life? You are everything in the world to me. You should know that.'

She took his face between her hands, swallowing simultaneously the last of the sweet and the lump in her throat.

'Do I know it? Have I any right to know it?' She spoke more to herself than to him.

'The right,' his voice was muffled on her shoulder, 'to

know what *I* know who am your lover and your love. Unless,' he raised his head, his fair young face, burnt red with the sun, had whitened leaving it a mottled pink, 'unless there is someone else?'

'Who else?' She put her mouth to his. 'Who but you can claim and take me? Unless,' repetition mocked him, '*unless* it were the Pasha!'

'No!' he sprang up, his fists clenched at his sides. 'Not him – not that – that —'

'Barbarian?' she interposed, a smile hovering. 'Are you jealous of *that*!'

'Of course,' he unfisted his hands to take hers. 'Of course I'm jealous. You sing his praises till I sicken. There never was so intelligent, so brilliant, so – Good God!' his voice cracked. 'All the ridiculous fuss and palaver that attends him is poured at your feet. How can you be flattered by his fulsome salaams and ostentation? You should despise them – and him. He is yellow – yellow skinned and yellow-livered.'

She gave a throaty chuckle.

'Have you taken upon yourself the medical knowledge of Meryon that you can know the colour of his liver?'

'I see.' He drew away from her, sulky mouthed. 'I see I'm just a joke to you – all my love, my worship, adoration —'

She covered her ears.

'Spare me the superlatives. I have heard them too often. They grow stale.'

'As do I?' Again he clutched her to him.

'Darling,' her voice and hands were a caress. 'There is only one of our quartet here who grows stale, and he is your familiar, Pearce. No, listen' – as he drew away, his forehead in a frown and a muscle moving in his jaw – 'I had meant to tell you this before, but I didn't want to interfere with a friendship that I thought to be necessary to you. I knew it was necessary to him who fastens himself on you for what he can get. Send him away. Let us be

113

rid of him. He is only an idler and encumbrance, battening on what your father allows us – allows *you*,' she corrected hastily. 'I have already sent your father a list of our expenditures.' (She omitted that she had left out the more extravagant of hers.) 'I didn't dare put down what Pearce has cost us. It is he,' she threw this at him with the certainty he would take it, 'who has turned you against me and put into your innocent trusting head these ideas about me and my interests here in Cairo. If he should go with us into the Holy Land as you know I intend to visit, heaven knows what mischief he will make between us and what he will cost us – or your father.'

His frown relaxed. 'You are only saying what I had sometimes thought. He is a born sponger but – after all we were at Cambridge together, and so I feel a sort of loyalty to him knowing he is hard up. And I thought the least I could do was to let him join with us. And – after all – he does pay what he can towards his expenses.'

'As much as will sit on a farthing.' She slid him her impudent grin, so like a mischievous boy's, and stretching her arms above her head, yawned widely. 'It is time for my siesta, and I've had my fill of Cairo now, so you need have no fear that I intend to compete with the Pasha's dozen wives. Concubinage *ad lib* does not appeal to me.'

She blew him a kiss from her finger tips, said: 'Remove that black scowl off your face. It doesn't become you. Do, my darling, cultivate a sense of humour. Life is too serious to be taken seriously. As for our – my,' she corrected, 'adventures here and everywhere, don't forget it has been prophesied that I am to be Queen of the Jews. Aha! That makes you smile. You are adorable when you smile – it makes you look about ten. So go and get your baggage packed. We will leave for Jaffa this week and then – Jerusalem!'

Much to Michael's relief they did leave for Jaffa that week after Hester had taken an effusive farewell of her 'dear friend' the Pasha. He, for his part, expressed his profound grief and disappointment at losing so illustrious a visitor and extracted a promise, which she never intended to keep, that she would return for a longer, if not an indefinite sojourn in this land which he had made his own, and – dared he hope – would be hers? This hopeful assumption as reported to Michael caused Hester much amusement but Michael none at all.

At Jaffa where they stayed a few days while making preparations for their journey to the Holy Land, Pearce, who saw that he was *de trop* and anticipating a tactful dismissal, left them to go his own way by a different route from theirs and so to England.

The arrival at Jaffa just after Easter found the town swarming with pilgrims on their way back from Jerusalem. The crowds, the babel of voices in various languages, the heat, the flies, the mosquitoes and the stench of the narrow filthy streets hastened Hester's determination to get out of it as soon as she came in.

A born organizer she took upon herself to make all arrangements for their transport to Jerusalem. Eleven camels were hired for their luggage and thirteen horses for themselves and their servants with two soldiers and a bodyguard of janissaries sent by the Governor of Jaffa, to accompany them through Arab territory where the Bedouins were always on the look-out for foreign travellers.

The British agent having been notified of the arrival of Lady Hester Stanhope, placed his house at her disposal, and received her with the deference to which she was now accustomed as the niece of Pitt.

Michael may have found travelling through the Holy Land with his 'more than wife' was something of a deterrent to a passionate relationship, since the men must be segregated from the women and he forced to share a cell in a Franciscan monastery with the doctor. The tempers of these two, never on the best of terms, were strained to breaking point at such unwelcome propinquity and both much relieved when the preparations for their journey were complete.

It was an imposing cavalcade that left Jaffa, headed by Hester on her Arab charger riding in oriental style with two grooms on either side. Her saddle and bridle were of crimson velvet, gold embroidered, bought in Cairo at the expense of Crauford Bruce, her father out-of-law. Her travelling habit, also bought in Cairo, was equally extravagant, an embossed satin waistcoat, red cloth jacket and trousers, and a white burnous. Ann Fry on an ass, and Michael and the doctor on horses, all wore Turkish dress. Poor Ann riding cross-saddle in trousers, had long given up all hope of heaven, having become one of 'those heathens in these outlandish clothes', which to her simple mind and her well-trained service as handmaid to the 'Quality', damned her to everlasting. Not but what she must have been comforted by the thought that she would be in good company with her mistress down below.

The country between Jaffa and Ramlah, their next halt, was rich in barley fields, and undulating lowlands, the road bordered with hedges that, had they not been of prickly pear and shrubs unknown to English soil, might have been an English lane yet there was nothing English in the sight of what the doctor thought to be a plague of grasshoppers covering the fields to right and left of them. On inquiring of a guide who answered in Arabic of which Meryon knew a little, he was told they were locusts causing devastation to the crops and ruin to the farmers. They passed trees and an isolated farmhouse, all of which looked to be mantled in a bright green cloak; and as they advanced they saw that the young wheat had been entirely demolished leaving only the bare brown earth. The sight was appalling.

'Locusts!' Hester shuddered. 'Was there not a plague of locusts when Moses brought the children of Israel out of bondage? History repeats itself.'

'Only,' Michael reminded her, as he ranged his horse alongside hers, 'we are not children of Israel, nor are we in bondage.'

'If I am not,' she laughed round at him, 'you are. Do you not always say you are enslaved by me? But if you wish you can be as free as that skylark.' She pointed with her whip to a small fluttering thing which, startled by their approach, soared upward into the blue from its nest under a shrub.

'He is not free,' Michael said following the flight, his eyes screwed against the sun's fierce glare. 'Already he is marked.' And in his turn he pointed to a circling hawk. 'See that – it's a buzzard.'

'Poor little lark! She can escape – she *must* escape! I can't bear it if she's caught.'

'She will be caught, and there is no escape once the hawk eye spots his prey. As it was in the beginning when you first looked at me.'

She laughed again, a very little, and with a twist of her lip rode on urging her horse to a gallop while her blood raced to a questioning beat. What *arrière pensée* lay behind that half jesting remark? Did he fret against the bit even as did this mettlesome young stallion until she gave him his head? Did he find her too possessive, too masterful? Was she the master, he the mistress? A whimsical smile broke again into laughter, unmirthful. 'As it was in the beginning. . . .' Or, when he pointed to that lovely doomed skylark, was he pointing to his end?

She slowed her horse to a jog trot. She had left the caravan some distance behind, with its camels, asses, janissaries and poor Ann, bumping along on her donkey. She had been cruel to be kind making the poor little creature wear trousers! Cruel to be kind to him too, who was her whole life's love. . . . Was he? Or was not the love of her life adventure?

Their way now led through a rough ascending path hewn from the rock of the mountain that replaced the gentle undulating valley and the spreading fields that had not suffered demolition from the locusts. It was nearing dusk; the sun's strength had lessened, and a slight breeze sprang up to dry the beads of sweat on her brow below the heavy burnous. She flung it off and let it hang by its cords at her neck. She was feeling tired, her bones ached. . . . I'm not so young as I was, she thought, dismally. I could ride fifty miles once and not tire.

A light, like a will-o'-the-wisp, beckoned on a hillside. She called to Michael who came up to her: 'Look! That must be a village. Ask the dragoman.'

It was a village owned, so the dragoman told them, by Abu Ghosh, the Sheik. 'But,' they were warned, 'the Sheik does not favour travellers or pilgrims in his domain where he is so greatly feared. They say he holds the keys of the gates to Jerusalem.' . . . It seemed he exacted a toll from all travellers to the Holy Land but, on perceiving the elaborate caravan descending the mountain path, the Sheik realized that these were no ordinary pilgrims. Hester in her magnificent Turkish dress, the splendid trappings of her horse heading the procession of eleven camels loaded with baggage, and mules, asses, and what appeared to be an army of servants, convinced him that this must be the Prince of some great European state.

The village they now entered nestled among terraced vineyards, fig trees and olive groves. Here the dragoman suggested they should encamp for the night. A suitable place to pitch the tents was found in a clearing, and the servants busied themselves in erecting the marquees, six of them gaily painted with flowers bought in Egypt at the expense of Bruce senior. All this increased the Sheik's impression that his visitor, if not a royal Prince, was at least a nobleman making the Grand Tour.

Abu Ghosh, hastening from his house, received Hester with fulsome salaams, and she having readjusted her hooded burnous and bundled her hair under it, presented him with the face of a young man of such remarkable beauty and so fair a skin that the Sheik was at once attracted as an Arabian Daphnis might have been to a ravishing young Damœtus.

When Hester introduced herself, whose name and fame had infiltrated even to these outposts of Arabia, he, realizing his mistake, at once insisted she and her entourage should do him the honour of accepting supper prepared by some of his wives. This consisted of a dish of minced meat rolled in vine leaves; vegetable marrow stuffed with rice and more mince meat of doubtful origin, possibly goat; a lamb roasted whole, and four rather ancient boiled fowls; a Lucullan feast served by four of the Sheik's wives.

At nightfall Abu Ghosh with his own bodyguards kept watch over the encampment against marauding robbers, and ordered a fire to be lighted to ward off jackals and hyenas.

The night was still and sultry. A moon like a large silver coin hung in the grape-bloom purple sky among a galaxy of stars.

Having sent Ann to bed on the canvas truckle that served each for a couch, Hester, for all the fatigues of the long journey, was unable to sleep.

She drew aside the entrance to their tent and stood entranced. Here she was at the gate to the Holy Land which she believed to be her destiny as prophesied that she should be Queen of the Jews, to instil into a nomadic tribe of Arabs, some said descended from the slaves of Israel in bondage, the word of Christ. . . . But what right had she, she asked of the star-laden night, to impose her beliefs upon those whose word was the Koran? Both East and West are God's. He is no respecter of persons or places. He who made male and female does not differentiate between race or creed and colour. White, black, yellow, we are all one with You! She raised her eyes to the high vault of heaven, shimmering in a silvery moon-haze. You up there and everywhere, even this – her foot touched a dry blade of grass – all are Yours even as those tethered camels yonder. She could hear a muffled munching, theirs or the asses who browsed in the bush? And the stamp of a restless horse – all of us and these God's beasts of burden, are one with Him, so why should I dare to take upon myself the lesson that Paul taught when he, blinded, saw . . . on the road to Damascus?

Sleep-forsaken she unfastened her night robes, and, half naked, let the cool night air embrace her.

Then, aware of the watchful Sheik, a ghostlike white figure looming near, she hurriedly closed the canvas.

In the adjoining tent, Michael and the doctor slept. She could hear a heavy breathing intermingled with the doctor's snores, not Michael's, he never snored. She was in two minds to waken him with whispers:

'Come out and let us lie together on God's warm earth'. . . . To love and be loved in our full consummation here in the land where the first of us were mated in what may have been their garden hereabouts. She had often wondered if original sin was the discovery of love between man and woman. . . . Love, a pretty word for the half-sister of lust. Was her love for Michael, his for her, just that? With my body I thee worship, which would have been said over us had we knelt at an altar before a priest of God. Hypocrisy! Yes, marriage in the world I have escaped is hypocrisy. These Arabs and Turks are lawfully entitled to their wives and concubines – as many as they can afford! Only, she bit back a gurgle of laughter, I, who ape the man that Michael and I might well be a David and Jonathan, cannot afford him as my concubine nor as my husband, nor can he afford me as a wife! How silly can one get in the moonlight. I'm moon-struck. . . .

Long she lay among cushions brought by the Sheik for her comfort on the truckle bed in her tent, seeing before her fastened lids a kaleidoscope of incidents, minutiae yet engraved in the archives of memory resurrected. Their first meeting, her surrender to him in that unforgotten night when she had known the uttermost fulfilment of ... love? Was it love? And what was love, brief ecstasies glorified by poets into some momentous transcendental imagery yet no more miraculous or transcendental than the mating of birds, and nothing so delicate. If she had not grasped greedily at youth and all youth's passionate desires to kindle a fire, never wholly fuelled until he came to her, would her life have been cast in a more static mould? ... Static! Who wants to be 'static'? Wifehood, motherhood or spinsterhood, any of which would have been her lot, to live and die unsatisfied, soured, incomplete. Whereas now ... she had been utterly completed, was the equal in knowledge of every matron in the land, or – of every whore! A chuckle escaped her. . . . I'm no romantic although I try so hard to be! What is romance? The frills upon the petticoat of a virginal young 'Miss' or a last attempt to recapture youth's vision of love before it fades into the lonely emptiness of age? Yes, age. Her eyelids quivered: opened. Her lips moved in silence, addressing a wooden post that upheld the entrance to the tent. . . . Some time or other he will see me as I am, much older than he in years, immeasurably older in wisdom, a cynic, hiding behind the frustration of my womanhood that should have been a wife and not – again that throaty chuckle, so like a boy's and so endearing to Michael – and *not* a male concubine!

A shadowy greyness crept through a chink in the canvas. Far off in the distance a cock crowed heralding the dawn. A horse neighed near by; men's voices called to the camels. Her mind's eye saw the slow dignified rise from their knees; the turn of a haughty inquiring head, the fixed smiling, leathery lips .. . . Why do camels always seem to smile so satirically, at whom? At their masters? At themselves ... or at life?

She slept at last.

THREE

The Holy City! . . . Riding at the head of that bizarre procession, wearing her elaborate male dress, she was as usual mistaken by the crowding natives for a beardless youth; a traveller from Europe judging by his fair skin.

With what reverence did she enter the gates of Jerusalem, undeterred by the arid uniformity of rugged mountains surrounding the city. Poised as if cut off from the world it stood in a circle of high walls with here and there an isolated church adding, as Meryon reported, 'to the gloominess of the prospect.'

Hester, not the least disheartened by these first impressions nor the gloomy prospect of the sacred city, and imbued with her faith in the prediction of a charlatan soothsayer saw only the fulfilment of her fate, Queen of the Jews to lead God's chosen people. . . . Nor, when a lodging had been found for her by the indefatigable doctor and which proved to be a few dilapidated rooms unfurnished of everything but bugs, was she at all deflated in her expectation that here she would find her Ultima Thule.

Michael and Meryon were lodged in another monastery where no woman could be received, since the assumption she was a woman had been verified by the doctor's assurance. That she could readily accept this separation from Michael, who for so long had shared her bed and board, did not improve his temper when again forced to be the room-mate of the busy, bustling, chatty little doctor who would read aloud by candlelight his voluminous notes of their journey through the Middle East. Michael was beginning to realize that travelling with his 'more than wife' was not an endlessly idyllic honeymoon. He may have found himself wishing he were a hundred, or a thousand miles hence, with a secret longing for . . . Paris. Yes, Paris! And civilization, gaiety, dancing girls, though to be sure there were those in plenty here if he could shake off the adhesive doctor and visit their haunts. . . . Perish the thought! Was he not bound in love and extra-marital vows to the one being who possessed him utterly? That was it. She did possess him.

He had too often said he was her slave, and she had taken him literally at his word. But let us face it, he told himself, he could not enjoy with her the same enthusiasm for this Arabian Night's entertainment on which he, blindfolded, had embarked. . . . These jabbering natives, their filthy streets, their revolting food and all the kow-towing and salaaming and ridiculous pomposity of Arab sheiks and Pashas with their harems which he was not allowed to enter; there might have been some relief from boredom if he were! As for their journeys along precipitous mountain passes on mules and donkeys, for no horse without risk to all their necks could undertake those perilous footpaths, while his Love rode ahead in her absurd trousers, and her poor little maid clinging to her ass, all of them flea-bitten, and no hope of a bath. . . . And: '*J'y suis, j'y reste,*' muttered Michael, itching and scratching where he lay on his wooden bed and stared at the star-pricked cavern of the sky through the narrow window of his cell. 'But I'll not rest here.'

He did rest there for a day or two because Hester insisted they should after their strenuous journey; but only long enough to visit the Holy Sepulchre with Michael, the doctor and Georgio, the Greek interpreter. The usual sightseers were there, dividing their interest between the grave of our Lord and the young 'nobleman' from Europe whose arrival was in everybody's mouth with arguments as to his rightful sex. Some declared him a royal prince, others a royal princess, and a few an Egyptian Bey travelling with his retinue to explore the Holy City.

Several monks received them at the entrance to take their fees for admittance, and preceded them bearing candles to light their way, and at the same time using canes and whips to keep back the ever-increasing crowds following behind. After removing their shoes at the request of the priest, Hester and her party were led to the chapel built over the Holy Sepulchre which was too small to admit more than the four of them and the priest. Silver lamps suspended from the ceiling illumined the interior, the walls decorated with tapestries, sculptures and holy pictures depicting the Stations of the Cross.

The Grave of Our Lord was covered with a marble slab. On this the doctor reverently placed strings of beads, crosses and religious emblems, as also did Hester and Michael, bought at the entrance from purveyors of such, pushing forward and clamouring in Arabic to be the first to sell their wares which were all of the most shoddy.

Georgio (short for Georgiaki), the Greek and a Christian, tore off his turban exposing a bald pate, for the Christian Greeks must have their heads shaved; and in devout ecstasy prostrated himself on the grave, beating his forehead on the marble till he was all but stunned, and on his brow a lump the size and colour of a plum.

Michael, product of strict Church of England and rather on the Low side, felt greatly embarrassed; more so, perhaps, because Hester habited in trousers in that Holy place was quite unconcerned at the wonder she had caused among the natives and the tourists. Some of these were Europeans, one or two were British and expressed shock and disgust, unaware of her identity more than that she was an Englishwoman. One old Colonel looked about to explode; and Hester, nudging Michael, whispered: 'I know that one – he used to come to Downing Street. He was married to one of my many second or third cousins. I forget his name.'

It was hoped, Michael hesitated to say, that he doesn't know yours, appearing as a male impersonator in here of all places, as if on a music-hall stage!

The next day they rode into Bethlehem along stony almost impassable roads under the frowning rocks of bleak mountains, until they came to a monastery where a monk told them he had fought under Bonaparte during the invasion of Egypt. When he had finished exploiting himself and his military adherence to the French, with some want of tact to the Englishmen as he supposed them all three to be, he conducted them down some steps to the manger where Our Lord, he said, was born. Nothing of this could be seen, so hidden under velvet coverings, brocaded satins, lamps, flowers, tokens, images, unless it were a dark hole immediately above and hewn from the solid rock.

As the party emerged they were surrounded by beggars and villagers selling crucifixes, more images, dead flowers, medals and rosaries. Some of these vendors of relics were half naked, exposing dreadful sores obviously painted and plastered on grime-encrusted arms and chests.

'If anything could make me an unbeliever this would,' remarked Hester as they rode away. The doctor seems to have agreed, for his notes of that excursion record it as: 'Disgust succeeds curiosity when we are conducted to view the print of the Virgin Mary's foot, the impression of Elijah's body where he slept and a hundred such sights which shock common sense and do no service to true religion.' ...

'What is true religion?' Hester asked, 'unless it be the Kingdom of God that is within us?'

More shock to the doctor who had dismayingly observed that her ladyship inclined to show too much interest in the ceremonies of the mosques, the devotion of Mohammedans, besides a tendency to believe in oracles, mysticism; and her adoption of male dress which was surely an indication of scepticism if not agnosticism

125

as also her illicit relationship with Mr Bruce, the doctor's dislike of whom did not decrease with close propinquity in monks' cells.

Without consulting her beloved Bruce, Hester supervised their departure from Jerusalem and, as ever to Dr Meryon's dismay, regardless of expense.

Acre, Tyre, Nazareth, Lebanon. . . . Hester's travels at this stage read like extracts from a *Baedeker* of a century later. Writing one of her numerous letters to Crauford Bruce, she tells him of her intention to move on to Damascus.

Neither she nor Michael had any idea that Crauford, who had subsidized the pair of them beyond even his, supposedly, unlimited resources, was nearing the bottom of his Fortunatus purse. It came as a shock to both to learn that Crauford complained of their expensive costumes for which he had to foot the bill, and all other expenditures; camels, horses, donkeys, mules and a retinue of servants, travelling as if they were Eastern potentates with her ladyship habited as such.

This gave Hester to consider how much longer she could support herself and Michael at his father's expense and if she could continue to put up with the incessant bickerings between Meryon and Bruce.

On arriving at Nazareth, Meryon and Michael having been engaged in another of their rows, consequent on again being lodged as cell-mates in a monastery, Michael left in a rage for Tiberius.

Hester, who had apartments in a house nearby, stood at the door to watch him mount his horse, his dragoman behind him on a mule, and a loaded camel with luggage enough for a month or – Good God! Her heart jumped – or a year? Or for ever?

'I'm off!' shouted Michael. 'I've had enough of your medico and —'

'Me?' she threw this at him in a tremble, shading her

eyes from the sun's glare that beat down on her uncovered head. 'Go on, say it. Go! And don't come back!' She could have bitten out her tongue as those words escaped on a rising wave of temper, and which he may not have heard as he put his horse to the gallop and was off in a cloud of dust.

Still standing there she watched the whirling dust kicked up by his horse's heels to obscure the plodding mule; only the camel with its load, and the driver seated among the baggage, could be clearly seen under the burning sky that showed a river of cobalt blue between the white-walled houses. Some urchins playing in the gutter scattered before the swift oncoming horse; and sighting Hester scampered up to her, their grubby paws outstretched for backsheesh. She turned from them and went into the house. What had she said? What had she done? Was he gone from her for ever? Did she want to lose him or was this his first bid for release? She had known, or had not dared to know, that he fretted at the chains that bound him. He had not said so, not in words, but she guessed he was tiring of the discomforts and incessant journeying from place to place in these strange lands that were so alien to him and so exciting and of such tremendous interest to her.

In the small living-room that adjoined the bedroom, sparsely furnished, its walls whitewashed and none too clean, cobwebs festooning the ceiling, the heat within was even more intolerable than without. White hot sun-shafts pierced the slats of the shuttered windows where flies swarmed. She dragged off her turban, its scarves clinging to her neck and shoulders, dampened with her sweat.

Unfastening her tunic and trousers she let them fall and threw herself down on the divan, naked. Her head ached damnably with intermittent little hammer blows. 'I'm sick,' she muttered. 'I've a fever.'

127

Reaching for a hand-bell on the table by the couch she rang for Ann.

'Bring me a cooling drink, and send for the doctor.'

'My lady is ill?' asked Ann in fright.

'Dying – I hope. Mr Bruce has left me. Gone. Don't stare. I'm not dead yet, worse luck. Citron water. Be quick. I've a formidable thirst.'

Ann brought the tepid lemon water and hurried across to the monastery. A lay brother, seeing a woman at the door, immediately closed it and spoke through the grille. Ann not knowing a word of Arabic guessed he asked what was her business.

She told him in English. Meryon, hearing her voice, came from his cell and spoke to the brother who opened the door to admit her.

'My lady is sick of a fever, doctor. Please to come. Mr Bruce has gone,' said Ann tearfully, 'he – has left her ladyship.'

'Has he indeed? Dear, dear, this is very distressing,' remarked Meryon with no evidence at all of distress. 'I will attend her ladyship instanter.'

'I am leaving here as soon as may be,' Hester said when 'instanter' the doctor appeared. 'I cannot stand this God-dam heat.'

Meryon blinked. His Methodist conscience would never be reconciled to her ladyship's unladylike and blasphemous language. That he perforce must turn a blind eye and deaf ear to her relationship with Bruce caused him much soul-searching. None the less he felt it incumbent on him to fulfil the medical duties for which he was paid. His patient's private life, he would have argued, was none of his affair.

A brief examination confirmed the opinion that her ladyship was suffering from a slight tertian fever as a result of a touch of the sun.

'I prescribe a complete rest for a few days, and that you take this' – from a bag he produced a phial containing

128

a pink liquid – 'which I will instruct your maid to administer every three hours.'

Suspiciously eyeing the potion: 'What is it?' she demanded.

'A prescription that I have adapted, as the great Doctor Culpeper recommends in his *Complete Herbalist* published in the seventeenth century and is still of invaluable use to the medical profession. As followers of the immortal Hippocrates —'

'What *is* it?'

'I have added some slight amendment to the simple described by the Master as an *electuraium e succo rosarum*, which is to say is the juice of the rose *diacydonium* and —'

'For goodness sake!' cried Hester, 'spare me the litany. I'll have none of your physic. Ann!' She raised herself on an elbow and called again, 'Ann!'

Ann came hurrying.

'My lady?'

'Pack everything now. Tell Georgio we leave here tomorrow.'

'Tomorrow?' echoed the doctor in a fluster. 'Madam, I cannot permit your ladyship to leave your bed for at least three days, or until the fever has abated.'

Totally ignoring this: 'I intend to visit Tyre and Sayda and then on to Palmyra. You can't keep me stuck here in this miserable hole. And at sundown this evening I will ride.'

'Madam!' expostulated Meryon, 'I, as your medical adviser must forbid —'

'Go!' she pointed to the door. 'I am my own adviser.'

Dismally Meryon went.

And: How, he asked himself, could he cope with so refractory a patient? He was a free agent. He could leave at a moment's notice. There had been no legal agreement. But how, if Bruce had gone, could he leave her here among these savage tribes and sheiks with their – God forbid – lustful intent, although she went in man's attire as less likely to be assaulted unless. . . . Conjecture uncomfortably paused. He was aware that these Biblical countries, notwithstanding their Holy associations, still practised the ancient sin of the cities of Sodom and Gomorrah. And not so ancient a sin neither, he reflected remembering his student days. Well, yes . . . And if her ladyship should be pursued as a youth in the masculine dress she chose to wear . . . he shuddered. No! However much he suffered from her obstinacy and wilfulness he would never fail her. Never! Not even were his salary unpaid as it looked to be with Bruce gone and no subsidies forthcoming from his father.

He went back to the monastery and shared with one of the monks two bottles of wine which the Father Superior had given him. He was thankful to find the monks good wine-bibbers.

Meanwhile Hester, prior to the doctor's visit had covered her nakedness with her shift. 'Not that he would notice,' she told Ann, 'if I were bare to my bones. To him I am just an anatomical study'. . . . She wondered if that were all she was or had been, with a romanticized flavour, to Bruce and those others who had desired her in the past and seemed to have no connection with this unbelievable present into which she had been voluntarily jettisoned.

'Bring me my bath,' she commanded. The bath, a wooden tub filled with brackish river water, was brought. Sundry foreign bodies floated on its surface including a dead scorpion: this, shudderingly removed by Ann. And when Hester had been sponged, dried, and clothed in her riding suit, trousered, booted, spurred, she ordered the horses.

As the day cooled and accompanied by Georgio, she rode out of the town taking a rocky path through the hilly tracts of the countryside. Reining in her horse she saw the violet misted range of mountains circling

Jerusalem and one peak reared above them nudging the sky aflame with the sun's cremation.

In the valley below, the terraced vineyards, olive groves and fig trees lay bathed in saffron light; and far in the distance she saw the fiery tinted sapphire waters of the sea that lapped the shores of Sayda.

'What sea is it?' she asked Georgio. 'Or is it a lake?'

'It is Galilee,' he said, 'a little small sea – it is small like a lake.'

'Galilee!' . . . She caught her breath. 'The gospels give us nothing of the topography of the Holy Land. Is this the Galilee where Our Lord first saw the fishers of men?'

Georgio signed himself and nodded his head. 'Our Lord's sea,' he said simply.

On the way back down that same path, bordered on one side by a rocky cliff, on the other by a sheer drop into a foam-streaked river, her horse, less sure-footed than mules and asses, stumbled on a boulder of stone, and fell.

Hester, her eyes on the glorious sunset, fine horse-woman though she was, fell with him. Up in a trice: 'See to his knees,' she bade Georgio who had dismounted and come to her. 'Is he hurt?'

One knee was bleeding. Together they pulled the stallion to his feet.

'I will ride yours. You lead him.'

'Is Lady hurt?'

'No, bruised maybe. Walk him carefully. . . .'

'Not since I was ten years old have I ever come off,' she told Ann, lying face downward in the bed while the maid rubbed her spine. 'If the horse is hurt I'll never forgive myself.'

Neither she nor her horse were hurt more than the stallion's cut knee, soon healed, but Hester was badly bruised.

'So that,' she said resignedly, 'delays me here a day or two. My backside couldn't stand a long ride to Palmyra.'

For Palmyra she decided would be her next halt.

She was laid low for three more days, and on the evening of the third day Bruce returned.

She had gone to bed and wakened suddenly to see him in the doorway. She thought she dreamed until she put out her hand to find his in her own, and he seated on the bed before she realized he was there, so swiftly and quietly had he come to her. The dying flame of a tallow candle revealed his face in shadow and the flickering light in his eyes, each holding a tiny spark.

'You!' she whispered, still but half awake. 'I thought I had lost you for ever.'

She was in his arms, his lips against her ear.

'I've been jealous – not of Meryon, that pedantic jabbering ass whom you foist on me in monks' cells, keeping me away from you as if you didn't want me – not of him but of *them* – these sheiks and emirs who bow and scrape to you, grovelling. Their adulation means more to you than my . . . my *ad*oration.' His voice broke. 'You would sooner live with savages who pour themselves and their gifts . . . their horses and their homage . . . at your feet than with me.' He buried his face in her bared breast. 'I couldn't bear,' she heard him say, 'to be put down for them. I'd sooner lose you than see you giving to them what I . . . what you have given me.'

Her heart turned over. She was dissolved in tenderness even while a sense of triumph overwhelmed her with that instinct of possession inherent from her autocratic father. He was hers! Utterly. She would have him always, never to be parted, only should *she* decide it were best for him to leave her, for his good.

'Undress,' she stroked back a lock of his hair, so childishly soft and almost flaxen, bleached by exposure to the burning sun. 'I'm waiting.'. . .

The candle guttered to its end. Through a slat of the shutters at the window crept a sliver of moonshine and alighted on his beautiful young naked body.

Satiated he was instantly asleep.

132

She yearned over him as might a mother for her babe whose suck had loosened from her breast.

'No,' she murmured, 'you will never leave me until another can give you what you crave of me and no woman can give you that but I.'

Cradled in her arms he lay, while her thoughts wandered. . . . All in her that was maternal as when she had cared for, guarded and protected her young brothers, had effected their escape from their father's tyranny enveloped him. She had loved her father despite his intolerable autocracy, his maniacal rages and neglect of her and those dear to her, more dear than any of her would-be lovers even him here in her arms with whom she shared the same delights of comradeship and passion and, knowing him weak, had strengthened him and for his sake had refused to be his wife in *less* than name!

She could not lay to his account the stigma attached to a relationship known to the world, her world which she had renounced, and all that her society demanded. Ostracized, spurned, relegated to the questionable status of courtesan, or yes, an intellectual *hetaera*. But we are not, she told herself, the ancient Greeks whose approach to love between man and woman was on an equally civilized par with the polygamous acceptance of these Arabs whom he calls 'savages'.

She had dozed off and was startled into wakefulness again by an uproar at the gate, with servants shouting, dogs barking, and the sharp metallic sound of a shot.

'Michael!' she shook him. 'Wake up. There's something going on outside. Wake *up*!'

Wide awake now he scrambled from the bed, flung on what garments he could find in the dark and rushed out as Ann, terrified, and carrying a candle, rushed in.

'My lady! Oh, my lady! Is it robbers?'

Hester, groping in the wavering light, pulled on her tunic and trousers. 'My belt! Where is my belt? Find it. I must have my pistols.'

The belt with its loaded pistols was found.

'My lady,' protested Ann, 'you are not going out to them? Oh, pray do not – listen!' Another shot was heard. 'They are shooting!'

But Hester had already gone into the courtyard to see a crowd of agitated servants, while in their midst was Michael yelling above the din in halting Arabic translated by Georgio:

'Hold! Don't shoot, damn you! He is a friend. Hold, I tell you. Disperse!'

He, whom Michael called a 'friend' Hester was astonished to see appeared to be an Arab with the fair bearded face of a pale and beautiful Christ, wearing the ragged travel-stained dress of a Syrian peasant, a tunic of coarse cotton, a striped Arab cloak, and bare legs terminating in shoes so worn that his toes showed through gaps in the leather.

'Allow me,' Bruce presented him as the servants slunk away. 'Mr Burckhardt, *alias* Sheik Ibrahim.'

'Your Ladyship's renown,' said the visitor in perfect English with the slightest trace of foreign accent, 'is in everybody's mouth from Constantinople to the outposts of this wilderness. My duty, Madam.'

He bowed with somewhat exaggerated courtesy that held a hint, could it be, she thought, of sarcasm?

'You are very welcome, Mr – is it Brackett?'

'My name is evidently less known to your ladyship than yours to me,' said he whom Michael had ushered into the house.

'I am sadly at fault,' Hester told him coolly. 'Living out of the world ...'

'I, too,' he said, 'live out of the world, or I should say rather in a world which is more my world than that I have left.'

By this time Michael had conducted him to the living-room. 'Pray, sir, may we offer you refreshments after your long journey?'

Servants were ordered to prepare a meal; and while, in voracious mouthfuls, their strange guest ate, he told how he came to be there in his dishevelled disguise. He had suffered the misfortune to be set upon by a hostile tribe with whom he was unfamiliar and who had bereft him of servants, camels and his horse, stripped him to the skin and left him to trudge through the desert on foot in search of a caravanserai or some hospitable natives to give him food and shelter.

And as he spoke of his travels she was mortified not to have known him for just *an* explorer but *the* renowned Swiss explorer, Burckhardt. She also felt that he regarded her own exploration of lands through which no European woman had ever before ventured, was as much a gesture of defiance against convention and to satisfy her thirst for notoriety, as was her flaunted liaison with Bruce that had shocked London society and made her more famous or infamous, than her equivocal adventures with Arab chiefs and Turks.

She resented his condescending attitude to her, particularly as Michael offered him the most deferential hospitality, invited him to stay at Nazareth as his guest, not hers; she having spent vast sums of her Government pension as well as Bruce Senior's money on gifts to the Pashas, Emirs and Beys who entertained her. She understood that they accepted Burckhardt with the homage and respect she had come to claim as her privilege, and for which, admittedly, she paid, while Burckhardt gave nothing in return for his lavish entertainment. Towards the end of his three days' visit and during the course of conversation, addressed almost exclusively to Bruce, he mentioned he was interested in the proposed excavations for certain treasures rumoured to be hidden at Ascalon.

Ah! She pricked her ears. A treasure hunt! If that were so then *she* would be first in the field.

'I, too,' she made him turn to her, 'am bound for

Ascalon and on that same hunt for hidden treasure of which you speak as rumoured, and that I know exists.'

A blatant fabrication. Neither Ascalon nor a treasure hunt had entered into her planned itinerary. 'I also intend,' she told him, disregarding Michael's elevated eyebrows, 'to visit the Druses en route for Damascus and Palmyra. I am anxious to become acquainted with that mysterious sect of people who inhabit the slopes of Mount Lebanon.'

Having surprised Michael with this, of which he had heard nothing from her and, as she hoped, sufficiently impressed Burckhardt, she sat back in her chair – they were at supper in the house lent her at Nazareth – helped herself to a date and passed the dish to their guest.

'If it is your intent,' said he – 'I thank you, madam, I am surfeited with dates, my sole sustenance plucked at the roadside after being robbed of all I possess – if it be your intent to visit Palmyra I suggest you abandon so hazardous a journey across twenty leagues of desert where you may be attacked by the Wahabiz always in conflict with one or other of the Arab tribes. Also, although the Druses are not a warlike people they are still semi-barbaric. And I must warn you they resent importunate visitors, especially Europeans.'

'Especially a woman, yes?' She gave him this with heightened colour, 'which makes my project all the more exciting and myself the more determined to venture across that twenty leagues of desert. I fear no Arab tribes. I am on best of terms with those I have already visited. I have a dozen horses in my stables, or rather my caravan, gifts from my various hosts who welcome me with overwhelming generosity. I think it was Queen Zenobia who was the first woman to visit Palmyra. I have no doubt my reception there will be as warm as was hers!'

He smiled into his beard.

'Your ladyship will doubtless be welcomed as triumphantly as was Zenobia fifteen hundred years ago.'

Sarcastic brute, she thought. It was evident he looked upon her as a society eccentric.

Later, when she and Michael had gone to bed: 'I find his vanity and his patronizing manner insufferable!' she told him. 'He is obviously a woman-hater if not a lover of men. I *will* go to Palmyra, and if you attempt to dissuade me or pay heed to him I'll go alone and without you or any escort other than the dragoman and my blackamoor guard – about seven feet high – who carries a sword to cut off the heads of intruders. So now you know!'

So now he knew. Useless to argue with or dissuade her against her will from any decision she would make. Incalculable creature!

Having seen Burckhardt on his way supplied with fresh clothes, a horse and money, Michael gave in.

Followed by a caravan of twenty-five mules, eight horses, baggage camels, servants, the doctor, and poor Ann on a donkey, they came to Sayda. There they lodged for the night at the house of the French Consul, where immediately on their arrival Hester received an invitation from the Prince of the Druses to visit him at Dayr-el-Kamar in the Lebanon.

She was immensely gratified.

'You see how all Syria knows of me!' She handed his letter, written in faulty French, to Bruce. 'He is sending me an escort.' She passed the ill-written screed to the Consul. 'I cannot quite read his scrawl. He is sending me camels, more mules, horses and servants. We shall have enough for an army!'

'Milady may require an army,' said the Frenchman dryly. 'These tribes are in constant war one with the other. You are fortunate that the Emir welcomes you to his territory.'

'I understood from Burckhardt that the Prince is a convert to Christianity.'

'Yes, madame, and so good a convert to Christianity that he puts to the torture any who, on suspicion, will

137

intrigue against him with his people. *Mais!*' he shrugged. 'Is this so different from the hanging of traitors in your country or the guillotine in mine?'

'But – to torture them!' gasped Hester.

Again that Gallic shrug.

'Such things go for nothing in Arabia where the Turks govern, as they have done for centuries past.'

'I don't care,' Hester told Michael who made further attempt to prevent her from visiting the Druses. 'The Prince is not likely to torture me, a British subject. You need not come with me if you fear he'll torture you.'

They left on the following morning. After about a mile from Sayda in the scorching heat along those rocky paths cut from the mountains, they descended to the valley at the foot of Lebanon.

The small capital of Dayr-el-Kamar was encircled by mountain peaks, snow-covered even in summer, the highest range reaching to some seven thousand feet above the lovely valleys with their date palms, verdant olive groves, orchards, and forests of cypress and cedars.

True to his written word the Emir had sent to Sayda as escort for the Lady, twelve camels, twenty-five mules – 'which gives us fifty!' declared Hester. 'How on earth can we fodder them?'

'On earth, of course,' muttered Bruce. 'They must graze the bush unless the Emir sends them nose-bags.'

'Only four more horses though,' she said, 'and a guard of seven soldiers – all pitch black! I thought the Druses were fair-skinned.'

'As they are, and possible descendants from the ancient Greeks or Romans,' put in the doctor, relieved to see soldiers whatever the colour of their skin.

The Emir's minister met them at the entrance gates mounted on a white horse and attended by four servants, also mounted. All along the narrow main street of the small city, the Prince's subjects were lined up to greet the daughter of the 'English Sultan', so word had travelled to them across the desert. Yet there were still some who believed the handsome 'youth' to be a prince for why should a princess ride as a man and wear a prince's habit? With much gesticulatory argument they discussed it as she passed.

The minister, who spoke a few words of French, intermingled with Arabic, explained how they had long anticipated her coming. Her Altesse would understand that the Emir was greatly honoured to receive and to welcome so notable a visitor whom all Syria welcomed (this a complimentary exaggeration) not only the daughter of England's Majesty but a daughter of England which country the Emir honoured as he honours the All Highest, the Sultan.

Very gratifying. If this were an example of the manners and customs of the mysterious and according to Burckhardt, semi-barbaric Druses, then how distorted could rumour be?

The minister conducted them with much ceremony to the house set aside for the Emir's guests. The prince's own palace stood on high ground and there, on the following day, the Emir received Hester and her two 'gentlemen-in-waiting' as Bruce and Meryon were taken to be.

Hester was immediately captivated by this distinguished good-looking man in his early fifties, with his long flowing beard and large curiously light mesmeric eyes. Little did she guess that he who welcomed her with such effusive grace would prove to be the most treacherous and merciless tyrant of his times. He had betrayed his people, adopted Christianity as a blind for his appallingly cruel methods of torture to any whom he suspected were disloyal to his suzerainty. Having escaped the vengeance of three successive Pashas of Acre who had sought his head for his attempted invasion of their territories, he eventually secured the throne of Lebanon, and pursued his reign of terror in the disguise of a benevolent parent of his subjugated people.

Never before in her travels had she met with such

overwhelming hospitality as offered her by this 'Prince of the Mountain' as he named himself. Not even in Constantinople had she seen such magnificence as that of the Emir's palace. The ceiling and walls of the courtyard were exquisitely painted by an artist from Turkey whose hands the prince cut off that no other but himself should enjoy his works of art.

The meals served to her in the house placed at her disposal, were prepared by the Emir's head cook, which she enjoyed more than did Bruce and Meryon who eyed with suspicion the dishes of highly spiced meat that might have been any animal rather than beef or mutton; more likely camel, the milk of which was given to them to drink instead of cow's milk. Moreover Michael was disgusted, which Hester was not, when in return for the prince's lavish hospitality she purchased a sheep to be given to the villagers and ordered the people to assemble in the market place, or in this case the bazaar, and to eat it roasted, as in England, she told the Emir's secretary, an ox would be roasted whole as a special treat for some celebration.

Watched by the three of them, Hester, Michael and the doctor, the loudly protesting sheep was brought and presented to the natives, not roasted but alive; then killed horribly, skinned and eaten raw. Men and women fell upon the bleeding carcase tearing at it with their hands and teeth, clawing out its entrails and within half an hour had devoured it, fat and all. The women were the greediest to get at the fat to swallow it in chunks as the tastiest portions. The fastidious Michael sickened at sight of the dreadful feast, Meryon was unaffected and launched forth on a diatribe concerning the atavistic reversion of humankind among certain savage tribes since the dawn of civilization. To Hester it was just another experience of which, in one of her letters to General Oakes, she wrote a full account.

After this and, not surprisingly, Michael decided to

take himself to Aleppo for a while, having had his fill of Lebanon, and tried to persuade Hester to go with him. 'I beg you,' he entreated, 'not to attempt to go to Damascus from here. You know that the Wahabiz are ransacking all the villages along the road – the desert is swarming with them – they have fifty thousand under arms, so Georgio reports. I won't let you go to risk your life!'

'Don't be a fool. What could the Wahabiz do to me? I am known to all the tribes in Syria. You see how well I am received by the Prince of the Mountain. He will protect me and mine. I have been treated with the utmost civility wherever I go by all the chiefs of the tribes. I start for Damascus so soon as we can arrange it. If you are afraid to come with me, then go to Aleppo and *stay* there!'

This was too much for Michael.

'Afraid! Not for myself but for you and your overweening obstinacy and pride.'

Although hurt to the core she looked at him soberly. He was the same yet not the same. All that she loved was there, adored, desired, generous to folly, kindhearted and worshipful of her, his most endearing quality. What had she then, that caused these frictions as trickles of water will widen a breach in a wall? . . . Her most powerful instinct, possessiveness, warred with her love for this boy who had restored to her all of her frustrated womanhood. If the only love of her life, John Moore, had lived, had she been given wifehood, motherhood, borne his sons . . . In a flash of insight it came to her that in Michael she had found compensation for the loss of that maternity with which she had guarded, loved, protected her young brothers. Or were her triumphant journeyings through lands unexplored by any other European woman also a compensation for all that she had missed?

She brought herself to tell him: 'Go, then, dearest, to Aleppo. I would not hold you back from what I know you need, a holiday away from the hardships you have endured in our travels among alien people which has not the same interest or appeal to you as it has for me. I should have been a man.'

'But I,' he said hardily, 'am no woman although you try to make me one. Once again I ask you, come with me to Aleppo. What peace of mind, or holiday, as you put it, would I find at Aleppo if I knew you were careering across the desert pursued by Bedouins or Wahabiz?'

'You need have no fear. I will be escorted by a dozen trustworthy janissaries and many stalwart soldiers which the Prince of the Mountain will send with me. I believe the Consul at Aleppo is a Mr Barker whom I met once or twice at Downing Street. He will entertain you. Go then, dear love, enjoy yourself and join me at Damascus if you wish.'

It was a mother telling her schoolboy son to take his holiday with a friend. He did not see it so; only at once felt contrite at her unselfishness and himself at fault. Swinging round on her, his cheeks flushed, eyes bright with a sudden moisture sprung to them, he held her face on a level with his own for she was as tall as he and: 'How can I leave you?' He was near to tears. 'I dread you taking this journey through the desert without me.'

'Dear heart, I would go with you and renounce Damascus just to be with you, but' – her boyish grin that he had always found so adorable warmed her words – 'but I am told that the sun at Aleppo or the water or the something, brings sensitive skins out in boils and I have one skin too few. I should hate boils on my face or – anywhere. I had one once on my – yes, I did! And couldn't sit on my backside for a month!'

He made one last effort to make her see reason.

'I am told that the country between here and Damascus is in chaotic confusion and revolt. Only yesterday I heard that the Pasha of Damascus has been murdered.'

'If you heard that from Georgio you can put a grain of

salt on his tale. He hates the idea of going to Damascus. He is scared to death of the Bedouins and Wahabiz. Take Georgio with you to Aleppo, and I will send the doctor in advance to find me a lodging in Damascus. The escort promised by the Emir will take care of me and I too will make every provision to guard you on your way. So go, and God be with you.'

She kissed him gently, a butterfly kiss that alighted on his nose.

He went to his room, his thoughts in a turmoil. . . . 'Every provision to guard him'. This guardianship! This silken chain that bound him as if it were of steel, unbreakable. Was this love, this entire submission to her whose body he had worshipped and with all his – or his father's worldly wealth – he had endowed! . . . 'O, God,' he groaned, 'what have I done to allow myself to be so utterly will-less, chained, enslaved?' . . . Yes, he had told her often enough he was enslaved and gloried in his enslavement. Was *that* love or a more englamoured physical desire for her than for the women whom he had paid for his pleasure? What was her attraction? Her courage? Her adventurous spirit, or that hail-fellow-comradeship found in no other woman, only in men? . . . He shirked further probing lest he discover hidden half-suspected truths: a strangled laugh came from him. Had she rendered him effeminate by reason of her innate or assumed masculinity? . . . 'It must end.' Again he spoke aloud; nor did he see the doctor, so silently he entered.

'Did I wake you?' inquired Meryon brightly, for Michael's chin was sunk on his chest. Both men were bearded now in accordance with the Turkish or Arabian dress they had adopted at Hester's insistence. 'An afternoon siesta is an excellent tonic for the nervous system.'

'I was not asleep,' Michael said while his jaw muscles tensed with the effort to control a desire to assault the cheery little doctor, whose effect upon him was similar to the bite of an inquisitive mosquito. 'And my nervous system requires no tonic more than a change of air and scene . . .' And, he almost added, persons.

'Which you will have,' Meryon beamed upon him in return for Michael's scowl. 'I am arranging for her ladyship's journey to Damascus. I will be going in advance to find suitable lodgings for her and for ourselves.'

'I will require no lodging in Damascus.' Michael got up as the doctor sat down. 'I go to Aleppo.'

'Indeed? I fear you will not care for the climate there. The heat, I understand, at this time of year, is most trying.' . . .

'If I required any more inducement to get away from here,' Michael told Hester when he came to say goodbye to her at sundown that same day, 'it is your chirping little sparrow.'

'My sparrow?' She glanced surprisedly around as if to see one hopping in through the window. She was seated cross-legged on the divan writing a letter.

'Well, isn't he? Or a parakeet – if parakeets do chirp. For a man, who I allow knows something of medicine, his platitudes and infernal pleasantries and god-awful cheerfulness and making-the-best-of-it and drinking camel's milk as if it were the finest Rhenish – Lord!' He clutched his beard. 'What would I not give for a bottle of it now!'

'The monks at Aleppo, if there are any,' she said, regarding him with her head on one side, 'may supply you with French or Rhine wine. You haven't done so badly at the monasteries so far. And I am sure Mr Barker has a good cellar. As for my poor Meryon – why should you so unreasonably dislike him? He is the most selfless, kindest and best-hearted creature in the world. What would any of us do without his unceasing care of us?'

'I know what I'd do with his unceasing care of me,' muttered Michael.

She said: 'I think I like you best clean shaven. You've an adorable cleft in your chin and that beard doesn't really suit you.'

'I'll shave it when I get to Aleppo. It was your idea I should grow it,' he said sulkily. 'To whom are you writing? I never see you indoors but you always seem to be writing letters.'

'This is to General Oakes to tell him how the people here devoured a raw sheep.'

He wrinkled his nose. 'Revolting. Take care in case your friends among the Wahabiz whom you may meet on the road to Damascus don't devour you! I believe half of them are cannibals.'

She laid aside her notepaper and carefully placed the inkwell on the floor. There was no table near to the divan. 'I must not upset the ink on the Emir's beautifully embroidered divan!'

It struck him as rather touching that she, in her trousers, tunic and turban and all the rest of the nonsense should, even at this moment, which he felt to be almost a crisis between them, show a housewifely concern for the Emir's belongings. She was saying:

'Darling,' looking up at him with those startlingly blue eyes that held a shadow of anxiety. 'You are not hurt, are you, that I go to Damascus and not to Aleppo with you?'

'Hurt?' He came to her and dropped beside her on the couch with an arm around her shoulders. 'Of course I'm hurt. You don't care that I am worried to death at your determination to run into danger in defiance of my advice.'

'Oh, my dear, you know I would give up everything – even my travels if I thought you really wished it. All I want is for you to be content and happy with me and my adventures which I believed you shared and enjoyed with me. You know I love you more than anything in the world, but —'

'But,' he drew away from her, 'you love adventure more than me or our lives together.'

'We share our lives.' She took his face between her

hands then let them fall. 'I hate to kiss your beard! . . .
Do believe that I am glad you are going to Aleppo,
although I can't bear to be parted from you even for so
short a time. But if later you wish to join me at Damascus
or Palmyra where you know I intend to go, then come to
me. Wherever I am I shall be waiting.'

He bent his head, said in a choked voice: 'You are too
good to me and too good *for* me. I'm not worth your love.
After all, you have given up everything for me. You refused to marry me and allowed yourself to be a pariah
and outcast from society so that I should be free to choose
my own life. You wrote this to my father. I was
devastated when he wrote to tell me – when first we
came together – that you would not marry me because
you wished me to be free to choose a wife – if I remember
what you told him in your letter – you wrote that you
looked forward to the time when you would resign me to
another woman more worthy of me than you are. As if
that were possible! There could never be another
woman.'

'Never? How can you tell? All things are possible – in
love.' She spoke with a tender calmness that belied the
furious beating of her heart. If he should take her at her
word, her written word to his father! He remembered it
after – how long? Two years and he still so young. A boy
in his twenties, and she in her late thirties.

'Go, my dear. Be free as the beautiful air you will
breathe at Aleppo – Oh! You have upset the ink!' His
foot had slid as he went to take her in his arms. 'All over
the Emir's exquisite rug!'

'Yes, and what a place to put an inkwell!'

Not such a good housewife after all.

'I must buy him another one,' she said. 'They cost the
mint.'

My father's mint, he did not say, and stooped to stop
the black and spreading puddle with his handkerchief.

He left her still writing her letter:

All I can say about myself sounds like conceit but others could tell you I am the oracle of the place and the darling of the troops because I can ride and because I bear arms. . . . The Dervishes think me a wonder.

*   *   *

The road to Damascus! . . . 'On this very road,' thus Hester's unnecessary reminder to the doctor who rode beside her at the head of the cavalcade, 'St Paul saw the Light. So let us not hurry. I must imbibe this loveliness.'

And lovely it was on that four days' journey through mountain passes.

Proceeding northward along the edge of a luxuriant valley they came to a village by the river where water melon fields bordered the steep and stony paths, and fruits of all sorts in season hung from the trees that lined their way unfenced and within easy reach of any hand that chose to pluck them.

'Not robbed by village boys as are our orchards,' remarked Hester, leaning from her saddle to reach for a ripe green fig. 'The Arabs would seem to be more honest than our people.'

'They go in fear of the Pasha,' Meryon said. 'They would get more than a chiding from the village constable as our lads would have if they so much as touched the fruit. They would stand a good chance of having their bones broken if they should dare to steal even a fig, to which your ladyship has just now helped yourself.'

'A fig for that!' said she flippantly, to cause Georgio riding behind her to look fearfully aside at the black and coffee-coloured janissaries armed to the teeth: her ladyship's guards. . . . But who could tell whom they served? The Lady or the Pasha? It was no uncommon punishment to cut off the ears of a plundering boy or man. Talk had it, which Georgio was nothing loth to retail to her ladyship, how a certain Pasha, predecessor to this present Sheik of

Damascus, had suspected one of his wives of infidelity with his minister, dragged her out of the harem and sliced off her head before the rolling eyes of the eunuchs and the horrified faces of the other wives peering through the lattices of the harem windows.

Toward evening they pitched their tents for the night in a level clearing, and the next morning Hester assembled her retinue and started off again to ascend Mount Lebanon. Here the doctor went on in advance to secure a lodging for her in Damascus while she and her followers pursued their way through fertile valleys circled by low hills, and taking a zig-zag path gained the summit of Lebanon. There, after a few furlongs covered with patches of snow unmelted by the sun, they made their descent and called a halt to fodder and water the camels, horses, mules, and refresh themselves. They then resumed their journey, and following the course of a stream came at last to the brow of the mountain that overlooked Damascus.

From that height the view of the beautiful small city bathed in the sun's fierce benediction gilding the white walled houses, was presented to Hester's enchanted sight as a casket of gold flung by a giant's hand to spill its contents at the mountain's foot.

Before entering the city's gates she was met by a messenger from the Pasha of Damascus to whom she had previously written of her intended visit to his domain. She had already been warned by her recently acquired interpreter, one Bertrand, a Frenchman, that it was forbidden on pain of drastic punishment, for a woman to appear in the city unveiled. To which Hester, who would always oppose any suggestion as to what she should or should not do, paid not the slightest heed and dismissed the discomfited messenger, interpreted by Bertrand, that as she was an Englishwoman Turkish customs did not apply to her, nor would she adhere to them.

'Madame,' Bertrand was in a rare taking, 'you run a

risque of the most formidable should you disobey the command of the Pasha. I implore miladi that she enter the city *en voile*.'

'I care nothing for the Pasha or his commands and I'll not enter the city *en voile*, and if he don't like it, I'll ride in as Lady Godiva!'

And spurring her horse she rode into Damascus barefaced.

Meryon met her so soon as she with her entourage passed through the gates. He, who had heard of the dire penalties inflicted on a woman should she appear unveiled in the shadow of the Mosque, begged her to cover her face. Whereupon he was, shockingly, bidden: 'Go to hell – you and Bertrand with your croakings!'

Whether it were that rumour had identified her as the daughter of the English king or because those who watched whom they took to be a 'noble youth', son of an Emir, mounted on a superb stallion, riding so proudly through the thronging streets, none raised voice against her. It was a triumphal entry.

Crowds followed to see her dismount at the door of the house Meryon had taken for her in the Christian quarter of the town. But after one cursory survey she decided she would not have it at any price.

'The outlook is hideous. There are no gardens, no views, and I'll not live among these Greeks and Armenians. Find me something near the river in the Turkish part of the town. I'll write to the Pasha demanding I be better housed.'

Purse strings were pulled. Crauford Bruce's money dispensed, and a splendid villa close to the Pasha's palace obtained to her satisfaction and, in consequence of lavish gifts offered to the Pasha, to his.

Her success with the inhabitants of Damascus was instantaneous. When she rode out with Georgio, her sole attendant, crowds hailed her as *Melika* (Queen) that she believed the soothsayer's prophecy was about to be fulfilled. Queen! . . . None now mistook her for a man, notwithstanding her trousers, turban and cummerbund stuck with pistols and belted with bullets. When she entered the bazaar the stallholders sitting cross-legged on benches crying their wares all rose to salute her, an honour paid only to the Pasha or the Mufti.

Writing to General Oakes of her adventures, she tells him:

> If I was to begin my history I should fill my paper with the honours paid me. . . . Arab chiefs tormenting me from morning till night all anxious to attend me on my journey to Palmyra. Everybody is surprised at my courage as above 80,000 Arabs will be on the march in a fortnight to their winter quarters, and I am determined to go into one of the largest Bedouin camps. . . .

She later informs the General of a report that 50,000 Wahabiz were within a four days' journey of Damascus. . . . 'But I do not believe it.'

She did not want to believe it. The report had come from a letter to the Pasha saying that at least thousands of dromedaries mounted by Bedouins were attempting an advance on the city having burnt and ransacked every village along the route. What really concerned Hester was that the Wahabiz, the most ferocious tribe of the Bedouins, warred with the Pasha and would join any party against him so that the roads through the desert would be teeming with marauders. . . . 'But should the worst come to the worst,' she wrote to General Oakes, 'I shall take fifty of my men and set off to my friend, Emir Bechir, Prince of the Mountain.'

Her alarm was unnecessary. There was no immediate uprising. The Pasha had taken the precaution to send a strong body of troops in readiness to attack the Wahabiz throughout the whole Pashalic of Damascus.

The officer of the troops invited her to inspect his soldiers, a thousand of them and fifty officers. This was considered a great compliment and though she confessed to such an undertaking as 'an awful thing', she came through it with flying colours to the admiration of the officers, and was presented by the Pasha with a fine little Arab horse to add to her stud of bloodstock. . . . 'And what to do with them all,' she complained to the doctor, 'if wherever I go I am given a horse! I can't take a dozen or more horses across the desert to Palmyra.'

'I advise your ladyship,' ventured Meryon, 'to postpone your visit to Palmyra while conditions here are so disturbed.'

'Postpone my visit? Not on your life! Mahannah, chief of the Anazès, is soon to arrive with forty thousand of his Arabs. He is outside the Sultan's jurisdiction so I could have him as my escort rather than the Pasha, so for goodness sake stop your incessant croaking. I'm sick of being told what I must or must not do. I'll send a message to Mahannah to tell him I await his pleasure as my escort.'

Meanwhile Michael at Aleppo hearing of Hester's enthusiastic reception and the tributes paid to her by Arab chiefs and at the military review which she inspected riding up and down the lines of saluting officers and men in her male dress, a cross between a Turkish officer's uniform and that of an Arab chieftain – she changed her costume two or three times a day to suit herself or her visits to her various hosts – Bruce decided to rejoin her at Damascus and see exactly what was going on. Moreover that she repaid in generous fee the gifts she received from the Pasha and other Arab sheiks caused him to wonder whether his father would withhold his allowance, and then where would they be?

The British Consul, Barker, was greatly opposed to Hester's intended journey to Palmyra and advised Bruce to do his utmost to dissuade her from crossing twenty leagues of desert with thousands of hostile Bedouins waiting to attack any caravan along the route.

Besides all this Michael was glad of the excuse to get

away from Aleppo. He had tired of the glamorous Orient, the beastly food, the incompetent servants and hoped, a doubtful hope, that he could induce Hester to abandon further adventuring and return with him to civilization and Paris: his Mecca.

Express couriers were despatched on sweating horses, back and forth from Aleppo to Damascus bearing messages of warning as to the dangers she would meet if she attempted so hazardous an expedition. Another of her letters to General Oakes complains that: 'Had Bruce and Barker made less fuss about my safety and let me have my own way I should have returned by this time from Palmyra.'

Then Michael, having started off for Damascus with Barker, fell ill on the journey. Hester, far too busy with her plans for departure to rush off and nurse her 'Dearest Love', sent Meryon to him, and stayed on at Damascus to receive the son of Mahannah el Fadel, chief of the Anazè Arabs.

Emir Nasar, eldest son of Mahannah, proved to be a delectable young man of five and twenty. He arrived wearing a rather dirty sheepskin, a satin robe somewhat the worse for wear, and a most engaging manner.

Hester, always attracted to men younger than herself, especially Arabian chieftains, many of whom were magnificent specimens of manhood, at once invited him and his retinue to a meal prepared in advance of his arrival. It was a sumptuous repast consisting of a mixture of English and Turkish dishes prepared by one Pierre, the French cook she had engaged recommended by the French Consul at Sayda. Much astonishment and some amusement were caused by the appearance of a *chef d'œuvre*, a huge plum pudding, manfully devoured by Nasar and his chief attendant whom Hester took to be his equerry. When the meal was over and coffee served, she and Nasar retired to her sitting-room in the villa Meryon had rented for her.

Nasar then in halting French interspersed with a few words of English and Arabic, told her that his father, having heard of her intent to cross the desert to Palmyra, had sent him to warn her against so dangerous an expedition if escorted by the Pasha's troops. . . . 'They, not of my father's tribes, are hostile to Mahannah who would be impelled to regard any escort of *son Altesse, la Princesse*, as an enemy, and —'

'I, an enemy!'

'*Mais non, Madame la Princesse, non! Pas Madame*, Star of the Morning' – this in Arabic or as much as she could understand of it – 'Daughter of the All Highest, the Sublime Sultan of England!' She let him believe it . . . 'But all who traverse the desert *sans* the permission of Mahannah will be *attaqué* by the armies of the Sultan of Turkey. Not *la Princesse*, Allah forbid! *Mais la risque* it is too great. The Pasha it is who is our enemy. . . .'

However, as he further enlarged, if she would trust herself to him, Nasar, the Lion of the Desert, as he modestly named himself, and to his father's faithful Bedouins, all of whom would lay down their lives for her, she would be safely conducted to wherever in all the Damascan territories she would desire to visit. On his life and the life of his father he swore it, his hand on his heart.

His eloquence and his beautiful dark eyes, no less than his evident admiration for her, won her over. She was always prone to flattery; and he made no attempt to disguise that he had fallen a victim to her still ageless charms. He had never met an Englishwoman at such close quarters. Those he had seen at Cairo, mostly wives of British officers or attachés at the embassies on his infrequent visits outside his father's domain, were, in his opinion, ugly as hyenas with their long teeth, long faces, and figures like sacks tied round the middle. But this houri, this Princess from England with her beautiful fair skin and a mouth – what a mouth! Red as it were painted. And her body! If he could but tear apart those Turkish trousers to find her as desirous as she was desirable! A lovely woman or – a youth?

Nasar had sampled various pleasures, both heterosexual and perverse. Imagination dwelled on erotically exciting delights. . . . Before he left he persuaded Hester to defer her visit to Palmyra until the spring. It would be inadvisable, he said, to cross the desert in winter owing to the cold winds and snow-storms. He went from her after exacting a promise that she would pay a private visit to his father, Mahannah, and discuss with him her journey to Palmyra under his protection in a few months' time.

And in the meantime Meryon had arrived at Aleppo to find Michael suffering from a gastric fever which soon responded to treatment. Then Barker took the infection, which delayed their departure for Damascus until both were sufficiently recovered.

On his way to Aleppo Meryon, at Hester's request, called upon a man of singular history and mysterious origin residing in a village on the outskirts of Aleppo. Purporting to have been descended from the Grand Master of the Knights of St John and Jerusalem at Malta, and born of the Piedmontese family of Lascaris, he claimed to be a Knight of Malta and follower of Bonaparte into Egypt. He had married a beautiful Georgian slave stolen from a harem, thereby losing what little social status he had gained from his exploits with Napoleon's victorious armies, and retired to Aleppo after frittering away his capital in loose living in Paris, Cairo and as far distant as St Petersburg.

This, according to his own glib account of himself to the credulous doctor, all ears for any tale told by one of the aristocratic nobility of France, Italy, or wherever.

Lascaris received the doctor in a humble cottage on the outskirts of Aleppo. The room into which Meryon was ushered had a floor of highly polished clay. The furnishings were poor, but everything was scrupulously clean.

154

Lascaris' wife had nothing left of the beauty that had attracted him and brought about her rescue from five men who had abducted her when, as a girl of fifteen, she went on some errand for her lord and master of the harem where she slaved. Again all this was taken in good faith by the gullible doctor who learned that Lascaris scraped a bare living as a schoolmaster in Aleppo.

Meryon spent two days at their cottage where he was hospitably entertained on such frugal fare as Madame Lascaris could offer. He found his host to be a man of culture, no mean linguist, and of an intelligence at variance with one who lived in such poverty-stricken surroundings with a fat, blowsy, native wife.

The kind-hearted doctor, snobbism aside, at once fell in with Lascaris' tentative suggestion concerning Lady Hester, whose renown had reached even to this wilderness, and how her ladyship so rightly named *Melika*, Queen of the Desert, was noted for her charity, that none in need of alms went from her empty-handed. This speech conveyed no inkling, of which the astute Piedmontese was well aware, having made it his business to know how her ladyship's reputed wealth was that of the merchant banker, her lover's father.

Before Meryon left, Lascaris offered himself to her ladyship as interpreter: 'Gratis, naturally, if I can be of any use to Lady Hester in her travels. I am bilingual in Arabic, French, English, Italian, with a smattering of Russian learned when I visited the Court of the Czar at Petersburg.'

So beguiled was the doctor by Lascaris' account of his adventures, no less than of his descent from the Knights of Malta and his direct ancestor, the Grand Master, that when Meryon returned to Damascus with his two convalescents, Lascaris and his wife went with him.

Hester readily agreed to employ him as her interpreter and liaison officer, not 'gratis' but at a munificent salary.

'He is worth it,' she told Michael. He was not so impressed as were she and the doctor with the ingratiating Lascaris who introduced himself as: 'Knight of St John and of Malta, with my humble duty, at your ladyship's service.' She was equally agreeable to accept his blowsy, fat unpleasant wife. Not until some time later did she learn she had been fooled, as had Meryon whom she blamed for the introduction to Lascaris since he was none other than Bonaparte's chief *agent provocateur* in the Middle East.

Nor did it improve her temper to hear Michael's repetitive, 'I told you so! The fellow is an enemy agent and it would be our duty to have him arrested.'

'And find ourselves without heads, decapitated by the Sultan's agents with whom he operates for Bonaparte?'

More frequent now were their disagreements, seemingly trifling wrangles, that would lead a false step to sink the unwary into dangerous mire.

'As for Lascaris,' she continued, 'the best we can do is to be on our guard and make what use we can of him as interpreter. He can't get much from me in any case. I am not at Downing Street now.'

Michael, still suffering from the after-effects of his fever, low-spirited, tetchy, took an instant dislike to Damascus. He and Barker were given the house in the Christian quarter of the town refused by Hester. There no man, unless it were a doctor, was allowed in the streets after dark on pain of death. This, one more grievance to be nursed by Michael as reason for severing their love bonds if such ties as theirs that held him chained, soul, body, and free-will, were love or ever had been.

Had it crossed her mind that Michael was come to the end of his tether and chafing to break loose, Hester would have dismissed the thought as result of her anxiety over his health and well-being, which she would not have admitted were of less account than the adulation of the crowds who hailed her as their *Melika*. But she too was tiring of Damascus, if not of Bruce, and agreed to his urge that they quit 'this infernal god-forsaken hole'. So she arranged for them all to winter in Hamah until the spring, when she would take the journey to Palmyra, her promised land.

FOUR

Hamah. . . . 'A very quizzical town on the Orontes,' is how Hester writes of it.

Here she was stationed during the coldest winter ever experienced for thirty years. The houses at Hamah were not designed for severe weather in a semi-tropical climate, and Michael still in a state of nervous irritability found fault with everything and every one: the servants, the food, the abominable climate, the doctor, Lascaris, his indolent fat wife and, in his heart but not on his tongue, with Hester.

The river overflowed its banks and flooded the rooms. He had to sit knees to his chin on a couch in the bed-chamber where the water rose up to his thighs. He must wade in it to get from one room to another, while Hester half-naked paddled through the ground floor rooms as if she were the child who went bare-footed on the common at Chevening tending turkeys.

'You have been treated too soft all your life,' she said. 'If you had been in the army as were my brothers, you would not have cared if you were up to your neck in mud – nor do I. I've been out in all weathers on the common at home in an old patched gown and clod-hoppers. Do stop grumbling and show some interest in this wonderful country and these people who might have come straight out of the Old Testament and are so different from us in our close little island, who know nothing of any world but ours. Do you hanker for Almack's and the clubs of St James's and the artificialities of the only life you've ever known? If so, go back to it! Steep yourself in the would-be intellectual patter and carousels of Carlton House and what's left of Georgiana of Devonshire's crowd – very few of them now since she died. Go back to the joys of dice and faro and drink your fellows under the table to be dragged to bed dead drunk if you are not already in bed with your best friend's wife. That's the way of life for *you* – not here among these simple folk who are unchanged since the time of Abraham!'

He turned a clouded glance upon her, critical, detached, as if her words had scarcely reached him. She stood between the door and his couch. Her trousers were rolled high up to avoid a soaking from the water that sucked at her legs.

Then suddenly his face changed, was fiercely red. His eyebrows lifted in a hint of mockery to the tendrils of blond hair on his forehead; and curbing the outraged retort that sprang to his lips:

'I see now that you have never known me,' he said with controlled equability. 'I am only what you would have me be in the likeness of *your* image. When have I ever been an habitué of the Carlton House-cum-Devonshire crowd? After all, you forget that I was only sixteen when I was sent on the Grand Tour – my first stop being Petersburg. Or that I was in the Peninsula but too young to fight during the campaign when Sir John Moore was killed.'

She flinched. Had he deliberately brought in that name, still an unhealed scar in memory?

'I forget nothing to do with you.' A well of tenderness surged up in her. She had hurt him. She knew that by his defence of mockery assumed against the stab she had dealt to draw blood.

'If I have made an image of you, my own dear,' her voice trembled, 'it was a false image and not in *my* likeness which is unworthy of you. I understand how life here' – she gestured at the water now, at last, receding –

'must gall you. But when spring comes again we will go away together.'

He was instantly contrite. Uncoiling his legs, he splashed through the flooded water to take her in his arms.

'My love, my dearest love,' he said brokenly. 'What a beast am I with my miserable complaints. *You*, so far above me, to say you are unworthy of *me*!'

She had not said exactly that but she let him think so.

He bent his head. She caressed his fair silky hair and placed a finger tip in the cleft of his chin. He had shaved his beard. 'You look about fourteen,' she said and kissed the cleft.

So all was harmony again.

'I'll bale this water,' he told her. 'These lazy devils won't do anything except loaf around and pray to Allah or Mahomet to send them the sun.'. . .

Before leaving Damascus she had planned a journey through the desert to visit Mahannah el Fadel, chief of the Anazè tribe. And leaving Bruce, the doctor and Barker at Hamah, she set off for the tents of the Anazès.

She took with her a few servants and Lascaris as interpreter, having rid herself of Bertrand. Snow had fallen on the desert where the furtive sun had not penetrated. In the scattered villages through which she passed, the natives turned out in astonishment to see a fair-skinned youth wearing a sheepskin pelisse and white robe, riding astride a mettlesome mare. She had relinquished her Turkish costume to appear before Mahannah in the dress of a Bedouin.

They had left the villages behind them and, on either side, the long stretch of desert lay in curves of lion-coloured sand rising to the crest of hills etched against a sky which, although wintry, was yet as deep a blue as that of an English summer.

At sundown the sky and desert, encrimsoned with the death of the day, were burnt in the sun's funeral pyre; a glorious sight to Hester's dazzled eyes to see the snow-capped distant mountains bathed in that fiery glow. The news had now reached the inhabitants of the desert that an English Princess was due to arrive on a visit to their chief; that she rode a mare with golden stirrups and that the Sultan of England had endowed her with a thousand sequins* and a bag full of magical herbs that could convert stones into gold.

These reports, in conjunction with the ecstatic account his son Nasar had given of the lady's beauty and her intention to abandon the escort of the Pasha in favour of the Anazè Bedouins, sent Mahannah hurrying to meet her.

He was a man in his seventies, short, crook-backed, with small crafty eyes but more elaborately dressed than was his son, in a curly-haired sheepskin pelisse over a robe of orange cloth and a black and white striped cloak, each shoulder of which was fastened by clasps of gold.

His welcome was effusive. Cringingly he saluted her as:

'*Salamet ya Melika* (Welcome Queen) *Salamet ya Sytt*,' translated by Lascaris as 'Peace be with you,' and more to the effect that Allah was gracious to send the Noble Lady to visit his humble self.

He had already been told by Nasar that she sought his protection on her intended visit to Palmyra instead of that of his enemy the Pasha of Damascus, and was flattered by the preference shown to him by the 'English Sultan's daughter' (she did not attempt to correct him) and invited her to a splendid banquet provided when the Emir learned she was on her way to his encampment.

That she should have attempted so dangerous a journey across the desert with but a few unarmed attendants increased his admiration, shared by his enamoured son who sat beside her at the rude board that served as table in Mahannah's tent of heavy black canvas. Although it was the depth of winter and snow lay thick

* An Arabian coin worth then about nine shillings.

on the spurs of the mountains, the heat in the tent where the Emir's sons and the chiefs of his tribes attended the feast, was over-powering; as also was the stench of sweating bodies and the rich fat-laden food offered to her and which she must eat to oblige her host, though it disgusted her to see them dig their fingers in the great chunks of roasted sheep swimming in melted butter made from camel's milk. There were no knives or forks. They all tore at the food with their hands, taking great lumps of rice from one large dish floating in fat. She too must follow example and eat as did they, and drink the coffee made with water from the desert springs and tasting of mud mixed with sand.

'A royal feast,' she bade Lascaris compliment Mahannah, who salaamed his gratification and prompted by Nasar persuaded her to stay a few days in his encampment with her servants and Lascaris, providing them with all necessities. This invitation she accepted as she wanted to see more of these Beduoins who were to be her protectors on her journey to Palmyra.

The next day, after having spent a fairly comfortable night in the tent assigned to her and waited on by two of Mahannah's concubines, she, accompanied by Nasar, saw and heard old men from the Euphrates singing their praises of ancient heroes learned from the tales of the Arabian Nights, sung in their quavering tuneless voices while they sat round their camp fires under cold starlit skies. She saw naked children, oblivious to the icy winds sweeping across the desert, playing outside the tents in the sand, laughing, shouting, happily. 'And happier than our children in England,' she remarked to Nasar, 'who at the age of six or seven are sent to work in the coal mines or factories.'

'We love our children,' Nasar said, casting fatuous looks at her from his velvety dark eyes. A likeable youth, she thought him and may have dwelled a trifle on the temptation of taking to herself an Arabian lover and to make Michael realize he was not indispensable, nor that she had lost her attraction for other men.

She saw the Bedouin women with lips dyed bright blue and scarlet nails as a hundred or more years later European women painted their nails that they looked to be dipped in blood; their hands were tattooed with flowers. Wherever she went conducted by Nasar, she was hailed as Queen. Men and women prostrated themselves before her, bowing their heads to the ground. She stayed three days and nights as Mahannah's guest and returned to Hamah to find Bruce in the sulks and not in the least interested in her glowing accounts of her visit and the homage paid her by the chief of the Anazè and his son. She flattered herself to think him jealous of her success with these 'barbarians'. He had written to General Oakes with whom he occasionally corresponded, not so often nor so lengthily as Hester, that she might be considering 'a matrimonial alliance with one of these Beduoins.' This could have been mentioned merely as a joke or it may have been an indication, as it likely appeared to the General, that either the rather well-worn affair was getting frayed at the edges or, far more disquieting, knowing the lady's devil-may-care disregard for convention, that there might be some truth in it.

The winter dragged on. Snow and sandstorms swept the desert; and Ann Fry, so long and patiently suffering, developed pleurisy. Besides all this came report of the plague which was sweeping along the coast to Syria although nothing as yet had been heard of plague near Hamah. None the less Michael seized on it as an excuse for them to return to Europe.

'You have surely had your fill of your Arabian Nights' Entertainments,' he said sourly, seeing her with that detached third eye which of late had seemed not to belong to his visual recognition of her or, come to that, of himself.

She was writing one of her numerous letters and

wearing the dress of a Bedouin chief she had worn on her visit to Mahannah. It consisted of a cotton shirt fastened with a leather belt; over that a pelisse of white sheepskin and long soft yellow leather boots. Seeing her there, her legs doubled under her on the couch in their bedroom, her head swathed, not in a turban but a red scarf bound with a treble row of cord made of camel's hair, she looked to him, ridiculous.

'Can't you take that thing off your head?' he asked her testily, 'and let me see your hair? I never see you without your head is muffled in a turban even in bed.'

'If you ever bothered to see me in bed since you sleep like a log here in this god-forsaken hole, as you call it, that seems to act as a narcotic on you but not on me – my mind is too active for natural sleep – you would know that I do let down my hair in bed. You used,' her eyelids quivered, 'to like my hair. It is still there if you wanted to see it. As for going back to Europe,' she poised her pen above the page of her letter, 'because of the plague a hundred miles away – if you are afraid of it, go by all means. Go back to London, Paris or Rome. I stay here until the spring and then I go to Palmyra. You can come with me or not as you wish.'

'It is not as I wish but as you wish. As it is and as it always has been.'

She said quietly to test him or to test herself:

'You are all that I need and want of life. I thought that what we are and have been together is shared as one and not two divided, striving each against the other. In thought, word or deed my wish is yours as it was in the beginning and as it will be unt . . .' her voice dwindled on the words, 'until the end.'

He went to her then and, sinking beside her on the couch, he pulled her close to him. The gold clasp on the shoulder of her absurd costume scratched his cheek. A spot of blood appeared and trickled down to her mouth as his held hers.

He drew away from her.

'You're bleeding! What have you done to yourself?'

She stared, surprised.

'Nothing. I've done nothing to myself.'

'It is the hurt I've done to you!' he cried. 'It is your heart bleeding for me!'

A bubble of laughter surged up in her.

'Darling! I never knew you for a maudlin sentimentalist. Hearts don't bleed – at least mine doesn't. It is too hard to take a scratch.'

He too laughed, unamused, not caring to be thought a 'maudlin sentimentalist', particularly as he had always professed to scorn sentimentality as did she. Taking his handkerchief he wiped away the drip of blood that smeared her lips, saying:

'This came from the pin of that brooch or whatever it is you wear here,' he touched her shoulder, and bending his head to her breast he whispered, 'I'm a beast. You know I will be beside you wherever you go – to the end of the world.'

'To the end of *my* world?'

She whispered it, and smoothing the tendrils of his girlishly soft hair she smiled a slow triumphant smile. . . . No, not now, not yet the dissolution. And if it came it would be in her time, not his.

*　　　*　　　*

Spring danced again along the banks of the Orontes where blossoms fallen from the almond trees floated on the waters of the river that two months before had overflowed in flood. The olive groves rustled in the laughing breeze to show silver linings in their grey green leaves; and the apricot orchards were gay with their shell-pink blooms. Bird song was riotous; the sun glorified the desert, now a parterre of flowers coloured like the mosaic floors of temples, and everywhere kids and lambs frolicked to

165

the piping of shepherd lads, 'that each one,' cried Hester, 'might be a young David in this glorious land.'

At last she could set off on her long delayed journey to Palmyra, with Bruce, Meryon, two cooks, four grooms and forty camels loaded with provisions. Both she and Ann Fry, a poor little wisp of her former self after her attack of pleurisy, were dressed as Bedouins; Hester as an Emir, and Ann as her servant. Michael resentfully was made to wear the same, but under his burnous he wore a pair of English trousers. The doctor, chaffed by Hester as 'no end of a quiz', had a pigtail which she said was a yard long and made of camel hair plaited and fastened to the crown of his head. All, with exception of Ann, were armed. Her ladyship led the procession, with Michael and the doctor very much a pair of also rans beside Nasar who, with his seventy Bedouins had come to escort her.

Lascaris and his wife were not of the party. He who had replaced Bertrand was ordered back to Aleppo to resume his duties at the school; this his excuse to Hester, much to her relief since she was now aware of his motive in his attachment to her service.

'But he got nothing out of me to report to France,' she told Michael, 'unless it be that I and my allies who would die for me and look upon me as their Queen and are prepared for any attempt from Bonaparte to invade Syria.'

Her allies! Their Queen! Michael ground his molars. It was wormwood for him to hear her boast of her conquests, not only of Mahannah and his son, 'But the whole bloody lot of them!' So did he unburden to Meryon. With the arrival of Nasar, when both were relegated to the background, he found the doctor no less aggrieved than he, a ready sympathizer, their mutual antagonism reversed into something close to friendship particularly on the part of Michael who felt himself regarded by the 'whole bloody lot of them', at the best as her ladyship's secretary, at the worst, her pimp.

Together they buried their hatchets in the wilderness

which for each had become a dead end; but Hester enjoyed every league of it with Nasar riding beside her, naming her his Pearl, his Sun, his Star, his Light of Heaven! All very gratifying to her yet for Michael, who overheard too nauseating much of it murmured in a mixture of French and Arabic, it turned his stomach to increase the belief, like a festering canker, that this great love of his life was no more than an illusion. Bitterly he gazed ahead at a mirage in the distance. The last few leagues of the desert that had been luxuriant with spring flowers had now become a wilderness, a tawny waste of sand. The sun had tricked vision to see a sweet and verdant oasis. Love. . . . Was Love also an oasis and, as one neared it inhaling its exquisite perfume, to see it vanish, lost in nothingness! A desert . . . he may still have been suffering from what was no more than depressive after effects of his fever. He dug his heels into his horse's sides and galloped on ahead of the cavalcade. To ride away over the edge of the world! But she would follow him and drag him back. . . .

That evening they pitched their tents in a lovely valley at the foot of the White Mountains, named for the perpetual snow on their highest peaks. Here a disturbing incident occurred. It had been Nasar's custom to come each night to her tent for orders. She and Ann, who was afraid to sleep alone, shared a tent, Michael and the doctor another. On this occasion when Nasar did not appear, Hester sent her Negro guard to bring him to her. Nasar sent back word, or as much as Hester's limited knowledge of Arabic could understand it, that he, Nasar, was the son of a prince and she but a vizier's niece. As such it was her duty to come to him, not he to her.

She was dumbfounded at this audacious message. What could he mean by it? Mere impudence or – revolt? The climax of a long nurtured scheme to beguile her with his flattery and, seemingly, passionate adoration to abduct her and hold her to ransom as the supplier of the cash she so liberally scattered? She guessed he believed it was she who had paid twenty-five thousand piastres,* for camels, provisions, and his escort.

She remembered that before Lascaris left he warned her against these treacherous Bedouins. Nasar and his father were feared throughout Syria for their plunder and their merciless raids. He had regaled her with horror tales of the atrocities committed by the Bedouins and that Nasar would stop at nothing, even murder, to gain his ends which was money and more money with rape thrown in by way of ballast.

What should she do? To ignore this outrageous impertinence – no! More than an impertinence, a challenge – might bring about further insult to result in immediate redress. If she did this she would lay herself and all of them open to attack. God alone knew what would happen to them then. She had heard mutterings among her own men that Nasar was in one of his blackest moods and capable of turning back and leaving their Lady in the middle of the desert. Hester had dismissed it as servants' gossip and their hope that she might be persuaded to abandon the journey to Palmyra. She knew her men were terrified of the Bedouins as they possibly had reason to be.

She decided to say nothing to Michael of the incident nor her fear of its consequence. She knew he resented her interest in Nasar and his absorption in herself which, to his disgust, she encouraged. He would welcome any incentive for revenge, and would attempt it single-handed if need be. For Michael's safety if not for her own she held her peace in the hope that Nasar would hold his.

She passed a sleepless night expecting any moment to find their encampment surrounded and she and all her retinue Nasar's prisoners. As to her own ultimate fate she had no fear of that. She was strong as any man or at least these Bedouins who with few exceptions were short,

* About £150.

stocky – yes, but no match for her own Arab servants unless they were too frightened to support her. She could, she assured herself, cope with Nasar even if he meant . . . No! Not that. She had toyed with the idea of a flirtation with the handsome young Bedouin chief but to allow him his way with her even were it her way, as an experiment only, would be a degradation for the niece of the great Pitt. . . . A vizier's niece, forsooth!

She dozed at dawn and woke unrefreshed with dark circles under her eyes and snapped at Ann who had slept through the night undisturbed, and bade her: 'Get up! Dress yourself. Don't lie there snoring' – Ann did, when deeply sleeping, snore – 'and then dress me. We still have a long way to go.'

On this, the last lap of their journey, Hester sent Meryon in advance to Palmyra to secure lodgings for herself, Bruce and her servants. And complaining that Ann snored she made her sleep in a tent next to hers. 'I want one good night's rest,' she told Michael, 'which I never seem to get with her snuffling beside me. She's been snoring and coughing ever since she had pleurisy.'

As Michael no longer had to share his tent with the doctor, he said he would come to hers. She refused.

'There is no necessity to let these Bedouins know of our relationship. Although they are polygamous they regard monogamy as practised in European countries as our lawful right and that any union not blessed by the Christian Church is a mortal sin. You travel as my secretary.'

'Your lackey in fact,' he rejoined and went off in a huff.

She fell asleep almost at once and was awakened by her Negro servant at the entrance to her tent. He carried a torch. His black face reddened in the lurid light of it showed the white gash of his teeth chattering with fright.

She heard a great commotion going on outside and managed to distinguish from his spluttering words in a mixture of pidgin English and Arabic that the encampment was surrounded.

'By whom?' She sat up in a daze. 'What is all this?'

'All this,' Bruce flung open the flap of the tent that served as a door, and shoved aside the Negro, 'are the Fayden Arabs, sworn enemies of the Bedouins. The horses have been let loose and they have been stolen by your precious Nasar who has absconded with all his men and left us to deal with the marauders. Probably in league with them to hold us to ransom and halve the money for our release! No! Stay where you are,' as she scrambled out of bed and was searching for her trousers, 'don't show yourself. Keep back!'

'I will not! . . . You,' to the quaking Negro, 'get the men. Tell them . . . No!' to Michael, '*You* get them. Station them at various vantage points. I can't make this idiot understand me.' All this time she was pulling on her clothes, had taken up her brace of pistols and was fastening her belt stuck with a Turkish scimitar in its leather sheath which hitherto she had worn less for use than ornament.

'Stay here!' shouted Michael. 'You are not to go out to them. I'll deal with the bastards.'

'If you go, I go or we'll both stay here and let the brutes take us. Don't be a fool! Get the men, and if they're too scared to fight we'll fight alone.'

There was no holding her. She dashed out after Bruce, and while he rounded up the janissaries and servants she marshalled those huddled in their quarters and too frightened to move until, brandishing a pistol, she threatened to shoot any who refused to obey her orders. She finally got them placed, armed with bludgeons and the muskets dealt them before they started on the expedition.

The night was starless. A pall of mist had fallen on the desert, deepening the darkness that, illumined by the torch flares, revealed the faces of the servants in a

170

demoniac glare. Their scared jabbering mingled with the snorting of camels, the braying of donkeys and the tearful cries of Ann who, in her night attire, had run to join her mistress and was hanging on to her burnous imploring her to come back into the tent.

'Go away!' shouted Hester. 'I've enough to do without you clinging to me. Go in and stay in!'

Bruce was firing pistol shots into the air hoping to lure the invaders from ambush; but still no sign of them.

'They are hiding!' he yelled to Hester. 'We'll go after them and get them out before they can get us. They are planning a surprise attack. They think to dupe us into believing it a false alarm. I'll bet you anything you like that this is Nasar's doing and I'll have his guts for it before he —'

His words were halted by a sudden uproarious clamour, not of fear, of exultation from the scurrying flurrying crowd that, in the darkness and the wavering light of the torches, looked in their white robes like dozens of frightened fowls in a farmyard. Then there emerged from clouds of sandy dust, still reddened by the flame of the torches, what appeared to be an army of men on camels and horses streaming out from behind the sand dunes.

'What the hell!' exclaimed Michael, and he raised his arm ready to fire. Hester stood stock still, her eyes on the leader of the troops mounted on a camel.

A shot from Michael's pistol fell short of him; sand spurted up and as the servants, crying frantic greetings, rushed forward to fall on their knees before the camel-rider, his voice rang out:

'Hold your hand, Mounseer Bruce. I have vanquished the *canaille*. They are the Fayden and have robbed you of your horses and the mares of la Princesse, but they are finish! They are – how you say – *mettre en déroute*, by me!' He made his camel kneel and dismounted. Advancing to Hester he knelt before her bowing his head to the ground. Michael, standing by, had all to do not to grind his heel on the neck of him he now recognized as Nasar.

'It is my privilege to have saved the Gracious Lady, Star of the Day, Goddess of the Night!' This effusion was spoken in Arabic, which, if Hester did not understand it, Michael did, and might well have caused him to drive his clenched fist into Nasar's face as he lifted his eyes to Hester's as if in rapture at sight of a celestial being.

'Filthy dago!' muttered Michael, surely the first conception of the word in common use a century later. Turning from the pair of them, his disgust and jealousy increased by Hester's gracious acceptance of this, to him, revolting deification, Michael made for his tent, there to fling himself down on his truckle bed pounding his fist into the canvas-covered board as if it were Nasar's jaw.

'Yes! And I'll break your bloody jaw,' he said, apostrophizing a hole in the tent through which flickered, like an evil eye, the gleam of a waning torch.

Hester had also retired to her tent after regally retreating from the genuflecting Nasar. Stripped of her burnous, trousers, pistols and all the rest of her paraphernalia, she prepared for sleep while allowing her mind drowsily to dwell on the night's events. How Michael, and she herself, had misjudged this excellent Nasar who, far from deserting her had hunted the marauders and saved her and her encampment from disaster and possible death. As for the thieved horses, Nasar had found and brought them back from the raiders. She had always believed in his loyalty and devotion, now proven. . . . Her eyelids sank and opened to a sound, the merest whisper . . . was it, or the rustle in the stillness of the first waking breeze of the dawn?

A whisper, yes! And in the murky greyness, a spectral figure, was revealed, whiter in its white burnous than the dim canvas of the entrance to her tent.

Advancing noiselessly he, whom she saw to be the object of her dreaming thoughts, knelt as before an altar.

'Madonna! *Melika!* Queen of my heart, my life!' His voice, no whisper now, was harsh with passion, the breath of his words in Arabic on her lips. 'I am prostrate before you, Noble Lady! Your courage has answered the test. I, your abject slave, dared to deceive you that I might not be deceived in my worship of one so far above me. You and all your servants, your,' he hesitated, 'your trusted secretary, Mounseer Bruce, all are safe from attack of the Fayden who are many leagues distant from this camp. Heaven has given me the grace to aspire for possession of the Star of all Creation!'

If barely half of this flowery speech, most of it in Arabic, were understood by her, his meaning was clear enough: that he had manœuvred a faked attack from a hostile tribe to gain her favour. She knew bravery to be one of the qualities most sought and admired by the Arabs, and that she had proved herself courageous in her masterly handling of what appeared to have been a dangerous raid rendered her, for him, the acme of perfection.

She was stirred in vibrant response to his passion. . . . A moment only while she yielded to his hot seeking mouth before the entrance to the tent was burst open with such force as to break the ropes that held it, and Michael, in his night shift, hurled himself at Nasar, too maddened with desire to be aware of his approach.

Seizing him by the throat Michael punctuated each blow of his doubled fist with:

'You bloody swine! You f . . . . ng sod! Take this, and this. . . . And this!'

The Bedouin, much the stronger of the two, and understanding most of these epithets hurled at him, was on the defensive rather than the offensive knowing himself in the wrong and that he looked to lose the twenty-five thousand piastres agreed in payment for his safe escort of the English 'Princess'. No matter that she, in her ripened maturity, half man, half woman, was as greedy to be taken as he to take, he must placate her pimp of a paramour. Wrenching free of Michael's furious onslaught and wiping blood from his nose that had suffered in the scrimmage, he said with inherent dignity and in his native tongue:

'Sir, infidel though you are, you would be justified in your assault upon me of the true faith were you not mistaken in my intent that I be guilty of violation of the sacred person of the All Highest Lady, niece of the Grand Vizier of England whom I am privileged to —'

'Cut the puffery!' broke in Michael, 'and get out of here before I have you torn limb from limb and thrown to the dogs, which you and your dirty lot judge to be the penalty for what you would have done and didn't do, you bastard – so get *out*!'

Nasar salaaming, and still with no decrease of dignity, got out.

'As for you,' Michael turned on Hester sitting upright on her crumpled bed in a kind of tranced immobility and as if unconscious of his presence. 'You've asked for trouble and you'll get it. And if you won't give up your lunatic adventures with savages, you'll find,' he added darkly, 'you'll have more trouble yet to come.'

To which she made no answer; only her lips moved as she murmured:

'May I die if more trouble yet to come to me won't come to you!'

*   *   *

Perhaps the greatest triumph of Hester's adventures was the welcome she received as she crossed the mountain pass leading down to the gates of the little lost city that lay among its ruins in the desert. It was fourteen hundred years since another adventuress, Queen Zenobia, the first woman explorer to visit Palmyra, had preceded Hester Stanhope.

174

As she and her entourage came through the Valley of the Tombs, so named for its ancient burial ground now nothing but a heap of fallen stone and rubble, a great cloud of dust was seen and a simultaneous report of gunfire heard. Hester, thinking this to be the herald of an enemy attack, ordered her men to prepare to charge and slowing her horse she loaded her pistol. Nasar, who despite he had been beaten up by Bruce the night before and carried its mark on his swollen nose, had thought better than to seek revenge on the Englishman and incur the possible penalty of having his head cut off which would have been meted by one of his own race for a like offence. He assured 'Madame la Princesse': 'These are no enemy, Madame. They are the people of Palmyra come to do you honour.'

Sure enough about fifty horsemen and as many men on foot emerged from the dusty distance. The Palmyreans had organized a tremendous welcome for the daughter of the Sultan of England, so word reported her to be and who had travelled thousands of miles from an island in the northern seas to visit them. The men who ran beside the horses were naked to the waist, their brown skins hung with cowrie shells and the teeth of animals, or possibly of men killed in warfare or for punishment.

The valley resounded with the deafening beat of kettle-drums, the firing of matchlocks, their shots coming sometimes singly or in quick sharp volleys, the bullets falling in the sand and sending up showers of yellow spray against the rocky boulders that might be the remains of what were once a Roman city's suburbs.

She had a sinking of her heart, not from fear of losing her life but lest she be lost of this, her Omega, the crowning point of her ambitious adventure should the shots claim her their target; or if Nasar, notwithstanding his avowed love for and devotion to her, sought vengeance for his thwarted desire by inciting the Palmyreans to an onslaught that might end in a holocaust. There was no trusting these semi-savages to judge by their war cries and the fearsome sights of them as they came within closer view, the hideous masks worn by some depicting frightful demons, or their faces painted in streaks of black, white and scarlet. This exhibition in her 'honour' could be the forerunner of an attack to take the 'Princess' prisoner, hold her up to ransom from the 'English Sultan', and if not paid the sum demanded she and all her retinue put to death, their tongues and eyes torn out – she had heard of their methods of torture – this might be Nasar's stratagem. She should have accepted the offer from the Pasha of Damascus that his men escort her. Too late now. . . . Was it? She stole a glance at Nasar sitting splendidly erect on his horse in robes of state, not the shabby sheepskin in which she first had seen him. And why, she wondered, had he not then appeared dressed as now like an Emir, the son of a great chief? And why had he not retaliated by fighting Michael or to call him out as would be the accepted satisfaction of an English gentleman; but he was not an English gentleman; he was a Bedouin whose laws were not our laws. They demanded bloody death for their satisfaction, even if they met their own death in what they deemed to be their right for insult and aggression.

All this passed through her mind even while she chatted to Nasar praising the performance as if he were the impresario who presented it for her benefit as Mr Kemble would present a performance for the Regent at Covent Garden. She turned her head to see Michael riding directly behind her. His lips were set in a thin hard line that he seemed to have no mouth. She knew that look as if he held within him a torrent which might burst forth with virulent words and action. He shared her thoughts to realize what this 'mock' battle might portend. She was stricken with remorse that she, even for a moment, had returned Nasar's passion which could well have been feigned, a cunning trick to trap them. Yet her innate vanity would not admit that his adoration amounting to worship was merely subterfuge to gain his ends. Money! To an impoverished tribe of Arabs money was their god, second only to Allah.

'Michael,' she called to him, 'come here. Don't ride behind me.'

He affected not to hear. He had ridden behind her for twenty leagues while she headed the procession with Nasar, and now that danger threatened she would have him at her side.

Their fears were unfounded. Whatever Nasar's motive, his intent was not apparent in the demonstrations with which the Palmyreans greeted her. They formed a fantastic bodyguard leading her through the ruins of the magnificent colonnade, past the crumbling temple of Apollo to the Arch of Triumph where Zenobia had made her entry named in her honour. And as Hester, the first European woman ever to ride under it, advanced there stood on the columns of the colonnade, as if carved in stone, a dozen of the most beautiful girls the Palmyreans could select, their lovely young bodies scantily robed in a single transparent shift. Then, while Hester and her retinue halted, they who had appeared to be living statues leapt to the ground and surrounded her in an orgiastic dance. Men and boys, taking hands with the girls, formed a ring singing songs of praise to the *Melika*. Six of the girls carrying garlands indicated, as interpreted by Nasar, that they wished to crown her.

She dismounted, and bending down, for the tallest of the girls could only reach her head by standing on tiptoe, she received the insignia of majesty. No matter that her kingdom was but a cluster of ruins in a desert, peopled by a tribe of poverty-stricken Arabs who inhabited what was left of a city built by Solomon in ages past and which thousands of years later teemed with Roman legions. The decay of a great empire of which this and its mouldering temple of the Sun god, its once magnificent Graeco-Roman colonnade, its columns still standing broken, crippled, the miserable mud-huts that were the dwellings of the entire population of fifteen hundred lining the way of her procession – of these she saw nothing. She saw, in her *folie de grandeur*, only herself fulfilling her destiny as prophesied by a crook fortune-teller who had foretold her glorification. Yes! . . . . She was glorified. . . . Queen! And already, as she remounted and rode, bowing right and left to the tumultuous cheers of the ragged, half naked crowd who acclaimed her, she envisioned her name carved on these stones to mark her coming as more than Queen, a female Messiah, the saviour of these simple worshipful desert folk, her subjects. She would rescue them from the ignorant and murderous tyranny of their overlords; she would raise them from poverty, their toil of labour in the sand, their sole means of livelihood being the product of the terraced olive groves, the date palms, the fig trees, and the distant waving fields of corn or wheat from such as Ruth might have gathered her stray gleanings. She would order the sheik that it was her wish – no, her command that a tax be levied on every traveller from Europe or from anywhere, whether man or woman, though she knew no woman would dare where she had dared. A thousand piastres at the very least for entry to Palmyra to view the ruins, and by so doing she would be the means of saving these, her people, from the hardship of their penurious existence. By her wise, tolerant and Christian rule she would live in immortality. Christian? . . . Was she destined to convert a whole race? Would her teaching extend beyond the desert to the very gates of Bethlehem, the Birthplace of the Word made Flesh, Queen of the Jews! And were these outposts of the world, her world as she had known it, to be her empire? Would she reign here for evermore or was all this – she removed her hand from the bridle-rein, gesturing the remains of the beautiful triumphal arch under which they were now passing, to

178

receive more wild acclamation – was it all a dream? Was all her life a dream, a chimera of her own self-deception?

She had been murmuring her secret thoughts low but not unvoiced. Dr Meryon who had come to meet her and lead her to the house, euphemistically styled, being but a stone floored hut that he had reserved for her coming, looked at her anxiously. A touch of the sun from over-fatigue? His ear had caught some of her half whispered monologue above the shouts of the populace and the clip-clop of horses' hooves along that narrow way. He shied at the possibility deduced from her mutterings, although her grandiose boast of conquering unconquered desert tribes was no new aspiration. He had heard often enough from her of the prophecy destined by 'Brothers', as he called himself, to realize she firmly believed in his charlatanism.

And seeing and hearing her now with her engarlanded crown – gone to her head with more than a wreath, the doctor glumly decided, he was full of misgivings. Her father's eccentricities had labelled him a lunatic among his peers, or alternatively genius. Which, queried the medical mind, was her inherent tendency? So narrow a margin lay between the borderline of insanity and sense if sense, as in this case, were megalomania? Only time, he conjectured, could tell.

The month Hester spent in Palmyra might have been interminably lengthened had not, as the doctor records: 'An unforeseen event hurried our departure.'

The unforeseen event, apprehended by Meryon, was this time a genuine attempt to besiege their encampment.

Four of the Fayden had come, ostensibly for want of water, to the environs of Palmyra where they had lain in hiding. But also four of Nasar's Bedouins stationed as guards on the look-out for intruders had seen them, and followed in pursuit to capture and take them prisoner. Nasar then ordered them to be stripped naked and held in close confinement with dire threats of punishment if they tried to escape. In the night two of them did escape, whereupon Nasar, according to the doctor, 'raved like a madman'. It was all that Hester could do to prevent him from seizing the sheik of Palmyra, an inoffensive old man in his dotage, believing, as Nasar told his 'Goddess' he had contrived at his captives' release.

'Gracious Lady, I care not for any danger that may come to me and my servants – we are all at your command. But this *canaille* – they have been sent to – how you say – *reconnoitre* to inform their sheik of their villain tribe that the Star of the Day is here in Palmyra, and they will descend upon us in *grandes armées*. They are fifty thousand camel and war horse to seize you and the monies they think the *Sytt* will pay them for her *liberté*.'

Ah! She saw through this, or thought she did. Nasar was anxious for her safety, not for love of her but for the wealth which he hoped to gain in rescuing her from a hostile tribe who would ransack the little city to rob her and him of his reward.

She wavered between mistrust and the attraction she felt for him and his avowed 'worship' that led him to risk his life to win her response to his ardour; his nose still bore evidence of that. . . . Poor nose! Let that be the least he would suffer in her cause.

'Madame, *je vous en supplie* that you return to Hamah *immédiatement*. If a stronger force than ours should overtake us' – this much she understood of his halting French and English – 'we must fall before them.'

Bruce was equally determined that she take Nasar's advice.

'Whether for his ends or yours, it is better we get out of here before the plague gets us.'

'The plague? What of the plague? It is a hundred miles away.'

'It is already in lower Syria and in Acre. There are

constant comings and goings of various tribes across the desert. Best leave here and go while the going's good.'

If for Hester the going were not good, she had to agree to go rather than delay their journey through the desert and risk possible contact with the disease. She therefore ordered their departure for the following day. She did, however, believe Bruce to be less anxious on account of the Faydens or the plague than he was to leave Palmyra on any excuse.

She was right.

He had now had his fill of Palmyra and of having to play second fiddle to a 'bloody dago', who by turning the other cheek had done him out of the satisfaction of a fight, more than to hand him a broken nose. He'd be damned if he'd stand by and see her for whom he had sacrificed his whole career and whose name coupled with hers was a sniggering byword not only in the London clubs but all the embassies of the Middle East – to see her befooled, swindled, lavishing his father's money and all of her own on a horde of savages, and herself glutted with their veneration as for Mahomet or Allah or whoever they fell down to glorify as they glorified her. . . . Good God! What did she think he was?

In some such fuming fashion did he rage as he paced the clay floor of the mud hut he shared with Meryon. There could be only one end to this preposterous, humiliating, nonsensical, degrading – the string of adjectives he spluttered to the mud walls was exhaustless.

The end though neither of them knew it was in sight.

*   *   *

Before they left Palmyra Hester had the gratification of seeing her name conspicuously carved on the portals of the entrance gates, no doubt at her suggestion, as a memorial of her visit to future travellers.

During the return journey through the desert there was

much disquiet among her servants who had it firmly that the Palmyreans' wild demonstrations of loyalty and devotion were but a blind devised by Nasar to gain her confidence that they might attack and take her captive for ransom, if not to kill them all.

When Bruce gave Hester this that he had learned with the reiterative warning: 'I told you so. Nasar is playing his Machiavellian game to beguile you with flattery and attempted rape thrown in,' she rounded on him fiercely.

'No! You do him wrong. He loves me even as you did – once.'

He looked at her curiously, wonderingly. How strange a mixture of masculine strength and feminine weakness was she who, like any young virginal girl or middle-aged spinster, could be so easily gulled into betrayal of herself to think that 'bastard's' cunning to get at her and her money was love! Useless to disillusion her. Such colossal egotism would never accept nor understand that this smooth-tongued tribal potentate, for all his smattering of western culture, was imbued with the first doctrine of Islam that placed woman on a lesser plane than man as his chattel for his sole use to beget him issue, either in multiple wifehood or concubinage, or, as in his approach to Hester, with simulated adoration for his own mercenary ends.

He shrugged away these crowded thoughts superimposed upon the sight of her in the hot narrow tent where the early sun stabbed through chinks in the canvas like thin brassy sword thrusts. They were wakened at dawn, for Nasar had said they must be on their way before the noonday sun caught up with them to delay swift travel. She stood before him booted, trousered, turbanned, looking years younger than her age, a Bedouin youth: the travesty of man with all of a woman's bewitchment. And suddenly he knew he hungered for her even here in this wilderness surrounded by chattering brown-skinned natives, here where death stalked behind their caravan, a deadly foe in the guise of a friend; and he must follow her, drawn, magnetized, even as that swine, that barbarous beast, had magnetized her.

He realized, with a grim sense of irony, that he too could be possessive. Not as was she, an autocrat to hold him chained, imprisoned, but with the possessiveness of a jealous lover or – a bitter laugh escaped him – or a leman.

He watched her buttoning her belt that held her brace of pistols. She took them up and slid them in their holsters.

'It is true, isn't it?' she continued, breaking in on his lengthy pause of self-communing.

'What,' he asked, 'is true? That I loved you once? Yes, it is true, but what is more true and oddly enough, is that I love you still.'

'Why "oddly"?'

She lifted her hands to fasten the gold clasp on her shoulder.

That the two of them standing there, she in her absurd Bedouin costume and he in his over a pair of English tailored trousers bought in Cairo discussing – as if in the intimacy of a London bedroom instead of a canvas tent, buzzing with flies and stuck in the middle of a desert – a relationship that for both had been slowly but surely disintegrating, struck him with a tragi-comical sense of incongruity. The fallen structure of all he had believed to be an overmastering passion throughout the whole of their outlandish journey was forcibly ejected in the hot retort of his resentment.

'After all is it *not* odd that I have to trail behind you and that lust-mongering son of a —'

His words were halted on her interruption of smiling indulgence.

'Dearest, you really are rather unintelligent about Nasar. I admit you surprised us – him – with me in what appeared to be a compromising situation, but you should make allowance for the difference in the blood and breed of a son of the desert – was that what you were about to call him —? Or was it,' she mischievously asked, 'an aspersion on his rightful mother, if he could know his mother among his father's many wives? Were you born of the desert as is he, whose ancestors and immediate forbears regard women as their inferiors – why even in China today a female child is looked upon at birth as a liability rather than an asset – you might also have been tempted.'

'The woman tempted me,' he murmured; ignoring this, she went on:

'I bear him no malice for following his natural instinct. That he conducted himself with dignity as a result of your attack when he had only to call his men to have you stripped and tortured, is more to his credit than to yours. . . . No, wait!' as he made an impatient movement, breaking in with:

'You're mad!'

'I am sane, saner than you who can see no farther than the hidebound ethics of St James's. Hear what I have to say. . . . That I embarked on my expedition to the East is because I believe I have a mission in life. I have tried to tell you this time and again, and I thought you were with me in my original plan of coming to this country. I had hoped to and I think I still can convert these people whom you regard as savages, to a more civilized way of life. They are *not* savages except in your view and the view of the western world. I believed and shall not cease to believe that I am destined to emancipate this country, to rescue it from the despotism and tyranny which has held its people in thrall since the Roman Empire possessed them, and now the Turks. You have seen for yourself how I have succeeded in commanding their respect and trust.

'Yes,' he said succinctly. 'I have seen. Such respect and trust that any day or night we stand to be robbed, murdered, and you, with all respect and trust, raped by —'

'My lady.' Ann, in her dress of a Bedouin manservant was at the entrance to the tent. 'Mr Nah-sir,' the nearest she could get to his name, 'bids me tell your ladyship and Mr Bruce that the horses are ready to go.'

'So!' Hester gave the scowling Michael her most dazzling smile, 'to be continued – if you and I may live to be continued – in our next.'

Fear of the plague which was raging along the coast from Acre to Tripoli decided them, on Meryon's advice, 'to continue in their next', at Latakia, so far the only place free from the scourge.

It was now apparent to both that they had arrived at the parting of their ways. Yet Michael made one last effort to save the wreckage of something more than an amorous interlude nearing its end; it was a tearing asunder of a whole slice of his young manhood's life.

He recalled a letter from his father written during their winter at Hamah. In it Crauford Bruce reminded him how Michael had pressed Hester to marry him, and that she 'so nobly' had said she would relinquish him to 'another thrice happy woman more worthy of him than herself.'

These heroics were later doubted by his father, who despite that of late he had professed admiration for Lady Hester, he never secretly approved of her, had in fact deplored the liaison in which his son had been so recklessly involved. But Michael, even while he guessed her love of power and adventure to be greater than her love for him, could not bring himself to contemplate a complete and final severance.

What was the alternative? Marriage? That from the first she had determinedly denied for his sake, or for her own? Or because of the disparity in their ages which could be equally a reason for the dissolution of their

185

present partnership, with the difference that each were free to separate by mutual agreement and without judicial intervention.

In another letter from his father, Crauford Bruce had made it clear that if his son returned to England with his mistress she could not be received by him, his mother, or any of his family. They would be ostracized by the world to which both by right of birth belonged, having forfeited all respect in contempt for the established proprieties.

Moreover his father, laying on argument with the heaviest trowel, hoped Michael would attain Crauford's fondest wish: a parliamentary career. . . . Even were he wedded to Lady Hester, niece of the 'great Pitt' (neither Crauford nor Hester could ever forget that) such influence as she might have implemented on his behalf before that fatal meeting at Malta and her fall from grace, was gone. Her very name, coupled with Michael's, spelt social ruin to them both.

Be damned to his career! He was pacing the bedchamber they still shared at Latakia in a white walled villa on the shores of the Mediterranean. Larger than any Hester had hitherto rented it had sufficient stabling for her nineteen horses. Latakia, described by the doctor as 'a very dirty town', was environed by numerous orchards providing fruits such as she had not seen since she left Europe: apples, pears, peaches, besides vegetables in abundance as grown in an English kitchen garden. But these attractions were of no account to Michael, more than to increase a nostalgic longing for England and – home. As for his future, she believed, or had made him believe as so often she had told him, that he would achieve a statesmanlike success if he had experience of a world beyond the narrow limits of London society. . . . What world? he asked himself, pausing to gaze out of the window that overlooked a courtyard surrounded by several rooms on the ground floor, and above them those that had been the harem, now set aside for the servants of their suite. And as he looked beyond to the sun-baked walls of the town and its distant harbour on which stood a decayed old castle carrying a tattered Turkish flag – was it *this* world of barbarians under rule of the Turks, knowing no laws other than possession by robbery, murder or rape!

He had yielded his ego besottedly submerged in hers, and now he would cut himself off from her as an axe fells a branch from a tree, yet the trunk remains. . . . As he stood at the window his eye caught sight of her coming from one of the rooms on the ground floor. She stopped to buy fruit brought by a small starveling boy. She took the basket he held out to her, and calling a servant bade him in her faulty Arabic to bring the child indoors and feed him. 'Poor little beast,' she added in English. 'He looks as if he hadn't had a good meal for a year.' In spite of the heat he was shivering as if with fever. 'No,' she told the man, 'don't take him indoors. He may be sickening for something. . . .Not, Heaven forbid, the plague!'

Michael left the window and sat hunched on the bed, his head in his hands. . . . Whatever happened, he thought with an agonizing sense of futility, he had known the fulfilment of all that his spirit had sought: the warmth of a union which was more than passion and all of passion's emptiness. A burning flame to light and – God help me! – he groaned aloud, to blight his eager questing youth. . . . 'I had not sought you if I had not already found you.' Where had he heard or read that?

So introspectively engrossed was he that he did not hear her at the door until she spoke.

'Why are you sitting there all doubled up? Have you a pain? One of your bilious attacks?'

He had been suffering from recurrent stomach trouble since his fever, which, as reported by the doctor, made him vomit after every meal.

Her concern for him was nothing lessened by this unromantic flavour; it may have been strengthened by

187

their mutual conviction they were truly, if illegally, bound.

'No – yes.' He lifted his head; his eyes slid from hers that expressed wifely anxiety. 'I have a pain but not in my stomach. In my heart!'

He seemed so much the little boy bringing his pain to a mother to be comforted that she was filled with an over-whelming tenderness, just as when Charles or James – especially James, always sorry for himself – would come to her even when she too, was a child, to show her a cut knee or bleeding finger to be bandaged, and the place kissed to make it well.

She sat beside him and drew his head against her shoulder, having first removed the clasp of her cloak lest it scratch him.

'There, then, there,' she said soothingly. 'I wish I could kiss the place and make it well as I used to for the boys. A heart ache needs heartsease to cure it. There's a little pansy flower called heartsease. I planted a bed of them at Walmer. There is none here.'

'No,' he echoed below breath. 'None here!'

She bent to the basket of fruit she had brought with her and put down at her feet when she sat.

'Have an apple instead.'

She offered one reddened ripely in the sun.

He took it from her, bit into it, and spat it out.

'Ugh! It has a maggot in it.'

She laughed lightly.

'As also must have been in the forbidden fruit offered by the first woman to the first man. Try this.'

She bent again to give him another. He pushed her hand away and got up.

'Hester.' He stood half turned from her to say in a throaty voice: 'I want us to be married. After all, you may think that in casting off the shackles of an antiquated social convention you are paving the way to a . . .' He was groping for words to clarify his meaning, aware of

188

his inadequate attempt to wean her from her inflexible belief that she had embarked on a Messianic mission to gain ascendancy and understanding of a savage people who regarded her with an almost deific worship – at least that is how she interpreted their salutations to her as 'Queen of the Desert, Light of Heaven, Pearl of Friends, and Standard of High Honour,' these the least of the eulogies showered upon her by the Palmyreans. But, Michael cynically surmised, these Arab tribes knew her to be the distributor of unlimited largesse and as the supposed 'Daughter of the English Sultan', hoped to benefit by her wealth which to them surpassed that of the Indies. How could he prove that conquest of this wilderness was a fool's paradise and her ultimate salvation lay in her life with him, legalized and received by his family and the society she spurned as – his wife.

Floundering, finding words at last to tell her, pleading: Hear me. Let me have my say. We are one in the sight of God or the Allah of your,' his mouth hardened, 'of your subjects, so why do you in your misguidance refuse to recognize the social principles which are yours by right of birth and descent? Why do you seek to break away from the ramifications of our western ethical acceptance of society?'

'What do I care,' she flung at him, her face aflame, 'for the ramifications of – what is it – "our western ethical acceptance of society"? I have never heard you so verbose as if on the hustings where you see yourself addressing your would-be constituents. Heaven forfend I should withhold you from your father's hope and your ambition – but do you ask, demand, that I should legalize that which is immoral in the "ethical" ramifications – you love that word, don't you – of a pleasure-greedy deluded hedonistic London bounded by Belgravia and Mayfair with its Saturnalian temple, Carlton House, and its High Priest, the Regent? Would you have me renounce what is to me a sacred ministry in a world forgotten since the fall

of the Roman Empire? Grant me at least the ministerial
endeavour to bring these people to a better understanding
of their right to live as men and not as beasts, ground
under the heel of Turkish tyranny. I begin to see a
method in my father's madness of his democratic – or as
he called it – republican idealism. Here, in this wilderness,
I follow in his steps.'

He was looking at her with something like horror, and
came close to her holding her arms in a fierce grip as if
to save her from the fateful doom, as he saw it, that her
overweening and misguided sense of power, would lead
her.

'Dear heart! Can you not feel what I am trying to tell
you' – loosening his hands from her arms he gave a little
deprecatory movement – 'although I am so immeasurably
your inferior in, as you put it, ministerial endeavour – all
I have to say now and before God, let it be the last and
irrevocable testament of my love for you, that either you
return to England as my lawful wife or stay here in the
desert alone. . . . No,' as she made to interrupt, 'I *will* say
what has been too long burning inside of me to say – there
is no life for us unless we live together in the sacrament
that you have discarded – holy matrimony.'

He did not see himself as she, biting her underlip to
hide its trembling saw him, as absurdly sentimentalized.
They both professed to abhor sentimentality. He only
saw himself, as still he was persuaded to believe, in love.
And she? No longer 'in love' but for ever loving him,
guarding him, salving with tender mothering unction, his
hurt – the hurt she had dealt him in denying him the cake
purloined from her cupboard so must he eat and have it,
too.

'My darling, that I refuse what from our first begin-
nings I made clear, not from my own selfish, and as you
think, misguidance, but for your ultimate good, your
whole life's future. We have been blessed with a union
that in its supreme one-ness is seldom the lot of lovers

whether married or, as the world where you would wish me to return would say, "living in sin". But it is now the time for us to go our separate ways. You, your way and I – mine.'

'You have chosen.' His face closed. It was as if in dealing him this, her ultimatum, she had demolished all between them that had gone before: the shared comradeship, the little silly intimate bickerings, the joyous readjustments, and the first surrender of her ungiven body to him in his submission to her overpowering dominance that had entirely possessed him to merge in one their separate entities, as has been the foolishly fond imaginings of lovers from time immemorial. . . .

Out of some far off vacancy she watched the shadow of love's sorcery recede and vanish. Love! The haunting phantom of life as lived in its reality and life envisioned, believing that a perfect union cannot be divided.

Something of this, inarticulate and unexpressed, flashed through her as she heard his voice, a stranger's voice, saw the cool calculating mask which was not his, or had it always been unrecognized and only now perceived?

'So be it,' said that voice; and turning, he went from her blindly.

She made to call him back, but her outstretched arms fell to her sides as her lips moved to echo his words without sound:

'So be it.'

None had heard of any quarrel to speed him on his way, for there was none. Nor was it necessary to make feasible excuses as to why he should have left her to return to England without any previous warning, briefly ordering the packing of his baggage, leaving such garments as his Turkish dress behind him which would not be required but must be kept for him if he should need them, suggesting he would come back. Georgio, who was to accompany him as far as Constantinople, had been given to understand that his master was only to be gone for a short time; and providentially, or coincidentally, a letter from his father arrived on the same day of that final break urging him to return on the plea, not only of Crauford Bruce's illness – he had been ailing for some time and made the worst of it to Michael – but because news had reached him of the plague that was sweeping through Syria and the Middle East.

On the morning of his departure Michael attempted one last effort to persuade her to go with him, not as his wife nor as his mistress, but as his travelling companion. She must, he begged her, see reason and not run the risk of infection by remaining in this plague-infected country.

That he had gone to such pains – if it did pain him? – to assure her that their mutual agreement to part would still hold good if she travelled as his 'companion', caused her a little laugh, and huskily to achieve a mirthless joke.

'If I did go with you I would go like this!' She ran her hands down her baggy scarlet trousers. 'Then there would be no mistaking our – or your – intent. None in Europe and certainly not in London would know me for a woman, although in mistaking my sex they might also mistake your interest in the Turkish young gentleman you brought along with you.'

He had gone pale. She saw him again as the sensitive beloved boy who had so loved her – once.

'Do you mean,' he cried, 'don't fool me, Hester, do you mean you *will* come with me as – as – anything you like. Forget all this, and come with me and marry me?'

She shook her head. She knew she was hurting him but not so dreadfully as she must hurt herself.

'No, Michael, no, I can't. I have no fear of the plague. It is unlikely I shall get it, nor does Meryon think it is the real plague – bubonic. He says this is merely the sort of tropical fever that does recur in the Middle East.'

She was trying to speak calmly, reassuringly, that he need have no scruples about leaving her here alone.

'You must never think,' he said with a suspicious moisture in his eyes, 'that I want to leave you. . . . After all you have given me every happiness I have ever known and ever shall know.'

That almost weakened her, yet she drew herself away from him who would have taken her, and held him hers for always.

But: 'Go, my darling,' she made her lips firm to say, 'I'll be behind you wherever you are and – God be with you.'

As once before when she had watched him from her window ride off to Aleppo before she journeyed to Damascus, so now did she stand to see him mount his horse with Georgio beside him, the proud-necked camel loaded with baggage, urged by its syce, patiently following along the narrow dirty street. She watched until the dust clouds and a dimness came upon her to lose all sight of him whom she knew she would never see again.

She died a little death.

PART THREE
Arabian Night

ONE

The plague had come to Latakia.

The first victim attended by Dr Meryon was the boy who brought a basket of fruit to Hester and collapsed in the courtyard where, as Hester ordered, he had been given a meal. Like fire the contagion spread through the town. Meryon urged her to leave without delay.

'The whole house is like to be infected. I beg your ladyship to go to Lebanon. I know of a convent at the foot of the mountain where you should be free from contagion.'

'Indeed I will not go,' she retorted. 'I have no fear of contagion. My servants are in a state of panic having been in contact with that poor little boy. How is he, by the way?'

'Recovering now. The fever was slight. It might even have been a form of dysentery. Nevertheless,' persisted the doctor, 'I do urge you to leave Latakia. Every day dozens of inhabitants are stricken with the disease.'

'In which case I shall remain here to help you who will have all to do attending the sick. I am told there are only two doctors within fifteen miles, and they must already have their hands full of patients. Besides, how can I go and leave my servants here without me? Would you have me desert, not my servants only, but those who look to me as their Queen? Who have crowned me their Sovereign Lady? No, my place is here with my people.'

Her people! Useless to argue with her for, since her parting from Michael, more than ever did she associate herself with the Arabs. Always at the back of her mind lay the conviction that her destiny was to bring these Arab tribes to a better comprehension of their place in life other than as serfs of the Turks. She had it firmly, her *idée fixe*, that her mission was that of a second Messiah or, because she had come to the land of the Israelites, a second Moses, Queen of the Jews, as prophesied, to teach them the commandments of Jehovah and not that of Allah or Mahomet.

Meryon hearing her talk in this strain as so often she did now that Michael was no longer there to hear her, began to doubt her sanity. And when she too fell sick of the plague and lay in a frenzy of delirium he feared not only for her reason but for her life. The doctor was himself overworked almost to death hurrying from one stricken house to another and consoling the bereaved. And then when the epidemic was at its height Meryon became a victim, not in his opinion of the plague which had devastated London in the reign of the Second Charles, but of an epidemical fever.

Whole-heartedly dedicated to his profession he rose from his sick bed to do the work, single-handed, of a dozen doctors and in a state that should have brought him to his grave.

Then Ann Fry was struck down by the same fever that had attacked Meryon and Hester. Her recovery was slow, and so soon as she, Ann, and those of her household who had taken the disease were themselves again, Hester decided to leave Latakia.

When Michael heard she had sickened of the plague and was at death's door he wrote from Constantinople to his 'Dearest Love', that he 'had been plunged into the deepest affliction . . . Good Heavens! If anything fatal had happened to you, I believe I should have gone out of my mind. . . .' He could not know that his 'Dearest Love' was almost out of *her* mind, not only as result of her illness but that he, at Constantinople and now travelling across plague infested countries, might also contract the disease. She sent letters after him to be received whenever he should arrive at his various halting places on the overland journey to Europe. These letters offer maternal solicitude for his health with minute instructions how to combat a temperate change of climate after the great heat of the desert. He is not to forget to wear a flannel waistcoat and must get Georgio to rub his legs, and if he has a cold he must take elder flower tea for breakfast or barley water gruel, and if constipated two teaspoonfuls of castor oil when going to bed. . . . Scarcely the letter of a lovelorn mistress, except after similar motherly advice she has one more word to add. . . . 'If it please God that anything should happen to me do not think of me with regret but consider that I have enjoyed a few moments of happiness that without you would not have fallen to my lot. God bless you, my angel.'

It is evident from her 'angel's' letters to his father, and also to James, that it was on Hester's insistence and not his that he had left her. He may have honestly believed it for, if absence makes the heart grow fonder, he gave Crauford Bruce to think the separation but temporary, especially as Michael was asking, as usual, for money to the tune of five hundred pounds. He had previously written to Hester that his father 'a man of great wealth' could well afford to make him an extra allowance of two thousand a year, one half of which he would give to her.

If the two thousand allowance to be divided between himself and Hester ever materialized to her benefit, there is a letter copied by her and now in the British Museum, proof enough that he had every intention of keeping his word.

He waited anxiously for further news from his 'Dearest Love'. None came. He wrote a long letter to James asking if he had heard from his sister since she had sickened of the plague. This put James in a rare state as it was the first he had known of her illness.

Ever since the outraged letter James wrote to Hester when he learned she was living with Michael as his mistress, flaunting her disgrace to the world and glorying in it, careering through the desert riding breeched and dressed as a man – and a Turk of all things! – James would have no more to do with her nor with him whom he believed had brought about her downfall. Michael's letter went unanswered. Yet now that he was really worried to hear Hester had the plague which was sweeping through the Middle East he wished for a reunion with the sister he had always adored, if the 'evil influence' of Michael, as he hoped, was at an end. He even contemplated journeying to those 'barbaric' countries, to bring her home with him to live as befitting her station in life and forget all that had gone before, providing, of course, she would never again set eyes on any of these Bruces, nor the scoundrelly Michael.

James, no longer the 'little brother' whom Hester had promised her uncle to 'care for and guard against bad ways,' was now Colonel the Hon. James Stanhope, very much aware of his position as virtual head of his family, for none of them regarded their eccentric old father as their 'head'; nor had James much use for Mahon who appeared to have but two interests only, the study of philosophy and expectation of the earldom at his father's death.

James was determined to rescue Hester from a life of sin, for heaven alone could tell to what abysmal depths of depravity she might sink left there in those desert towns among a horde of savages. She might even – God forbid! – enter into a form of marriage with one of those sheiks, who from all account had paid her marked attention, showered her with gifts and, if talk which had floated from the embassies at Cairo and Constantinople could be credited, she had already received more than 'marked attention' from another of them discovered in her tent by Bruce in *flagrante delicto*! . . . James fretted himself sick dwelling on horrific possibilities, particularly when he heard that Michael, far from inconsolable and returning as the prodigal son to the fold of his father at

Hester's 'insistence', had found consolation with a lady at Pera.

Letters from this lady, written in French so that her nationality was uncertain and whose name, as she signed herself, was 'Theophanie', wrote that 'the time which had passed without his telling her he loved her – eight whole months – seemed endless.' How that time when he was telling her he loved her had been passed, we may conjecture by his ultimate reply while spending that two thousand pounds, and possibly Hester's half of it as well, in Vienna where another lady who, when he moved on to Paris, may have found time to be equally endless since he had told her he loved her.

He did, however, find time to write from Paris to 'Theophanie' that she was . . . 'The only woman worthy to replace my guardian angel. I told you I admired a woman whom I regarded as a superior being. . . .'

While he made no secret of his love in the desert with 'a superior being', he tells his 'dear Theophanie that distance and absence can only strengthen his love and admiration for her.'

One hesitates to think that the same sentiments were sent to other ladies in Vienna and Paris, but it is evident he spent a considerable amount of his father's money enjoying himself in both these cities before he eventually arrived home.

As for Hester, the loss of him who for five years had filled her life was nothing lessened by the fact that she had been prepared for it. The agony of separation, now that it had come, was worsened by the knowledge that he so soon and so easily could be consoled. She must have heard, as all news concerning him was brought to her by Barker in constant touch with the Embassy at Constantinople, of his affair with the lady of Pera, if not with others.

Her empty nights were tormented by vicarious fantasies of him in another woman's arms; fantasies that jeered at her broken love, mocked her deprivation of a mate no longer hers but any woman's for a passing interlude. Was that all she had meant to him? A passing interlude of sexual desire? Did her body no longer delight him? Or did her age, so many years older than his, at last begin to tell that he must see her as she was?... Her mirror, into which she shrank from looking, spoke too harshly of the truth; her recent illness had left its mark. Mercifully he had not seen her ravaged face, as she now saw it. Only her eyes, their lovely colour still undimmed, remained of the face he once had loved. Her skin, so clear and fine, had lost its fox-glove tint, was sallow, sickly, faded. Her figure, always boyish, which he had professed to admire, was thinned and skinny; her features sharpened. Where now lay her attraction, if any; should she in her turn seek consolation?

'You're like a beautiful boy.' Had he said that or was it Camelford who likened her to Ganymedes?... Camelford, gone, dead. John Moore, her one and only true love, dead. Was she also dead, living with the ghosts of those who had loved her, desired her, a shadowy procession passing through the corridors of her sick fancies? Even here, in these desert lands, Nasar, to whom she might have surrendered had Michael not appeared at that crucial moment.... Was Nasar dead, no more to her now than a shadow?

In her debilitated state of health, such in-dwelling resurrections of her life with and before Bruce, had told on her highly strung nervous system. Her servants bore the brunt of her frequent outbursts of uncontrollable temper when she would rage at and dismiss them for some trivial fault. Her maid, Ann Fry, whose own nerves were at breaking point after all she had suffered in her devoted and uncomplaining service to this tyrannical mistress whom she had followed in dreadful days and nights across the desert, living in filthy disgusting tents and houses, expecting at any time to be set upon by thieves, violated, murdered, she too came in for her share of her lady's frenzied brainstorms. Poor Ann, and poor Meryon, who also had to contend with his patient's neurotic behaviour which, he was persuaded to believe, as symptomatic of temporary mental aberration inherited from her republican father, 'Citizen' Stanhope, said by his peers to be mad.

At last she agreed to Meryon's persuasion to leave Latakia. 'This damnable, filthy, stinking hole', for which she insisted *he* was to blame for having brought her there, and thankfully did the doctor remove her and her household to Mar Elias near Sayda.*

*   *   *

The Convent or monastery of Mar Elias, dedicated to St Elias and no longer housing the monks was in formidable disrepair. It stood half-way up Mount Lebanon and had nothing to commend it other than its view of the Mediterranean on the Syrian coast; a barren, lonely spot ringed with rocky mountains as sterile as the slope on which the convent stood.

Hester travelled there by boat that the doctor found to be 'very roomy and comfortable'; an agreeable contrast to the Greek ship which had wrecked them on a rock in the Aegean Sea. But on arriving at Sayda they found the monastery that had been so long unoccupied required complete redecoration, and in the meantime a house had to be found by the tireless doctor until Mar Elias should be ready to receive her.

This unexpected delay before she could be settled in what she had hoped would have been a permanent home did nothing to improve her temper. 'The disputes between her and her maid,' wrote the much tried doctor in his diary, 'and Lady Hester constantly in a passion makes me quite miserable. . . .' Something of an understatement for

* Originally Sidon: Biblical.

both the doctor and Ann were made almost suicidal by her ladyship's constant 'passions'. When at last the monastery had been rendered habitable there was further cause for complaint from Hester, not altogether unjustified.

A disused chapel adjoined the house of one storey, the walls of which were discoloured and stank to heaven. The reason for this was later discovered to be the burial place of one of the Greek patriarchal monks who had been embalmed, not very efficiently, some few weeks before. They had sat him upright in an armchair inside the wall. The men dared not take him out and bury him somewhere else lest they incur his wrath and be cursed to everlasting; so he stayed and Hester must put up with him, smell and all.

This decided her to seek yet another dwelling-place and Meryon was despatched to find her one.

A village a few miles distant, still higher up on the Lebanon range was suggested by the doctor, the air being cooler than at Sayda for the sun was now hot as Hester's temper. But she, having had to wait so long to get into the convent, changed her mind and said she would *have* to stay at Mar Elias whatever its condition and with the patriarch stuck there in the chapel wall.

'For what use have I of a chapel?' she demanded of the doctor. 'Block up the door and burn the place down – with the old man inside it.'

And when at last all was ready to receive her, and the 'old man' still seated in his armchair, the chapel not burned down nor the door blocked up, she again refused to live there. But she had to stay until another house could be found. She remembered that Emir Bechir, Prince of the Mountain, by whom she had been so hospitably entertained two or three years before, owned the territory bordering the village of Mushmushy. To him she applied for permission to rent a house in that village and received a grudgingly non-committal reply.

Whereupon she told Meryon she would pitch her tent on the mountain if he could find no better place for her to live than 'in this stinking hole!'

The better place to live had to be in Mushmushy* where, with or without the Emir's permission, she could retire.

'And become a recluse,' she conveyed to the doctor. 'I intend to study astrology and devote myself to the betterment of these ignorant people, my subjects, through the knowledge of the stars.'

'God grant me patience,' prayed Meryon. And set about to put a second house in order. This also required substantial redecoration and entailed more delay. Meanwhile the plague had spread through Syria to seize upon the isolated village where the convent of Mar Elias stood.

The fear of the plague again infecting her brought a recurrence of Hester's 'passions'. She raged at the doctor: 'You're an unfeeling brute! You're *all* unfeeling brutes. You don't care a damn whether I live or die. None of you cares!' She hoped the plague would take her and the whole lot of them. . . . 'As for you!' rounding on the wretched Meryon, 'if you had the spirit of a louse you would have knocked that damned Fry flat before you allowed me to be insulted by the slut!' This, because Ann, poor worm, had ventured to turn with tearful remonstrance: 'Oh, my lady, I beg you to control yourself. I do my best but there's no pleasing you,' sobbed Ann. 'Your la-la-ladyship would be ber-ber-better suited with one of those ber-black slave women th-than me. You can swear at them and they,' snuffled Ann, 'ca-can't understand you. I can – and I'd ber-best be leaving my lady and ger-go.'

'Yes,' yelled her lady. 'You *can* go – to hell!'

Ann took fright for where should she go and how? To

* Meryon's spelling of it which appears more correctly to have been Mishmushi.

journey back to England alone across those plague infested deserts on a donkey and then in an awful boat –
that would be hell indeed.

'Oh, no, my lady, no!' she clutched at Hester's caftan,
'I can't leave you – pray don't send me away.'

'Then you can stay here with the old man in the wall
for company and make a list of all our movables and
baggage until I want you – if you're still alive in this
stinking morgue.'

And so the day of departure for Mushmushy was fixed
but because Hester declared she must halt at every station
on the way, tents had to be pitched all along the route. At
the first station her ladyship fell into another violent rage,
this time with Pierre, her French cook who had provided
her tent with a wooden bedstead, that, although thought-
fully prepared for her, was not what she had ordered.
'Idiot! I told you to take it to the next halt – not *this*
one!'

'*Mais, miladi* —' ventured Pierre, pale, and dreading
what would come next.

'Don't *mais* me!' came next; and taking a heavy stick
which she used when having to walk up the rocky paths,
she beat him – 'bastinoed him unmercifully,' according
to Meryon. Some peasants working nearby came to see
what all the noise was about. The doctor, confessing to be
'much discomposed,' as he feared the men would prate
in the village of what they saw and heard, 'endeavoured',
he says, 'to tranquillize her.' . . . 'For God's sake calm
yourself. Here are strangers', which mild attempt to make
her see reason served only to make her see red. While
Meryon, exhausted, left her to it.

'I was dropping with sweat and agitation. There was
no tree to lie under and nothing to lie upon, while from
the door of her tent her ladyship abused me and called
me names. . . . So I mounted my ass and went back to the
village.'

Meryon had also decided, as did Ann, that he could no

longer endure his lady's passions'. 'But,' reflected he, 'no treatment however unjust, could authorize me to desert Lady Hester. . . .'

The next morning he sent her a letter by one of the servants at Mar Elias in which he told her he had retired from her presence the night before to avoid a second indignity and repetition of a scene that could only aggravate her ladyship's condition. He was now desirous of returning, 'and had the honour to be her ladyship's very faithful and humble servant'. . . .

What was the secret of her hold upon these creatures in her service? That no matter how much she 'abused and called them names', beat them – her dragoman, a French Levantine, was similarly 'bastinadoed' as was the cook, Pierre – yet they were still always her 'faithful, humble servants.' Was it a something which those who for a time had loved – and left her: Granville, Camelford, Bruce, who had found in her so endearing a childish quality, which for all her unfeminine dominance that could 'bastinado' an offender, threaten at pistol point a tribe of marauders, swear like a trooper, abuse that most tolerant and gentle of gentlemen, the willing martyr Meryon, and the next minute would burst into tears and beg forgiveness for her 'hellish temper'? Not that any of her lovers were treated to more than a taste of her 'hellish temper', unless it were Camelford who may have come nearest to a bite of it when she flew at him with a riding crop. Yet it is recorded she was ready to humble herself to the humble, could not do enough to atone to Ann Fry for having left her at Mar Elias alone with the smelly old walled-up monk. She sent for her, coddled her, made her take plenty of exercise, drink lots of milk, if only asses' or camel's milk; and get some colour in 'your poor little peaked cheeks. You mustn't be so thin.'

So now all was calm as after summer storm.

But the calm and peace of Mushmushy soon began to

pall. She must be actively engaged on some exciting new exploit, which was presented to her by a chance allusion to a name forgotten. . . .

Ascalon! The name evoked a memory of her meeting at Nazareth when she entertained the explorer Burckhardt at dinner. She remembered how he had seemed superciliously to denigrate her adventurous travels as the eccentricities of one of those 'lunatic Stanhopes' for which, looking back upon that visit, she could only believe was the reason for his cavalier reception of her as his hostess. When he spoke of hidden treasure at Ascalon she at once fabricated her intent to find if there were any truth in the rumour of which she had said she was well aware. While at Latakia, just before she had been stricken with the plague, she again heard of hidden treasure at Ascalon but now, with more concrete evidence, she had been told of a manuscript relating to this so-called treasure held by some Italian monks who had all particulars of the actual site of its burial. But before she could make further inquiries she fell ill and was unable at that time to follow up the clue, which she now determined to do.

While she was planning how to start negotiations, a letter, long delayed by reason of the plague, arrived to tell her of the death of her sister Lucy. . . . Little Lucy! Another death, another loss, the sister who, although she had not seen nor communicated with for many years was of her own blood. Heartbrokenly she grieved. If only she had not left England, she would sometimes tell herself, cut off from all she loved – but no! Whom had she left to love now Bruce was gone? Griselda? But there had never been much rapport between the two.

More than ever now must her mind be diverted from dwelling on the loss of those whom she had held most dear. She had taken a dislike to Mishmushy. She would go back to Mar Elias, and from there she would make inquiries as to how she could get to Ascalon and begin her search for hidden treasure.

Chance offered a solution. His Majesty's sloop *Kite* had put in at Sayda from Constantinople. She sent word to Captain Forster of the *Kite* to call upon her, and of him begged a favour. Could he ask permission of His Excellency, Robert Liston, the British Ambassador at the Porte, that he provide her with a warship that she might examine the ruins at Ascalon, where, with the permission of the Sultan, she proposed to search for the hidden treasure known to be buried there.

Captain Forster was staggered. He had heard much of Lady Hester and her astonishing adventures and her hazardous journeys through these outposts of civilization; of rumours that she had taken to herself an Arab chief as lover, if not had entered into a form of marriage with him; that she had lived openly on her travels with young Michael Bruce to the scandal of her name and his. . . . While exhibiting shock when such tales were circulated among his mates in the wardroom, Captain Forster was none the less intrigued to be met face to face with the notorious niece of the great Pitt who had held place of honour at Downing Street and now paraded herself dressed as a Turk. He could scarcely believe his eyes – although he had been told that she masqueraded as a man – when she received him in her trousers, her caftan, her turban, her embroidered belt stuck with a sword, and – good Lord – a brace of pistols!

Finding the Captain passably good-looking and not having seen a visiting Englishman for months, let alone a young one, she who had regained her health and with it her physical attraction enhanced by the Turkish costume which she knew was vastly becoming – and one of the reasons she chose to wear it – she made him charmingly welcome.

Regaled with the wine of the country, the best to be obtained which was not saying much, but when liberally imbibed he was ready to agree to her request. Neither he nor any man could resist her when she was bent on capture.

The result of this visit was the return of the Captain in his *Kite* to Constantinople with a message from the lady to Mr, afterwards Sir Robert, Liston. His Excellency must have been amazed as was the Captain when he had first heard of Hester's proposition, but not having met the lady he was free from predacious beguilement. The message entrusted to Captain Forster suggested that his Excellency approach the Sultan for a permit to conduct excavations at Ascalon and to discover the secret treasure hidden there. The proceeds of the expedition, after all expenses had been paid, were to be handed over to His Sublimity, the Sultan.

Mr Liston, recently appointed as Ambassador to the Porte, was in somewhat of a fix as to how he should deal with this fantastic project. And when confronted by the Captain, whose *Kite*, seen through the windows of the Embassy gracefully afloat on the waters of the Bosphorus: 'Who,' his Excellency demanded, 'will be called upon to finance these excavations?'

'Her ladyship,' the Captain had been led to believe and hesitatingly reported, uncomfortably expectant of a severe reprimand for bringing so audacious a proposal to the Ambassador, 'considers that the British Embassy at the Porte should be held responsible for, er, for all expenses incurred including safe conduct to Ascalon in one of His Majesty's ships, mine, er, actually,' was Forster's finale to this overture.

'Good God!' Blond, pink-skinned and young in his early thirties for so important a position, Liston had not yet learned how to mask his reactions to any untoward procedure under diplomatic imperturbability. Flushed to the colour of an albino beetroot he let forth an explosive: 'The woman's crazed! I – my – Embassy, to finance on behalf of my Government, a hare-brained crank to go digging for a non-existent treasure – or at best a lot of mouldy coins dumped there by piratical Spaniards. I'll be hanged if I consent to any such foolhardy – Damnation!' Banging his fist on his desk he had upset an inkwell. 'Now look at this!' He struck a bell to bring a junior attaché. 'Send a footman,' he told him, and to Forster: 'Tell her ladyship I'll have none of her or her bl—' he checked the epithetical adjective on the tip of his tongue and substituted lamely – 'foolish excavations.'

'Sir,' accustomed to command a man-o-war, Forster recovered command of himself to reply, as primed by Hester in event of opposition: 'Her ladyship feels that such a gesture on the part of the British Government in presenting the Sultan with precious relics of an ancient world, which she is convinced she will unearth, is bound to cement a more friendly relationship between the Turkish Empire and Britain besides adding prestige to our country and —'

'Clear up this mess,' interrupted Liston at the entrance of a footman. 'And you can take from me to her ladyship, who seems to be as crazy as her father, that it is impossible to land a ship on the coast at Ascalon. . . . Yes?' at the reappearance of the attaché with a sheaf of papers for his signature. 'Refill the ink pot,' this to the footman: and to the Captain: 'So let that be the end of it, Captain Forster. I will bid you good-day.'

But that was not to be the end of it.

She would never admit herself defeated in any undertaking on which she was determined. To Ascalon she would go and not all the King's Embassies nor the British Government could hold her back. She would go and would return with a million pounds' worth of gold bullion and priceless treasures to be offered to the Sultan. This she believed to be a *coup de grace* that would not only consolidate a friendly relationship between the

Sublime Porte and Britain, but establish herself as Ambassadress to Syria.

Her first move in this direction was her return to Mar Elias with a chastened Ann in tow and Meryon, thankful to see her restored in some degree to a more normal state of mind. To be interested in no matter how wild a goose chase, digging for gold or whatever at Ascalon, was preferable to her alternate outbursts of uncontrollable temper or frenetic delusions.

'But how,' the doctor tactfully inquired, 'as the venture will prove costly, does your ladyship propose to meet the inevitable expense incurred? Have you any guarantee from the Porte that the Sultan would be willing to finance the expedition?'

'None at all,' he was cheerfully told. 'I demand my expenses from the British Government.'

'Yet I understand,' persevered Meryon, 'that the Porte has not granted your ladyship the assurance of —'

'I don't want their assurance. I shall send my bill of expenses to Liston at the Embassy, even if he refuses to pay having already said he can't supply me with a ship. But I am certain Captain Forster could have landed his sloop at Ascalon and so save me a long and much more expensive journey overland. I know the Captain was ready to conduct me in the *Kite*. I had him in my pocket.'

Meryon blinked.

'Yes,' she said with her mischievous grin. 'I suppose you think I'm off my head. They all think that. Bruce, Liston, my brother James – he thought that the moment I set foot in the desert simply because I, a mere woman, choose to be a century in advance of your masculine hide-bound conceptions of what the female of the species should be – a child-bearing mammal. And don't look so shocked like an old maid who has found a naked man under her bed. I am an old maid – to all appearance that's to say – but I'd not be shocked to find a man naked or otherwise under my bed or under my petticoats! And if

I can't get the money out of Liverpool and his old women at Westminster – they've had no leadership since my uncle was lost to us – God rest his precious soul – then I'll have it put in the London newspapers that they have refused to finance me. I'll expose them. I'll let them know it is my *right* to conduct a diplomatic mission, not for *my* honour and glory but for Britain !'

Having thus expressed her intent, which the doctor knew it useless to oppose, preparations for her journey went apace. Beaudin, her latest French interpreter and dragoman was sent to find the safest route via Acre through the desert, and Meryon to Damascus to negotiate for a caravan of camels, more horses, mules and provisions.

In the meantime Mar Elias buzzed with ominous talk of the arrival at Stamboul of one of the chief officers of the Sublime Porte attended by a formidable retinue of armed troops. This was thought to be the forerunner of a raid to confiscate property or an arrest for some misdemeanour that could entail the putting out of eyes with red hot pokers, the tearing out of tongues, or decapitation according to Sublimity's decree.

Meryon and Beaudin returned both in sorry case, the former having been lost in a snowstorm had to sleep in a wretched roofless lean-to under his horse for cover. And Beaudin, whose mare was stolen, had to walk most of the way until he begged the loan of a horse from the Governor of Acre.

At Mar Elias they met with a commotion, the household running helter-skelter chattering with fright and all in anticipation of immediate arrest, torture, imprisonment or worse. In the courtyard, uniformed mounted Turks strove ineffectually to quiet them, and Meryon and Beaudin at once suggested the cause of the disturbance.

'This means, milady,' said the dragoman, pale and trembling with apprehension – he had some previous knowledge of what this descent from the Porte might portend – 'that the Sultan has been informed of your ladyship's project and put – how you say? – his heel to stamp her. Yes?'

'No. The Porte has sent these,' she gestured the mounted officers – 'these gentlemen at my request.'

'But your ladyship,' this from Meryon only slightly less pale than the Frenchman, 'how did you manage to send for these – gentlemen? Neither Monsieur Beaudin nor myself were available being to and fro from Acre. I must entreat you to go indoors and take cover. There is certain to be shooting. I cannot allow your ladyship to be exposed to any such risk.'

'There's no risk unless to yourselves. The *Zaym*, the Sultan's emissary, brings a message from the Sultan that he is entirely in favour of my expedition. He has sent this lot – these gentlemen —' she hastily substituted, 'led by the *Zaym* as my escort and has promised to grant me authority over the Pashas of Acre and Damascus to conduct the excavations.'

Meryon could scarcely be assured that these promises, if promises they were with no written guarantee more than the honeyed words of the *Zaym*, that the Sultan was prepared to bear the expense of the excavations at Ascalon, nor the caravan which Hester had been told would be placed at her disposal; but, as ever he must bow to her command.

She started the next day for Acre and, in compliance with orders from Constantinople, was given the honours paid only to princes. And why not, when she had been acclaimed Queen of the Desert and received as British Ambassadress? (Self-appointed.)

In addition to her own six tents she was supplied with twenty more, one of which with its curtains of green silk decorated with golden stars was 'the acme of elegance' according to Meryon, much impressed to learn it had been used by the Princess of Wales during her scandalous tour of the Holy Land. This 'elegance', however, did not compensate for the fact that before the caravan and tents had caught up with Hester who rode ahead, she and Ann had to sleep in a cow-shed.

But nothing could exceed the luxury which eventually escorted the *Melika* seated on a palaquin drawn by mules under an awning ornamented with two golden balls. 'Could this,' she inquired of the doctor with a giggle, 'be intended as a phallic symbol from the Sultan?' Yet Hester, after two hours of it, insisted on riding her own mare to Haifa, their first halt, no easy journey at the beginning of the rainy season. As they neared the coast a terrific storm sprang up from the Mediterranean. The tents that had been pitched beyond the town were blown inside out and looked like gigantic inverted umbrellas. Many of them fell upon their occupants. The animals – there were Hester's own six horses and the twenty sent by the Sultan besides the troop of cavalry led by the *Zaym*, and a dozen or so camels – all frantic with terror at the gale that looked to be a tornado. The camel drivers were on their knees grovelling in the dust and praying Allah to preserve them. Hester's tent collapsed on top of her; Meryon and Beaudin rushed to the rescue, dragged her out and found a tent that was approximately dry. There she and Ann, the latter in hysterics, passed the night, with Meryon and Beaudin patrolling in shifts outside the entrance to guard her.

When the storm was at its height the doctor staggered through the teeth of the winds to the dinner tent leaving Beaudin to keep watch on Hester. Meryon found, huddled in a corner, a ragged dishevelled individual with straggly unkempt hair, wild tormented eyes and only one hand. The other had a wooden stump with a hook attached to it. He greeted the doctor in cultured French and launched forth on a diatribe of awful prophecies concerning the ultimate fate of 'the Emperor'. Which Emperor? . . . Meryon, buffeted by the storm for hours, rain drenched, no servant within call, no food within sight, no *Zaym* –

he too had deserted the encampment and sought shelter in the nearest village – thought for a moment he was the victim of hallucination brought on by sheer fatigue.

'Do you allude to the Sultan or —' could this extraordinary visitor be a messenger from the Porte who had fallen into the hands of robbers, bereft of all his belongings, his escort fled, and himself tortured? Any horror could happen to anyone in these barbaric countries.

Just as he was about to probe with further questions, the stranger slunk away muttering: 'The doom of France is near. . . . The Emperor will be conquered and the conqueror is a man of iron. . . .' Or so much as Meryon understood it.

Mad, mad, he told himself, we are all mad to embark on this hare-brained adventure.

He had half made up his mind a dozen times to quit the service of his lady of whose eccentricities and exacting demands he long since had had more than enough. While he prowled in search of food, he had eaten nothing for several hours and then only a handful of dates, he speculated on how and when he could break away from her whom he had served so faithfully and with so meagre a salary; but that was a minor point. She was his patient and as such, in duty bound, also because of a true affection for her which all who served her had, as witness the patient enduring, uncomplaining Ann Fry. 'So how,' murmured Meryon, 'can I ever leave her, unless she decides to return to England?' Bruce had left her, he was in Paris the doctor had been told. Hester wrote to him frequently and received very few letters in return. . . . Ah! He had come at last upon the remains of a joint of camel flesh, a flagon of wine, a dish of dates, no bread, no utensils to eat with, but it was not the first time the doctor had to tear at food like 'these savages'.

'Dear me, dear me,' he sighed as he munched, digging into the unsavoury tough meat with his teeth and spitting out the gristle. What, he cogitated, will be the end of us, and what did that demented fanatic mean by the end of France? France is all but ended with Bonaparte imprisoned on Elba! ...

He drained the last of the wine from the flagon and, seeing the first grey finger of dawn probe through a hole in the canvas, he went back to the encampment where Beaudin sat in a puddle of rain, his head on his knees and fast asleep.

'A fine guard you are!' exclaimed Meryon, shaking him. 'Wake up! You will catch your death of cold if not rheumatics sitting there in your wet clothes. Go change into dry things and round up the men. We should be on our way within the hour. The sun is rising. I will attend to her ladyship.'

Hester was awake, and Ann had been sent to fetch her riding kit which had been left in the marquee.

'Did your ladyship sleep?' asked the doctor.

'Not a wink, what with the neighing of the horses, and the snoring of the camels and Ann – I couldn't tell which snored the loudest – oh, go and tell the cook, if you can find him, that I want my breakfast.'

'The rain has ceased and the storm abated, so I suggest,' said Meryon, 'that we proceed as soon as possible.' And he hurried away to find the cook.

When he returned he told Hester of his strange encounter.

'Poor creature, he is certainly demented. He vanished – I could see no trace of him – he went quite suddenly after prophesying doom to France. I gather he is a Frenchman of some education, but he gave no name nor could I tell whence he came. He is certainly in need of medical care whoever or whatever he is.'

'I can tell you who he is and what he *was*,' Hester said, taking a handful of dates; her breakfast had been brought to her consisting of muddy coffee, damp bread and sodden fruit. 'I saw him wandering about the encampment when you and Beaudin had gone to Acre. His name is Loustenau and he is or was a general in command of the Mahrattan troops at Poonah. He distinguished himself in those tribal wars, was decorated by the Rajah, and acknowledged by the French government as a useful *agent provocateur*.'

'As was also Lascaris,' the doctor dryly reminded her, 'in whom you placed implicit trust.'

'I repeat only what General Loustenau told me,' Hester tartly rejoined. 'All this occurred when he was much younger. He has since suffered great misfortune. The Rajah in gratitude for his service rewarded him with jewels, honours, and wealth, but he used his money in unwise speculation and lost it all. He said he had been offered one of the Rajah's most beautiful concubines as wife and Loustenau offended him by marrying a French girl who gave him several children. Only one of them, a son, is believed to have survived, but he doesn't know if he's alive or dead. He lost a hand in one of his military actions and the Rajah gave him a silver stump of which he was robbed. He said he had lost everything and is a wanderer on the face of the earth. I am deeply sorry for him and ordered to have him clothed and fed, he was in rags as you saw, but before the servants could do so – anyway most of them were hiding from the storm – he disappeared. Do you know the first words he said when I met him crouching from the rain by one of the tents that had collapsed? He said: *'Madame, le moment que je parle, l'Empereur Napoleon a échappé de l'Ile Elba!'*

'And you believe all this?'

'Yes!' Hester threw the core of her apple at him, barely missing the doctor's head. 'I do believe it. I know a liar when I see or hear one, and this man is no liar nor is he mad, as you seem to think. He is no more mad than you or I.'

'Which, in your ladyship's case,' said Meryon, does not prove the poor gentleman sane. But this he did not say aloud. What he did say was:

'He professes to have the gift of second sight in

prophesying Napoleon's escape from Elba, which is as improbable as it is impossible. Bonaparte will be far too well guarded. I beg your ladyship not to spend your sympathy upon imposters.'

'He is no imposter, and I intend to take him as a member of my household. He has gone from here now, but he'll come back.'

Meryon profoundly hoped he would not.

They arrived at Ascalon on April the First, 1815, than which Meryon refrained from remarking, save to himself, a more appropriate date could not have been chosen for a fool's errand.

And a fool's errand it was.

No expense had been spared by the accommodating Sultan, from the gaily coloured tents and the elaborate marquee with its gold-starred curtains retained for Hester's use to receive guests. There was a large dinner tent where she and her attendants could have their meals, but a hut had been reserved for herself and Ann as it was forbidden that women should sleep in close proximity to the tents of the men. Ann also must never appear unveiled; this according to the law of the Mohammedans, and must, Hester told her, be enforced, rather than offend the Governor of Acre, Mahomed Aga, commanded by the Porte to supervise the excavations. There was evidently no reason to doubt the co-operation of the Sultan's good intentions, to aid and abet her to the best of his will and his exchequer. But, again Meryon refrained from offering a damper to his lady's enthusiasm, by reminding her of the cliché that hell is paved with good intentions.

The expenses for which someone would have to pay were from the first, formidable. Every day a hundred and fifty workmen, peasants from the fields or neighbouring villages, were commandeered to dig with Meryon and one of the Governor's *aides-de-camp* acting as overseers.

Hester, mounted on her favourite black ass rode up and

down, supervising and giving orders to the workmen, translated by Beaudin.

Among the ruins, reported to be the birthplace of Herod, stood a small building, evidently once a mosque, of which the sole inhabitant was an elderly sheik much alarmed to see a troop of Turkish cavalry headed by a fair-skinned young man riding an ass and dressed as a Bedouin chief. On being told the reason of their arrival and of their encampment, with its brightly coloured tents that Meryon remarked resembled a Derby Day at home, the sheik at once offered his services to join in the search for the treasure which he had heard was hidden there; and he pointed to various places where other excavators had in the past attempted to seek but never found.

'We,' Hester said, her optimism undaunted by Meryon's discouragement, '*will* find and give to the Sultan the treasures which by right are his, since he is paying for it all.'

'Quite so.' The doctor was cold, Beaudin hot and suffering from slight fever and the effects of sitting in the pouring rain at the onset of the adventure, with severe pains in his joints, nothing bettered by another heavy downpour that impeded the digging for the first day.

'*Poisson d'avril en verité,*' he muttered, as he tramped back to the tents, sharing an umbrella with the doctor.

On the second day of the dig, three or four feet down, some foundations were laid open. Great excitement on the part of Hester convinced she had come upon the first discovery of the coveted treasure, particularly when a Corinthian capital and three fragments of marble were unearthed.

'The treasure is not left here by Spanish pirates!' she cried. 'This dates back to ancient Greece.'

Further digging in the merciless sun that followed the rain, brought to light two small earthenware vessels,

220

some fragments of pottery and two or three human bones. Hester was delighted.

'There is evidence here of untold wealth buried since aeons before the birth of Our Lord.'

But the workmen were whispering among themselves, and when Beaudin was asked by Hester to know what they were saying, he told her they had come upon a ditch which had recently been dug by Mahommed Aga, Governor of Acre. This gave her uneasily to think that others might have been there before her, and in all probability had found all that was worth finding. However, she would not be put off by that, if only to prove Meryon a cross between doubting Thomas and Job's comforter and to admit her right and he wrong.

After two more days of strenuous work in alternate blazing sun and downpours of rain and hail with the mud of unearthed soil up to their knees, the excavators uttered loud excited cries to bring Meryon hurrying to the dig. Hester on her ass was there already.

Making a trumpet of her hands, she shouted: 'They have found the treasure!'

The doctor confesses, in his laborious account of it, that he felt exultation at the sight of a 'relic of antiquity'. The relic of antiquity, being a marble statue dragged up by ropes from where it had lain, six or eight feet below the ground with the remains of the pedestal on which it had stood.

Meryon was now ready to allow himself at fault in having doubted the success of the venture; Hester gleefully triumphant. No matter that the figure was headless, had lost a leg and an arm, it represented, according to the doctor, a god or a king, Alexander if not Herod who was said to have had a palace here. He made a sketch of it while further digging discovered a broken marble pavement and the remains of a Corinthian column.

'Here is treasure indeed!' he exclaimed to her ladyship, who seemed not so delighted with the unearthing of a mutilated statue of uncertain origin as with the possible discovery of million pounds' worth of hidden gold, which had been reported from the various visitors who had come to see the excavations but even more to see the lady who, dressed as a man, was an English princess and ambassadress from England searching for treasure to hand to His Sublimity.

She was certain of success, particularly after the descent upon the site of several so-called astrologers, soothsayers, and other sorts of charlatans laden with magic spells, crystals, and all such paraphernalia to prophesy good fortune and glory to the Queen of the Desert, chosen by the Prophet to pour at the feet of His Sublimity, the Sultan, the lost treasure at last retrieved.

There was no end to the flattery, homage and wizardry offered to 'the Queen' and received with gratification and ample reward to the self-professed descendants of the Three Wise Men. There were three who acted as spokesmen and chiefs of the gang, leading her to believe them the reincarnation of the three kings who had come with gifts to the stable where the Child lay in His Mother's arms.

She would believe anything.

But after four more days of fruitless digging she decided to give up, disheartened. Yet the sight of the sweating peasants, half naked in the broiling sun and demanding to be paid by the Pasha – as she had understood, but requesting more from her or else would down tools – decided her to call a halt and resume excavations later in the season. She must humour them at all costs.

Then suddenly, before she had voiced this decision, and after the discovery of the headless statue which Meryon considered to be worth its weight in the undiscovered gold, as a 'relic of antiquity', he was horrified to be told:

'What do I care for antiquity? I came here for one purpose only. If treasure is to be found I will find it, if not now at some future date. It is written in my stars. As

222

for that' – she had dismounted from her ass and gave a contemptuous kick to the marble torso of 'that' where it lay among the earth and dust and rubble when hauled up from its bed – 'it may or may not be an antique or a carven image of Herod, Alexander, or a god or goddess – No, obviously *not* a goddess! Or it may have been dumped there by some aspiring seeker who has filled it with gold and is coming to fetch it – Ah! Wait a minute.' Meryon shuddered wondering what further sacrilege she had in mind.

The further sacrilege she had in mind caused more dismay to the doctor.

'Order the men to break the thing into a thousand pieces. We'll soon see if it's filled with gold – or not!'

'Madame!' Beaudin who had no interest in these activities other than to receive his wages and his share of the treasure, if any, which he doubted, was almost as shocked as the doctor. Whether genuine antique or not it must be worth money for the marble alone. '*Mais, miladi, pour casser* – to break it – *nom de nom!*'

'I'll nom de nom you! Do as I tell you. Take half a dozen of the men and have them smash the damn thing to bits. Then we'll see what we will see.'

What they saw when they had smashed the 'damn thing' to bits, marble splinters flying, great chunks falling beneath the hammer blows was nothing. Absolutely nothing.

'Then take up all the pieces and throw them in the sea,' commanded Hester.

Tears of rage and disappointment sprang to her eyes; she turned away regardless of Meryon's attempt to stay this final act of: 'Vandalism, madam! You have committed an inexcusable act of vandalism. For pity's sake keep at least the arm, the leg —'

'I'd smash you with it for tuppence!' she muttered; and mounting the waiting ass, she stayed to watch the men gather up the remains of Herod, Alexander or whoever, and went with them down to the shore. Meryon was greatly agitated to see the last of this 'relic of antiquity', sink in its broken pieces of marble into the blue tideless deeps of the Mediterranean.

'Gone for ever,' moaned Meryon. 'A priceless relic – that this act of vandalism can never be forgotten in the memory of virtuosi.'

'Virtuosi my —' Hester refrained from shocking the good doctor further by uttering the inelegant expletive on the tip of her tongue.

When the last fragments had been flung into the sea, she left the men to go their ways with the doctor gloomily behind her on foot, and went back to the encampment.

Saddened, discouraged, lost of faith in the three wise men's prophecies of wealth and glory, she bade Ann: 'Pack everything. We return to Mar Elias, and from there . . .

Where would she go from there ?

Only God and the Fates could tell.

Neither it seemed could tell. God remained indifferent to her prayers for guidance, and the Fates – she could no longer trust the Fates. They had deceived her once too often.

At Mar Elias where the blocked-up door of the chapel and the burning of aromatic pastilles dispelled to some extent the odour of the defunct Patriarch, Hester was undecided if she should or should not return to London. No! Never. To be ostracized, a pariah, an outcast who had sinned against the unwritten commandment: 'Thou shalt not be found out.' That the greatest sin of all !

With cynical amusement she considered the effect of her arrival at the Bruce mansion in London or their country house, Taplow Court, where Bruce, after his sojourn in Paris and Vienna, would be received as the prodigal son, having rid himself of her whom his father regarded

224

as a Jezebel, and who, if not yet thrown to the dogs, deserved to be.

No, London, England, was closed to her whose name had become as infamous as that of the much maligned and even more eccentric than herself: the unfortunate Caroline, Princess of Wales. Hester had heard how the Regent's wife with her motley crew had toured these very lands where Hester was crowned Queen; and how the poor lady attended a ball at one of the European Courts naked to the waist with a pumpkin on her head. The Desert Queen felt a certain sympathy with the future Queen Consort of England. We have both kicked over the traces of convention, she told herself, only the Princess is more courageous and more *out*rageous, than am I, in that she has a royal position to consider and I have none, at least none that would be considered of any account in our civilized – save the mark! – society. But if England were impossible, what of Cyprus or Greece, or Malta? No, never Malta of too tender memory.

She wavered between this and that plan, where to go and what to do with the remainder of her lonely frustrated existence, yet she was too much in love with life and Hester Stanhope to indulge in masochistic self-pity; and now she must suffer another if less humiliating shock than the failure of her treasure hunt.

A letter from Robert Liston at Constantinople gave her clearly and firmly to understand that the British Government would on no account stand responsible for the expenses incurred at Ascalon.

As for the Sultan and his extravagant caravan, horses, mules, camels, servants and those luxurious marquees – 'Heavens above!' she raved to Meryon, 'how have I been deceived. How can *I* pay for it all? It must have cost hundreds. *Some*one must pay.'

'Not the Sultan, I fear,' was the doctor's discomfiting reply.

In desperation she wrote to Barker at Aleppo asking

for a temporary loan. Never must she contemplate borrowing off Michael, who had not yet kept his word that half the two thousand a year promised by his father should be hers. But he had agreed, through Coutts, her banker, to allow her six hundred a year, not yet forthcoming and not enough even with her twelve hundred per annum government grant, already spent, to cover her expenses. As for travelling to Europe – out of the question. She had not the wherewithal to take her there, and not one of His Majesty's ships would now be allowed to give her transport. Here at Mar Elias she must stay and economize as best she could .

But Hester had not inherited her father's parsimony, indeed much the reverse having had her fill of cheeseparing at 'Democracy Hall', the rags of clothes she had been made to wear and the tending of turkeys rather than Stanhope should have to pay a boy to do it. She did, however, reduce some of her staff; yet as always generous when she knew of deserving or, indiscriminately, undeserving cases, she took into her household the old derelict, General Loustenau. He had presented himself at Mar Elias soon after her return: and as she had promised when she met him at the encampment en route for Ascalon, she at once offered a home to the friendless exile whose sorry tales of misfortune, piled on *ad nauseam* to one whom he, the cunning old devil, recognized as incurably gullible where her sympathy could be touched.

She found a new interest here at hand to engage her imagination, and who, like the soothsaying humbug 'Brothers' before him, prophesied that she would reign as Queen of the East. Much of that prophecy had already been fulfilled; and now with a religious mystic, as he purported to be, installed as her personal prophet, she swallowed everything he told her. She was destined to be the bride of the Messiah at his second coming. She too would ride on an ass at his side to the Holy City. . . . Had she not an adorable black ass, pure bred, that she loved as she

226

loved her two favourite mares? A most knowledgeable ass who did everything but talk, and he too would talk, she had no doubt, a possible descendant of the ass of Balaam.

All these auguries, accompanied by incantations, crystal gazing and the prognostication of the end of monarchical rule in Europe, when all men would turn to the East and to the white woman who had been chosen to lead them to a Utopian world of her making, were handsomely rewarded. Such lavish subsidies greatly diminished her present slender means and caused Meryon much anxiety, not only and far less on his account than hers, for the good little doctor would sooner forego his salary than that she should be embarrassed.

The summer sweltered on in burning heat. Hester languished and was prescribed complete rest and to stay in her room darkened against the glare of the sun. Meryon may have seen the deleterious effect upon his patient of the 'General's' necromatic visions with which Hester was obsessed.

Barker's loan relieved her of immediate financial worries until there came to her other more disturbing news. This time it disastrously concerned Michael. In October of 1814 when all fashionable London flocked to Paris he was there too.

He had spent some enjoyable weeks or months in Vienna where he had written to his Theophanie; but if he found other consolation in the Austrian capital Hester had not heard of any certain successor to herself until his arrival in Paris.

In Paris he became acquainted with Princess Moskowa, the widow of Marshal Ney; and also with another charmer, la Duchess de St Leu. To the avid gossip of the English pleasuring in Paris when Napoleon was safely, as believed, imprisoned on Elba, Michael's name had been coupled with both these ladies, in particular with Madame la Princesse. It was the talk in the salons of the

227

ton that Michael Bruce had been inveigled into a promise of marriage with the widowed princess or if not to an unofficial honeymoon in Italy. As for Madame la Duchesse de St Leu, with whom there could be no question of marriage since she already had a husband, there was sufficient evidence to warrant suspicion of a *liaison* in frequent visits to her house at all hours of the day and night. All this eventually came to the ears of his *belle amie* in the desert, who had written to tell him she was 'very oppressed and unhappy' signing herself 'the Nun of Lebanon'. She was to be more unhappy when she heard of the ladies in Paris who were enjoying his company as much as he enjoyed theirs.

But besides this knowledge from various sources, bringing reports of her ex-lover's feminine interests, came more and most shattering news.

Michael was in prison in Paris on trial for his life!

*   *   *

What now of the oracle in her home foreseeing the fall of Empires and herself crowned with sovereign splendour? Never a sign that her best beloved faced death on the greatest of chargeable sins – High Treason! Against whom and how could he be guilty of treason? No treason against his own country, surely, in a land with whom we are at war?

'No longer at war, *chère Madame*,' said the General, reclining at ease in her living-room at Mar Elias with a dish at his elbow of *Rahat Lahoum* known in English as Turkish Delight and greatly cherished by the General's sweet tooth. 'I have had news, much delayed, but brought at last to me by special messenger.'

'What messenger?' She was always insistent on chapter and verse for any news to do with the war.

He waved his stump. The wooden one and its iron hook she had replaced with a substitute near to the original in silver as supplied by the Rajah, and procured for the 'Prophet' in Damascus at considerable cost.

'What messenger?' he repeated, his eyes under wrinkled lids, with their heavy shelved grey brows above them, gazed fixedly into space. 'I receive my information not of this world, *ma reine*,' he had gauged her satisfaction at this mode of address, 'nor yet of yours, Majesté, until the High Powers with whom I am in constant *rapport*, ordain it.'

In this past year he who had but little English, could now converse with her more or less fluently in her own tongue.

He leaned forward to lift on his knee a large black cat. Hester had of late adopted a half dozen strays, male and female, two of the latter having been delivered of kittens; one litter of nine in Hester's bed, the other – 'Dear me!' tut-tutted Meryon when he found a heap of blind sucklings in *his* bed.

'These creatures of a psychical clairvoyance excessive,' remarked Loustenau, 'were adorés – how you say worship – by les Egyptiens anciens, for example the goddess with the face of the cat, Sekhet!'

'Did Tom,' short for Thomas Aquinas, queried Hester referring to the occupant of the General's knee, and the father of a prolific progeny, 'tell you we are no longer at war with France? I know you augured correctly when you told me Napoleon had escaped from Elba before anyone in the whole of Britain knew it, but how do you know the war is ended?'

She had not yet heard the news of Waterloo, which Barker, her chief informant, had not received until weeks after the event. Reports from England, even to the consulates in distant British outposts, travelled slowly in the days before the horse of iron had replaced the horse of flesh, and steamboat travel was as yet a rarity.

'The secret things belong unto the lords, my gods,' was the obscure reply. 'And this son of Sekhet,' he stroked the

229

purring Thomas Aquinas, 'conveys to me the news of this – and other worlds beyond us.'

Hester, as usual, implicitly believed him.

How Michael came to be imprisoned in Paris on so dreadful a charge, drove all other worries from her mind. She at once set about to inquire into the case. Nothing mattered to her now, not the failure of her treasure hunt, nor her increasing debts, nor the Messianic prophecies of her ultimate glory, all faded into insignificance beside the awfulness that had befallen her 'Dearest Love'.

She wrote innumerable letters; to Michael first of all offering to come to him in Paris if she could be of any help in saving him from so dire a fate. She wrote to the recently restored King of France and sent a copy of her letter to her cousin, the Marquess, afterwards Duke, of Buckingham, whom she had not seen nor corresponded with for years.

What the recipients of these singular epistles must have thought of them, if they were ever received, is uncertain. We cannot believe that Louis XVIII could have been gratified by the rhapsodies of Lady Hester in praise of the conquered Bonaparte in his living death on St Helena and full of invective against the Allies of whom she writes:

> . . . They have violated the laws of nations to the utmost by deluging France with foreign troops and degrading and imprisoning a man acknowledged King by every power in Europe! . . . The Grand-daughter of Lord Chatham, a niece of the illustrious Pitt, feels herself blush that she was born in England.

That the niece of the 'illustrious Pitt' who, when at Downing Street, had witnessed the subjugation of Europe by Napoleon, self-crowned Emperor of France; she who had shared the constant threat of invasion with the British whom she now reviled when all Britain was rejoicing over the victory of Waterloo, might have inclined Dr Meryon, had he known of these letters, to fear as he often had reason to think, that she suffered from inherited mental derangement.

Meryon gathered from hints she had dropped that Bruce also admired and sympathized with the arch-enemy of this England that gave her 'to blush' for being her birthplace.

It seems Bruce had got himself into this serious trouble due to a mistaken knight-errantry, having aided and abetted the escape of Count de Lavalette who, at the restoration of the Bourbons, had also been condemned to death for High Treason.

Whatever the result of Hester's intervention on Michael's behalf and the pages of letters to him, to her cousin Buckingham, and to his Majesty, the King of France, whose secretary may have consigned them to the rubbish heap unread, we know nothing. All we do know is that Michael came out of what might have been a calamitous climax to his Parisian adventures with no worse penalty than a few months' imprisonment, and which earned him more adoration from his various inamoratas.

But with the ladies of Paris who had engaged his attention amid much speculation and talk, he soon was finished; and, as he writes to his father, he also is 'finished' with Hester. This decision must have been exceedingly agreeable to Crauford Bruce, himself now involved in serious trouble. The banking house of Bruce and Co. was on the verge of collapse.

Michael is possibly a trifle conscience stricken for his desertion of her from whom he had broken the chains that held him victimized for these four years in the desert. Her voluminous letters upraiding him for his neglect of her, and his failure to pay her the agreed allow-ance on the strength of which she had overdrawn on her banker Coutts, had gone unanswered.

'Notwithstanding the fine promises you have made have vanished into thin air,' she wrote, 'I still feel a great solicitude for your happiness. . . .' This before she had learned of his imprisonment, when all recriminations were forgotten in her anxiety to save her 'Dearest Love' from disaster and a dishonourable death.

Then, at last, she hears from him. Michael has managed to squeeze out of his father before the final crash, three hundred pounds to hand over to Hester.

One can hardly blame Michael for being unable to keep his promise of financial aid to her whose personal extravagance surpassed even his own; nor that he could be held responsible for the fiasco of Ascalon if the British Government had refused to have anything to do with it and left her to foot the bill.

She is 'overjoyed' to receive his letter which took several months to reach her. She 'hopes her tears could blot out what she wrote in an agony of mind. . . . But now, thank God, all these misconceptions are done away with'.

There are pages of it, in which it is hoped her 'Dearest, Dearest B,' having 'done away' with her found the time or the wish, to read, and is followed by two more, in similar strain, the last of which ends:

'Farewell, my once dearest B! I must call you so no more.'

TWO

'*Et tu, Brute,*' murmured Hester.

Ann Fry, in tears, fell on her knees before her lady in the room that overlooked the courtyard where a drooping date palm wilted in the glare of the July sun. Hester, seated cross-legged on a divan and divested of almost all her clothes except a thin cotton shirt and muslin trousers was smoking a long amber-handled pipe.

'So,' smiled Hester, 'you summon up courage enough, my poor little worm, to turn on me?'

'No, my lady, no! I'd ner-never turn on you – I ler-love your ladyship,' blubbered Ann with her knuckles in her eyes.

'Love?' Hester puffed a volume of smoke to make Ann cough and add more streams to her already streaming eyes. 'What is love? A vapour like the mirage you see in the desert and think it water to quench your thirst and find 'tis nothing but dry sand. There is no love save self-love. Do you know that?'

'Yes, my lady – no, my ler-lady,' bleated Ann. 'I ler-love you more than anyone else – not myself. I have ner-never loved myself or I wouldn't have sta-stayed all these years in this der-dreadful country with these der-dark gentlemen and all their – their porcupines.'

'Their *what?*'

'Their per-porcupines, my lady as not being their wives.'

'Ann,' said Hester almost herself in tears and half in laughter, 'if I can bear to let you go I could never replace your malapropisms. . . . Porcupines! Dear life!'

'Yes, my lady,' said the submissive Ann quite at a loss;

and, gazing dumbly at the smoke haze that veiled her lady, she found voice to say:

'I will of course stay with your ladyship until you are suited.'

'Much obliged, I'm sure,' Hester removed the pipe to tell her. 'Am I to be suited with Fatouma, my black girl who smashes a dozen cups and plates of fine porcelain a week, and gives me to drink the ass's milk from my bath after I have bathed in it?'

'She thought, my lady, that is what you ordered not understanding your ladyship's language,' strove Ann apologetically on Fatouma's behalf, remembering the howls of the slave girl when chastised for this and other offences.

'Then I am to be waited on by half-wits or deaf mutes and speak to them in signs? Think again, Ann. Picture me here deserted in the desert – no pun intended – there's the doctor throwing out hints every day for the last twelve months that he is homesick for England and his family. He'll be the next to go and leave me here surrounded by natives and murderous enemy tribes.'

'Oh, my lady, no!' squealed Ann, horror-stricken. 'Can the doctor not persuade you to go back to England with him?'

'To England with him?' cried Hester. 'To that fog-bound miserable island inhabited by fox-hunting drunks and the hell-rakes of Carlton House? And swarming with the poor wretched down-trodden slaves of the Haves who batten on the starved flesh of the Have Nots? My father was regarded as a lunatic because he upheld the French republic, and let me tell you,' Hester leaned forward to tap the bowl of her pipe against a massive brass spittoon, 'I will never return to England. I dislike the English and their Government. They have had *no* Government since my uncle, the great Prime Minister Pitt, was lost to us.'

Pressing the tobacco of her pipe down with her thumb, she resumed: 'But if you do leave me I will send for my good Williams, your predecessor, who is at Malta with her sister – Yes!' She started to her feet, as the idea rocketed into her mind. 'Yes! That's what I'll do. I'll have Williams here with me and you will stay until she comes. . . .'

So that was it, to the satisfaction of all concerned including Meryon; he may have been thankful that Ann had paved the way for his own longed-for departure.

Before the arrival of Williams, however, Hester who found time pass haltingly slow, was soon to be engaged with another great adventure; or it might be termed a crusade in the interest of a certain French officer, Colonel Boutin, of the Engineers. He had been sent by the Emperor Bonaparte on a mission to Syria, and Hester first made his acquaintance in Cairo. They met again at Sayda, at the house of the French Consul, and Boutin had latterly been Hester's guest at Mar Elias. Her preference for and sympathy with France against her own country was very shocking to Meryon, and may have finalized his decision to leave her.

It was during a visit from Boutin to the convent on Lebanon that he told Hester of his intention to cross the hitherto unexplored Ansar mountains inhabited by the most savage and dangerous of tribes.

She attempted to dissuade him from so hazardous an undertaking but her persuasions went unheeded. He was determined to go, and go he did, despite the warnings of the 'Prophet', Loustenau, dismissed by Boutin as *un coquin fieffé* – an arrant rogue.

The arrival of Williams and the departure of Ann filled in a time lag that followed the final break between Michael and Hester. Williams who had known and served her as personal maid and confidant during her girlhood in England was a welcome change from Ann Fry. Hester had given Ann instructions to initiate Williams in her duties in this strange world in which Ann, poor soul, had suffered so many hardships during her enforced exile.

235

Williams must have wished she had never set foot in these desert lands inhabited by – 'savages, I do assure you, Miss Williams,' Ann confided, when giving her successor accounts of the horrors entailed by long journeys – 'on a donkey from one dreadful place to another, living in tents and no servants except blacks and natives.'

And of her ladyship's violent tempers, 'Much worse, believe me, my dear Miss Williams, than you could *ever* have known. And the food! Never so much as a good fresh egg – no cow's milk, only camels' milk —'

'Camels' milk!' gasped Williams.

— 'or asses' milk. She bathes in asses' milk and as for the servants, they are born slaves most of them and bone lazy and as for thieving – you daren't leave anything lying about, not a handkerchief even or they'd have it. You'll never learn their barbarous language neither, and just look how she makes me dress!'

Williams looked, and paled.

'Gracious goodness, Miss Fry. Do you mean her ladyship *makes* you – I thought you were wearing these awful clothes and trousers – like fancy dress – because they are the custom of the country.'

'So they are, but not for ladies, Miss Williams. These are gentleman's – I should say *men's* clothes. It is what the Shake's gentlemen wear.'

'The Shake's?' wonderingly echoed Miss Williams.

'Being the Arab word for lord in our Christian language,' explained Ann, thankful for the first time in six years for this unburdening of complaints and grievances to one of her own kind. 'They pronounce it Shake – that is how they say it. But they have so many names for lords and gentry here – a Meer and Patcher, and I'm dressed as a Shake's valet. My lady dresses as a Shake herself and they all take her for a man but I have to go veiled always because one isn't safe to walk about among them heathens,' Ann contemptuously sniffed, 'if you are unveiled and they can see, even if dressed like this, that

236

you are a female. They'd as soon rape you – pardon me, Miss Williams, one gets outspoken in these savage parts – as look at you. But my lady, she don't wear the veil, they all take her for a gentleman anyway until they know.'

'How,' queried the shrinking Miss Williams, 'do they know?'

Ann pursed her lips and opened them, drawing nearer to say with a rolling eye at the flimsy curtain that hung at the entrance to the room: 'They think nothing of going to any wicked length to find out.'

'To find *out*!' came the inevitable echo.

'One of them Shakes,' Ann was now enjoying herself hugely, 'he came to her ladyship's tent when she was in bed.'

'In bed!' chorused the scandalized Williams.

'And if Mr Bruce hadn't come upon them, well – there's no knowing what would have happened. Mr Bruce didn't half go for him, I can tell you – such a to do! It was all over the camp, all speaking of a fight and questioning of me in their language so I couldn't have told them anything being good as deaf and dumb to them heathens, not speaking Arab or whatever it is they do speak. They've not so much morals as our Thomas – our tom cat, Miss Williams. Only think, they all of them, the gentlemen, I mean, have half a dozen or more wives and lots of the other kind too, what my lady says are their concubines as in the Bible. I used to think,' giggled Ann, 'they was something to do with porcupines. This whole country, believe me, is like a stew. How one keeps one's decency is a marvel. But her ladyship won't stand for any bad behaviour. If she catches them black girls doing what they shouldn't, stealing, or breaking her china, or – you know – funnycating with the men – excuse me speaking plain. And there's no sort of privy in these places. Quite disgusting in a camp to see the men – no decency at all – and if my lady gets her back up against any one of them she'll beat them, the women *and* the men. She takes a stick to them but nothing'll teach them manners. How I've stood it in this outlandish country all these years only because she has a way with her that makes you love her even at her worst when she turns on you and in spite of her vile tempers, and now, if you believe me, she's taken to smoking a pipe.'

'Never – a pipe!'

Almost more shocking was her ladyship's smoking of a pipe than the adoption of gentlemanly dress and the visit of 'one of them Shakes' to her lady's tent.

'It began with an ordinary gentleman's pipe, and now,' said Ann with relish, 'it's a hookyouah what the Turks smoke. Don't have a blue fit if you see her ladyship sitting cross legged on a couch puffing away at it. And I warn you, Miss Williams, she'll make you dress like she makes me. She says it is to safeguard your,' Ann blushed at the word, 'your maidenhead she calls it.'

That Miss Williams managed to adapt herself and her maidenhead to her new situation with as much patience and uncomplaining martyrdom as did Ann and the faithful doctor, does confirm Ann's declaration that her lady had 'a way with her' in spite of her exacting demands, her bullying, and unreasonable rages, that those who served her, loved, honoured and obeyed her even as did Michael. And after the final break he still and always insisted their parting was of her choice, not his.

When Ann, in floods of tears, at last departed she was loth to leave the mistress she had so long and loyally served. Meryon, who intended to accompany her had been delayed. He must wait until the arrival of another doctor from England to take his place. In the meantime Hester found something of more serious moment to divert attention from domestic upheaval.

It was now some months since Boutin had left to explore the Ansar country; and no news concerning him had come to Hester whether or not he had succeeded in his hazardous mission. She began to be anxious; and when told that a watch purporting to have belonged to Boutin had been sold in the bazaar at Damascus, her suspicions were aroused. She felt certain that some dreadful fate had befallen him.

At once she started inquiries and sent three of her men, disguised as pedlars, on the track he was believed to have followed. They returned with facts beyond all doubt: that the Colonel had been robbed and murdered, and his two Mohammedan servants with him.

Her first move on behalf of the Colonel, who had been one of Napoleon's most trusted and courageous officers, was to approach the French consuls of Damascus, Tripoli and Acre, but none was willing to become embroiled with the savagely fanatical Ansaris.

Hester, always the crusader to fight in the cause of the wronged and oppressed, and, as 'Ambassadress in Syria' as she chose to call herself, sent a message to Soliman Pasha of Acre and Bechir requesting that he send an army to avenge the assassination of Colonel Boutin. But the Pasha was as reluctant as the French consuls to risk engaging an army in guerrilla warfare with the murderous Ansaris. Soliman backed out of it tactfully by reminding the *Sytt* (Queen) that it was impossible to send an army into the high mountains at this season of the year, as the ways would be snowbound. It was then mid-winter, so she must wait until the spring.

It was during this impatient time of waiting that she heard of the death of her father, 'Citizen Stanhope'. It cannot be said she unduly grieved for the parent who had turned her out of doors and, for all he cared, rendered her homeless. She had hoped her father would have provided for her in his Will, but he left her nothing. Yet she had her ten thousand legacy from Charles, which amply could have paid for the Ascalon fiasco had not money run through her hands like water to plunge her in debt again.

When winter passed and there could be no more excuse on grounds of bad weather she determined to avenge

Boutin's death. Dressed in her most gorgeous robes and accompanied by an extravagant retinue of servants, all paid for in advance of what she expected to have from her father's estate, she set out for Acre.

Once more she bearded the lion – a very tame lion – Soliman Pasha, in his palatial den. He received her with flattering welcome and expensive gifts, yet gave her little more than the doubtful promise that he would send troops to scour the Ansari mountains, discover the perpetrators of the crime and punish the murderers of Colonel Boutin.

But she was not to be put off by words and gifts with no concrete evidence that her campaign would be supported. She was out for blood and would have it.

Soliman Pasha gave in; he could scarcely do less when she threatened him with trouble from the Porte and the French Government if he refused to comply with her demands. In the end the Pasha agreed that Mustafa Aga Berber, the Governor of the district, should take command of the expedition.

'Under my command,' was the *Sytt's* ultimatum.

'Under the *Sytt's* command, naturally,' agreed the harassed Pasha.

'No, my lady, no! I beg you to consider —'

'Consider, consider! Fiddle-de-dee! I go with and in command of Mustafa's army and you go back to your suburban villa in the London I loathe. Your parents must be longing to see you.'

'Indeed they are, and I them,' retorted Meryon, this a few days before his departure for England. His successor, a Doctor Newbury, having arrived at Mar Elias, Meryon attempted to dissuade her from undertaking what must surely be the maddest of all her adventures.

And at this eleventh hour with his arrangements made for the journey, his baggage sent in advance, his parents joyfully expecting his return after his long absence, he would have abandoned the homecoming to remain with and protect her from what might prove to be the most perilous enterprise of all. It must have been a severe wrench to leave her with whom he had been so closely associated all these years; she who had wilfully opposed his advice in all matters whether medical or personal; who had raged at and insulted him in one breath and the next moment would come like a penitent child tearfully asking his pardon. Not only was this severance from the ties that bound him to her because of 'that way with her' which kept Ann Fry her willing slave and had held Michael utterly possessed even though he had found other loves, so did the little doctor find it hard to tear himself away from this imperious, insolent, hot-tempered yet strangely lovable creature that he now must plead:

'How can I leave you here alone to embark on this dangerous hazard on which you are bent? You surely cannot think of commanding in person Mustafa Aga's troops, and your*self* to engage in war against those savage Arab tribes?'

'How else should I command an army of vengeance against the murder of one who was my friend and a distinguished officer of my allies, the French?'

Her allies, the French! . . . Meryon had always deplored the laudations she heaped upon France and as the admirer of Napoleon, whom, the doctor feared, she regarded with almost that same reverence as, in the past, she had reverenced Bonaparte's fiercest antagonist, Pitt.

'As your ladyship will have it, at your peril.'

And so we find her mounted on her white stallion at the head of Mustafa's troops to lead them with her better knowledge of that mountainous country, facing danger at no matter what risk to her life. She was determined to accomplish that which not all the Ambassadors, the consulates, nor the Grand Seigneur himself could have effected, the conquest of the murderous Ansaris.

'Vengeance is mine!' she cried as, watched by hordes

of frightened natives who thought they saw in the *Sytt* a celestial being, a goddess, or a god incarnate – her sex was still and ever would be uncertain – leading an army into battle dressed in the elaborate robes of a Turkish chief. They all knew and feared the Ansaris who would come down from their mountain fastness to pillage, burn and rob their homes, rape their helpless women and kill their men. Prostrate in the dust as she passed, they homaged her as their heaven-born deliverer.

Mustafa, in command of the expedition, had sent word to her that he marched at the *Sytt's* bidding and only at her direction. But not content was she to direct from a vantage point of safety; she must be in the forefront of the fight, the general commanding the movements of the troops.

It was a marvellous spring day. The desert had changed overnight from an arid waste to verdant growths of green that shone, interspersed with patches of bright yellow sand that it looked to be a vast carpet of burnished copper set with emerald. As she led the advance troops Hester's spirits soared. She was elated at the prospect of fulfilling the destiny to which she believed she had been called.

Entirely fearless, she rode into danger to storm the savage enemy in their stronghold behind those towering rocks with a sense of exhilaration never experienced since, when at Chevening, she rode to hounds in her girl-hood to the admiration of the M.F.H. and all the rough-riding boisterous squires.

Behind her the picked men from the garrison at Acre mounted on swift-footed camels, rode in massed forma-tion; and leading them their officers on magnificent horses. The sun struck dazzling light from their lances and the gold clasps of Mustafa's cloak. He rode beside her, his face stern, his eyes, under the jewelled turban staring steadily before him at the rolling plain, less verdant now as they neared the rugged line of mountains violet edged against the deep turquoise sky.

Mustafa spoke little English, some French, but Hester, in all the time she had lived in Arabia and Syria, had not mustered sufficient Arabic to converse fluently with the natives nor to understand their different dialects.

And now the character of the scenery had changed; they were coming to the ascent up steep conical shaped hills, while in the rear the camels followed in single file twisting in and out of the narrow rock hewn paths. Suddenly Hester's horse swerved, and looking down she saw a pile of bleached bones, a human skull and more of them heaped against the boulders; a grinning grotesquery of yellow fang-like teeth.

She shuddered. 'Is this a warning to invaders of the Ansar territory?' she asked, speaking more lightly than she felt. Mustafa turned, smiling into his grizzled beard.

'Zay are dose who come *en avance* to us, Madame *Sytt*. Not so good – how you say – victory as we do come. See, *Altesse*,' he raised his hand pointing upward. Behind them the troopers and camel-corps halted. She, too, reined in her mount. Mustafa his. There, in the distance high above a strip of sand, and peering over slabs of rock, a row of red-turbaned heads appeared like scarlet blobs of blood; and then, at the sound of a harsh bugle, those heads rose up revealing a line of coffee-coloured figures, some almost naked, the others in tattered caftans.

Mustafa's voice rang out giving an order to his officers, who in turn repeated it along the line, and before Hester had gathered breath to realize that at last she was in for it up to the neck, and no retreat had she wished to, which she didn't, the men of the Ansaris, some on camels, some on foot streamed out from a gorge on either side of them. It was as if some volcanic eruption had been spewed from the yellow earth's bowels.

Unheedful of Mustafa's entreaties, '*Sytt*, *Altesse*, I muss' pleass to ask *s'il vous plaît retourner* – my officer – he will escort miladi —'

243

'No! Never. I'll not go back. I stay, I am in command. You have agreed to act under my direction.'

She spoke in English which he feigned to have misunderstood, for he rasped out what he took to be her order to his leading officer, and glancing back Hester saw that the troopers were stationary and the line of camels kneeling, their graceful long-necked heads moving right and left in a curiously human inquisitive fashion.

'Why don't you advance?' demanded Hester. 'Why do you halt? What are you waiting for?'

'It is zat l'enemie, ee do arrive near, yes? So den we go for to kill eem. We are ze more strong zan eem.'

She had to give him that, for they had come to the end of the narrow path which now considerably widened to show, far out on either flank, an oncoming advance of the Ansaris, dipping and rising among the sand-hills. It was evident that Mustafa, no soldier, relied on the advice of his officers and that their policy would be to draw the enemy into firing range, for the Ansaris were virtually unarmed save for out-dated muskets and blunderbusses, robbed in their raids.

Suddenly some dozen or more camel-men appeared on the brow of a sand-hill, their leader a white-bearded old fellow in a tattered jibbah, gesticulating wildly. In an instant his followers, uttering savage yells, galloped up on either side of him. Even at that critical moment Hester wondered at the swift speed of their camels that seemed to be as well trained as her own. But what arms had these Ansaris? . . . She saw they carried swords, and some tall wooden poles roughly made and topped by spearheads shining in the firce sun's rays like a miniature river in full spate; she heard the sharp ping-ping of bullets firing wide of their mark.

'*Avance!*' she shouted, and in English, 'Charge! Tell your men,' this to Mustafa, 'we must attack them now before they attack us.'

Without waiting for his order she spurred her horse

forward, riding hell for leather into a delirium of sight and sound, but was immediately out-distanced by Mustafa's troops and the following camel-corps. They crashed down on the Ansaris who were closing in from all sides around their leader. In vain he looked to be marshalling them into some coherent discipline. Unused to combat with an experienced army they fell into instant confusion. It was a massed epilepsy of hideous gorilla faces, maniacal, demoniac; of tossing frenzied arms and shrieks and awful battle cries, a holocaust of death, of dying bodies, trampled under horses' hooves amid the deadly aim of musket fire from Mustafa's troopers seen through a haze of yellow sand dust.

Hester saw their leader fall from his camel, his long white beard red-stained. 'Stay!' she cried. 'We do not slaughter the old. Send the stretcher bearers to him.' There were camels loaded with all necessities for attending the wounded. Her voice was lost in that raging maelstrom and the angry clatter of bullets against rock. The Ansaris out-numbered by hundreds of the Pashalik army, their leader gone, the sand soaked with the blood of their tribal brothers, were in maddened convulsive retreat.

Where now their reputed courage in merciless raids on the homes of law-abiding villagers, the murder of men, the rape of women, the slaughter of children – a massacre of innocents who lived by the word of the Koran and the Prophet? Of courage these fanatical Arabs had none when running the gauntlet of that inexorable onslaught sending volley after volley at the fugitives, snarling, howling in their flight like rabid dogs.

Some mounted on camels shambling over the broken ground wheeled their terror-stricken beasts to fire obsolete blunderbusses at their relentless pursuers. Others on foot, stumbling, crawling, falling, their red turbans indistinguishable from the pools of blood in the golden sand were, to Hester's exulted fancy in the excitement of the battle, like poppies in a field of English corn. She was torn with pity, not for the wounded stragglers, but for the bleeding agony of their patient beasts, the open gash in a camel's side, its heart-rending groans. . . . 'Enough !' she cried. 'Cease fire. Enough, I say !'

But not yet enough for the revenge of Boutin's murder. She would not be appeased until she had ransacked the villages of the Ansaris, recovered Boutin's stolen property and restored the homes they had ravaged.

Back at Mar Elias she set about to finish off her campaign. She commanded Mustafa to invade the Ansar territory, to burn their huts as they had burned and pillaged others who had been devastated as she would devastate those dreaded pagan tribes that strove for the ruin of Islam. She would not be content 'until' – she swore it – 'the heads of Boutin's assassins shall be brought to Damascus.'

Fifty-two villages were razed to the ground, three hundred men and some women killed, and the fame of her campaign spread throughout all Syria. She had basked in the triumph of achievement and the proud title bestowed upon her as 'Protectress of the Unfortunate.' Nor were the French backward in their gratitude to her for avenging the death of their compatriot. She received a grateful vote of thanks from the French Foreign Office in Paris and a congratulatory letter from Burckhardt in Cairo. He, the celebrated explorer who had been robbed by Bedouins, left stranded and offered hospitality by Michael when he and Hester were at Nazareth, had offended her and injured her pride by belittling her own explorations as a self-exploited amateur in search of notoriety. And now he admitted in writing, that her 'spirited and dignified conduct' – which is something more than *he* has ever done, was her inward comment when reading this, for all his fame in exploring these lands where I have lived among my people who have crowned me their Queen. *He* has never led an army into battle. . . . And reading on she saw that he allowed she had taught the Egyptians and the Syrians 'respect for the English character'.

It is likely Barker and other English consuls could scarcely have shared Burckhardt's views of the English character as exemplified by an Englishwoman who sought so bloody and ruthless a revenge for the murder of one French officer once, the enemy of Britain. But Hester gloried in the success of her 'Crusade' that had slaughtered hundreds of men, burned and devastated their villages, and sent their heads to Pasha Soliman. He may not have been so delighted as was she to see these bleeding trophies from the *Sytt* impaled on his palace walls.

*   *   *

The success of her bloodthirsty campaign against the dreaded Ansaris, while earning eulogistic approval from the French Foreign Office and the Pashalic of Damascus, was not so favourably received by the English visitors to Syria. They could not have been particularly proud of her partisanship to him who had fought with Bonaparte in his long drawn out struggle for the supremacy of his cosmopolitan Empire, a struggle that only ended on the field of Waterloo.

He whose life was rotting away in his prison island of St Helena, may have heard tell of the eccentric Englishwoman's warm admiration for him and her abuse of her native country as she wrote to her cousin, Buckingham, expressing her 'contempt of all the statesmen of the present day who have brought ruin to France.' ...

Such sentiments when reported, as without doubt they must have been, could not have endeared her to her victorious fellow countrymen, they and whose allies cruised the Levantine coast in their luxurious yachts and sailed into the harbour of Mar Elias.

The many who had heard of, and some in her former

life had known her, were curious to meet again the notorious Hester Stanhope in her mountain fastness on Lebanon but she would receive no English visitors.

Since her complete subjugation of the Ansaris they, strangely enough, had made no attempt at retaliatory offensive; on the contrary they now regarded her with awe, a supernatural being to be feared and reverenced as one endowed with powers from the Prophet. She too was more than ever inclined to believe in the prophecy of the quack fortune teller 'Brothers', substantiated by the auguries of that other soothsayer, Loustenau, battening and fattening on her bounty.

Was she not crowned Queen of Palmyra, and yet to be crowned Queen of the Jews? And now there came a third wise man, one Metta, recently employed as her steward at Mar Elias. He claimed to be well learned in mystic lore, had a certain education and possessed a magic book from which he would read to her in Arabic; and although she understood not much of it, she gathered, when he translated it into approximate English, that:

'A European woman will live on Mount Lebanon and will obtain power and influence greater than a Sultan's.'

'Wonderful!' rhapsodized Hester. 'My power, my influence *is* greater than the Sultan's. All sheiks do me honour. They always have from the moment I set foot on this hallowed mountain!'

Salaaming his homaged agreement, Metta, the cunning old rogue, with an eye to his lady's purse and expectant reward, piled it on *ad lib*.

'The Messiah will follow the white woman's coming. She, mounted on a horse born with a saddle, will ride into Jerusalem beside Him.'

A horse 'born with a saddle' was already in her stables, the foal of a beautiful mare, a gift from Emir Bechir, a near neighbour who had welcomed her when, some years before, she had visited him in his palace at Dayr-el-Kamar. Bechir had presented her with the mare's pedigree purporting to descend from a horse bred by King Solomon; but when she told him of the prophecy concerning the horse born with a saddle on which she would ride into Jerusalem at the side of the Messiah and indicated that the foal had a hollow back – actually a deformed spine which looked exactly like a Turkish saddle – Bechir laughed her to scorn.

He was not now so charmed with the redoubtable Lady Hester, acclaimed by his subjects and those of his fellow sheiks as 'Queen'. She had caused an infinity of trouble throughout the Mountain and with the Druses, his own people, who looked upon her as their sovereign chief. She could not know, for her oracles would only tell her of a golden future to earn them a golden reward, that she was stirring up a hornet's nest for herself in the not far distant future.

After the departure of Meryon and the success of her 'Crusade', as she regarded her defeat of the Ansaris in revenge for Boutin's murder, life seemed very flat and uneventful. She missed Meryon more than she would have thought possible. His successor from England, Doctor Newbury, was a poor substitute for her good doctor who with such incomparable patience, had listened to her egocentric rodomontades, to be retailed in his memoirs for posterity.

Dr Newbury, with ill-concealed boredom, endured her lengthy diatribes against the Allies delivered through the stench of her tobacco smoke. . . . 'They have violated the laws of nations by deluging France with foreign troops. I will never return to England *nor* Paris where I had thought of meeting my dear brother, Colonel Stanhope, for I, the niece of the illustrious Pitt, could not stomach to see those ministers of ours strutting about doing mischief and rejoicing in the defeat and degrading imprisonment of a man acknowledged King by every power in Europe. That England, which was once *my* England and who employed her valiant troops in the defence of her

249

national honour, has exposed to ridicule and humiliation a monarch who might have gained the goodwill of his subjects if those intriguing English had left him to stand or fall upon his own merits. You will tell me that the French army – the bravest troops in the world – would not listen to the voice of reason, and you think I will believe you. Never! If a humble individual like myself can inspire thousands of wild Arabs with confidence in my integrity and sincerity, could not a King – a legitimate King – guide that army to which he owed the preservation of his power, now despised, imprisoned in a living death!'

All this and more Newbury was forced to hear until he, a loyal patriot who had been on the battle field of the immortal victory that brought peace to war-ravaged Europe, and had given his medical skill to tend the wounded and the dying, could hear no more.

'Madam, I, likewise a humble individual, have witnessed the valour of the French armies and have treated with equal impartiality those who fell at Waterloo, must also give my gratitude and praise to the English and allied troops for their amazing, I may say, *inspired* valour that vanquished the enemy whom you call a "legitimate King". Napoleon was no more a "legitimate" King than is your ladyship a legitimate "Queen" of these wild Arabs whom you dominate by your self-confidence and, admittedly, your well-intentioned efforts to bring them to a better understanding of our western civilization.'

This was the lighting of a fuse to set her ablaze. That this undistinguished doctor whose medical qualifications were but little higher than those of an apothecary should dare to criticize *her* opinion on the development of European events, and more especially in regard to English policy, at once brought a heated retort.

'Those who do not care to hear the truth which I always speak openly had better have nothing to say to me. As one of the most intelligent Turks who was of the

Divan at Constantinople said, as I was told: "It is not that Napoleon is so great, but that other crowned heads are so *little*!" And since you, Dr Newbury, are imbued with the ignorance and duplicity that has brought ruin to France, I will waste no further words of mine upon *you*!'

This was the beginning of Newbury's end as medical attendant on her ladyship. Henceforth, until he left Mar Elias a few weeks later, he did have nothing to say to her except it were strictly professional. He continued to listen to her interminable monologues, and one night, unable to stand any more of it, of her, and the stink of her pipe, he feigned a swoon. Hester, always concerned for the welfare and health of her dependants, at once rang for Williams to restore him. She told the maid his faint was due to his concern for 'the deplorable state of European politics and the cruel, the *dastardly* imprisonment of the Emperor Napoleon'. She had firmly convinced herself of this and nothing would alter her opinion, no matter how abhorrent to Newbury and others of her compatriots.

Although she saw Newbury go with no regret she had now no English member of her household with whom she could converse, or rather soliloquize aloud for hours on end. Williams, a devoted and admirable maid, was not an adequate substitute for Meryon or Newbury to whom she could express her iconoclastic opinion of European and British policies. There were few European visitors in the months after Newbury went, to call on 'the Nun of Lebanon' as she named herself. They who came out of curiosity to see the far-famed Hester Stanhope had seen and heard enough of her to give exaggerated side-splitting accounts of the 'Queen of the Jews'; of her obsession with astrological mysticism, in which she had of late become immersed, surrounded by bogus 'magicians' and sooth-sayers who cadged on her, cashing in on her belief in their humbugging persuasions that she was divinely inspired in her mission to lead and to convert the pagan Arab tribes from heathenism to the Lord Jehovah.

That she had any true belief either in Judaism or Christianity was uncertain. As foretold 'Queen of Jerusalem' she was bound to believe the Messiah had yet to come, for she chose to misinterpret the words of John the Baptist 'There cometh one after me,' ignoring their application to Our Lord. It would seem that her religious faith, if any, was a medley of the Christian, Jewish, and Mohammedan. Yet while relentless against her enemies, following the Mosaic tradition of 'an eye for an eye, a tooth for a tooth' as witness her vengeance on the Ansaris for Boutin's murder, she had a Christian's love and pity for those in need. Her generosity was boundless. None came to her in want and went from her unaided. She spent lavishly on herself and her household, but never at the deprivation of her bounty to the poor, the aged, and the sick. She conducted her self-appointed sovereignty much on the lines of an incipient Welfare State. Little did she guess in these distant lands where, by her dominant and aggressive personality, she ruled with the iron hand that in something over a century the England she had renounced would unknowingly adopt the very seeds she had sown; whether for good or ill time alone could tell.

It was the French visitors, aware of her partiality for their dethroned and defeated Emperor, who saw in her that quality of greatness eulogized in later years by the poet-statesman, Lamartine. Notwithstanding his ardent Bourbon sympathies, Lamartine, when he visited her in her isolation, wrote panegyrical impressions of the 'discourse of this extraordinary woman, this Circe of the Desert'. . . . He saw her as he saw himself a fatalist, 'expecting the Messiah like a Jew, and worshipping Christ like a Christian.' Her 'discourse', to which the poet listened with keenest interest, he described as 'lofty, mystic, well-sustained, connected, forcible. . . .' There's no end to the hosannas heaped upon her, and not, one may believe, because of her sexual attraction, although

Lamartine, poetically licensed, dwells upon 'those personal traits which years cannot alter. Freshness, colour and grace depart with youth, but when beauty resides in purity of expression, in dignity and majesty, it does not pass away. It eminently characterizes the person of Lady Hester Stanhope.'* All this, had she read it, would have been nectar offered to her self-deification. But when Lamartine called upon her and pronounced his name, she told him bluntly she had never heard of him.

Yet long before Lamartine had glorified her name to resound throughout France and the England she despised, another Frenchman was beguiled by the magic of this 'Circe of the Desert'. He was a young French diplomat, the Vicomte de Marcellus, who during his journey through the Levant discovered, to his lasting fame, the Venus de Milo. In seeking out Hester Stanhope, he, a bud of the flowering 'Romantic' age that blossomed from the blood-stained battle fields of France and flourished abundantly in Paris, was immediately attracted.

He saw in this mysterious being, sexless, epicene, a beauty not of this world with her exquisite fair skin and those wonderful blue eyes; and poured out fulsome praise of her as he reclined in a bower of her garden at Mar Elias.

She had transformed the dreary sepulchre that housed the Patriarch, still stuck in the disused chapel wall, into a miniature palace, yet too small to house all her many servants. The surplus were lodged wherever room in the village could be found for them.

The divans in her arbour were spread with tiger skins; she had a passion for these procured from India at great expense and sent some to General Oakes. Her exotic surroundings and her colourful dress, the gold-embossed turban, the short embroidered jacket with the open-throated shirt revealed the rounded creamy neck and a tantalizing glimpse of the valley between the hidden

* Lamartine's *Souvenirs pendant un voyage en l'orient.*

253

breasts. Marcellus might have hoped to see more and, disappointed, could not know if she were indeed a woman or the beardless youth who had struck wonder in the hearts of the Arab tribes when she first appeared among them.

He, as was Lamartine, had been enchanted with her 'discourse'. She had learned much from the two 'wise men' of her household, besides their claim to the foretelling of her future. Loustenau had studied the history of the Mohammedans and the religion of Islam, and imported something of his knowledge to her.

For hours on end Marcellus listened as did Newbury, but with more charmed attention, to her accounts of the religious beliefs of the Arabs before Islam. She told of the low state of civilization in pre-Islam days, and how she had been chosen to instruct and convert the scattered tribes of the Mountain to the true belief and revelation of Mahomet. 'But,' Marcellus was assured, 'I am not a Mohammedan although I read and delight in the Koran. Nor am I a follower of Judaism more than that I believe in one Almighty God who has sent me here to fulfil the mission ordained for me to ride at the side of the Messiah on His second coming. I have a foal born in my stables with the sign of the sacred saddle on her back. It is on her that I will ride when called. They name me the Prophetess here in the Mountain and as such I do believe in and follow my vocation.'

He did not see her as ridiculous; he saw her as she saw herself, a visionary endowed with sublime grace. Others may have thought her mad; many did who had not the patience to listen to her self-glorification.

Marcellus stayed a few days at Mar Elias, but when pressed to prolong his visit he apologized for refusing with the excuse that he must attend a diplomatic conference in Jerusalem. He may have had more than he could take of the ridiculous if not of the sublime. Had he accepted her invitation to stay longer at Mar Elias he might have attempted to overcome her apparent sexual *naïveté*, assumed in the guise of a nun-like Mother Superior. He may or may not have heard of her association with Bruce and the rumour of her marriage with a Bedouin Sheik, noised abroad in the consulates as the backwash of the Nasar *affaire* which could have had more serious or perhaps a more binding result than accounted for by Michael Bruce and a Bedouin's broken nose.

So Marcellus departed with the unspoken thought that: '*Elle est une créature a part qu'étonne et tout que charme, mais l'esprit est toujours le dupe du coeur.*'

He might yet have hoped, when she asked him to return (which he never did), that she would have offered him encounter on a lower, less sacrosanct, plane. But she offered him nothing more than the escort of two servants and a couple of pure-bred Arab mares.

Since Michael had left her it was as if the flower of her passion for him or any man had wilted and died, shed of its blossom as in a dead orchard.

She could not know that he who would restore her faded love and bring to her a second blooming was even now upon his way.

THREE

No premonition, no astrological foretelling from her two personal 'Magi', installed in her convent on the slopes of Mount Lebanon, warned her of the coming of a son in search of a father. Or, if the father had known of his coming, he held his peace nor spoke of that which he may, or may not, have believed was written in her stars.

The barren wastes of loneliness that followed each new exciting adventure in which she sought to forget the years with Bruce whom she could call no more her 'Dearest', had left her always unsatisfied, ever seeking the completion of her destiny.

Her endless bounty to the poor and those in need whom she housed, fed, clothed, and subsidized far beyond her means, drained her resources to their dregs to plunge her deeper into debt, yet she would never withhold help to those who looked to her in faith for charity. But neither faith nor charity were recompense enough for loss of hope. And for what, in her secret heart's recesses did she hope? For what vague unwhispered longings to recapture from the wintered ashes of remembrance a dying spark that would rekindle the warmth and fever of her youth and all youth's glowing crises and suspenses and brief ecstasies before day's sunset orbed to downward dark?

The travellers who came and went on short uneasy visits left her friendless and alone with only the faithful Williams to bear her company in the long winter evenings. The two old men, Loustenau and Metta, sat together in their own apartments drinking late into the night. They had nothing to say to her nor she to them when their mystic crystal gazing and bogus prophecies were done. Or, by way of variation from her predestined glory, they would tell of disasters, earthquakes, famine, wars, not unlikely in that country of her chosen life.

As for an earthquake foretold by Loustenau, that did actually and coincidentally occur at Aleppo; but at the time of Hester's waiting for the Delphic oracle to be manifest in more than dreams, she still must wait.

It was on a night of thunderous storm that wracked the mountain, and rainfall drummed at the windows of the convent, while between deafening thunder claps could be heard the howl of jackals in the forests on the higher peaks of Lebanon. Hester was with Williams in the sitting-room when some commotion without, the clatter of hooves in the courtyard and a man's voice calling: '*Holloa! Qui est chez soi!*', caused Hester to say:

'Go, see who is here. It may be a traveller seeking shelter from the storm.'

Williams laid aside her sewing but, before she reached the door, one of the servants announced the arrival of a visitor wishing to speak with the *Sytt*.

'Bring him in.'

He was brought in; a tall well built young Frenchman, wearing European dress under a drenched sheepskin from which the water splashed in little pools on to the polished floor. His hair, flattened wet to his head, dripped down his face with the rain like tears. None the less Hester, quick to note him handsome, was at once intrigued.

He apologized for his intrusion in the accent of Marseilles rather than of Paris; and in French she answered him.

'Monsieur is very welcome. My men will have your clothes dried for you and your servant – I thought I heard two horses. You are attended?'

'Madame is too gracious. Veritably my servant is almost drowned, as am I.'

She ordered a fire to be lighted in one of the guest

257

rooms and the visitor's servant taken to the domestic quarters. It was now nearing midnight. The staff, including the cook, were gone to their beds either in the convent or their lodgings in the village; but Hester did not scruple to have those who worked in the kitchen roused and made to prepare a meal for the travellers.

Metta, still in session with the General, was called to attend her guest; and when supper had been served to him and he dried, warmed, and asleep in his bed, Hester was given further proof of Metta's psychic vision. That this might have been the bibulous effect of inferior Lebanon wine did not discredit her belief in the singular pronouncement, accompanied by discreet hiccups, that:

'The son who would come in search of his father is here. His father – hic – awaits him. It was ordained – hic – in the stars of the *Sytt* that are one with the father's son. As it was in the beginning and will be – hic – unto the end.'

He bowed himself out, slightly tripping on the mat as he went.

She was immensely stirred and restless for the morning when she would see and hear more of this stranger who had come to her out of the storm and whose father awaited him. . . . His father. *Who* was his father? One of her household? Not possible. None of her staff was European except . . . Loustenau! Not Loustenau surely?

It was.

The next morning so soon as the Captain – Captain Loustenau, late of l'Empereur Napoleon's Imperial Guard – had breakfasted, Hester greeted him with polite inquiries after his comfort and hoped he was recovered from his unfortunate night's journey. She then sent for the General.

The meeting between the two could not have been less enthusiastic on the part of the father, nor more boisterously affectionate on the part of the son who, on his own

258

account, had been seeking his parent for these last five years.

'Eh, well,' was the laconic greeting of the General, disengaging from his son's embrace, 'you have been long enough to arrive, isn't it! I have awaited you like everything since the lamented fall of l'Empereur. In effect, you are here and here you will rest, to live and,' he raised a bleared eye heavenward, 'to die.'

'No talk shall be of dying!' Hester, also in French intervened on behalf of the young man, who seemed to be somewhat dashed by this cool reception: 'Monsieur le capitaine has found his destination and it is my pleasure to suggest he makes his home chez-moi, chez' – correctively – 'chez nous, mon général, if agreeable?'

'Perfectly, miladi,' concurred the General, and:

'Enchanted, miladi,' said the Captain, bowing nose to knees. 'Madame is too amiable.'

She left the two of them together and went about the daily routine of ordering her household with a sense of elation. It was as if the eternal miracle had come to pass again, and never known since she had first surrendered her ungiven body to a lover twelve years younger than herself and now awakened from nepenthe to a lifted new horizon.

Love! Was this love, this feverish expectancy that brought with it urgent reminder of the one great passion of her life? He, who had fallen at Corunna to leave her questing, never finding full resuscitation until in this reincarnated image of – John Moore!

Not the tone of his voice nor the colour of his hair which was dark and Moore's light, but the turn of his head, the grace of his walk, the tall lithe muscular frame and the cameo-fine bone structure of cheek and jawline, all of this she felt to be so like and yet unlike, for he was young and Moore, had he lived, would have been old – older now than she in her middle forties was to this other, young enough to be her son.

Must it be for ever so that she could only find her satisfaction in youth when youth had passed her by?

She held herself within herself until, or unless, she were sure that her craving for possession, that powerful instinct which had dominated Michael, would force him to accept her. No adept in subtlety she must be subtle in her approach to him, for: 'What's on my lung must come out on my tongue,' was one of her slogans oft repeated to Meryon and to the ever devoted little Williams, who suffered dreadfully to see her lady railing at the native servants, beating her slave women unmercifully, swearing and raging at the men for their slovenly ways – she who had horsewhipped one of them, a Negro, for scratching his fleas while serving her at dinner – all this and more did Williams see and still adored her mistress.

During the interim before the arrival of the younger Loustenau, Meryon, unable entirely to sever his connection with this woman whom he had served with that same devotion that she, unaccountably, inspired in all her dependants, heard from the ever faithful Barker, British agent at Aleppo, that Lady Hester had a recurrence of the severe cough that had attacked her after the plague, and returned always with the winter.

Meryon, having taken a post as personal physician to one of Hester's former admirers, Sir Gilbert Heathcote, asked leave of absence for a short vacation and took himself off on the long journey to Syria.

He found that her ladyship, to the dismay of the puritanical doctor, was again in the throes of an *affaire*. He who had never become reconciled to the 'illicit' association with Michael, must now witness a successor to the once detested Bruce who was, it appeared, to be even more in her ladyship's favour than 'that other'.

The convent of Mar Elias being too small to accommodate her numerous staff and this latest addition to it, the young French Captain, she decided to rebuild a dilapidated house at Djoun higher up in the mountain.

The workmen were already engaged on the process of reconstruction when Meryon arrived. Captain Loustenau was to be given his own suite of rooms, his father to remain at Mar Elias, and the son to be employed as her ladyship's secretary, which admirably suited the lazy, dilettante, out-of-pocket, out-at-elbows Loustenau. Not now, be it understood, was he either out-at-elbows or out-of-pocket being handsomely endowed by the Lady of the Mountain.

If Meryon thought to see her changed from the report sent to him by Barker of her hacking cough and general debility, he must have been pleasantly surprised. He saw no sign of debility. She had always looked younger than her years, even before she had adopted Turkish dress, that the Syrian peasants still mistook her for a young man if they did not recognize their *Sytt* galloping up the mountain on one of her Arab mares, the filly 'born with a saddle' now full grown, or its mother. These were Hester's pride. She had never ceased to believe she had been chosen to ride into Jerusalem on one or other of them beside the Messiah on His coming. But time was racing on and yet He had not come. . . .

That she appeared to be in excellent health and did not cough more than the smoke caused by her 'infernal pipe', to the disgust of Meryon, gave him to think his medical attention was superfluous. She no longer required the constant anodyne of tobacco to divert the sluggish undertow of memories past from the exhilarating current of the present.

It was on a morning when the harsh winter had reluctantly conceded to the spring, that she went with the Captain to see the work of reconstruction to the house at Djoun. This she had arranged to rent from a Damascan merchant on condition that all the improvements she had made would revert to him or his heirs.

She rode the filly and Loustenau rode its dam; a great concession this, for none, not even the grooms – they each had their own groom – was allowed to mount them, regarded by Hester as sacred. She had named them Laila and Lulu, the one grey, the other chestnut, and they were exercised on leading reins. Only Hester ever rode one or the other.

The house on the fringe of the village at Djoun stood on a cone-shaped hill of Lebanon overlooking a luxurious valley and surrounded by weed-grown gardens. She visualized a transformation; to make of that wilderness a replica of the grounds in the long ago days at Walmer. She intended to convert the neglected lawns into a labyrinth of walks interlaced with arbours, thickets and trellises under masses of roses, honeysuckle, all kinds of English flowers.

Shading her eyes from the sun that turned to gold the silvery piles of cement and stone and the bronzed torsos of the sweating workmen, she said to Loustenau in English, which she was teaching him:

'Much as I dislike the administration of my country's government there is no land that can give us such sweet and lovely flowers. Here' – she glanced aside at him sitting upright, the perfect horseman of the Imperial Guard and wearing a European riding suit which she had tailored for him in Damascus – 'when the desert after the sand storms of winter breaks into blossom, they live for one day and are too full blown and exotic for my liking. All except the lilies of the field. You remember that "not Solomon in all his glory was arrayed as one of these." Only they aren't and were never lilies, they are anemones. See!' She stooped from her saddle, but not far enough to reach a small red flower just emerging from the bud. 'Here is one that has strayed from the slopes yonder.'

He, taller than she and long in the back, bent to pluck the floweret. In doing so his hand brushed hers: the slightest contact for a held moment while she fused to his touch, and her cheeks beneath the white turban

262

that hid her hair were flushed, not with the flame of the sun.

He, straightening, offered her the flower and again their hands met and lingered together before, within seconds, they escaped as if to tempt and not to take the first seedling of desire.

There was a tension of silence between them as they turned back to Mar Elias along the winding road that led to the village. The gold-sliced shadows on the mountains trembled in a drifting transparency of sight and echoing sound. The busy murmur of Arabs toiling at their work, the ring of hammer blows on stone, mingled with the champing of tethered camels patiently awaiting their drivers to goad them back to Djoun and to return with the heavy loads of cement and brick and mortar until work should cease at nightfall.

That evening, when the moon had risen to hang like a silver coin caught in the branches of the cedars of Lebanon, she sent Williams to Loustenau with an invitation for dinner. As a superior employee, nominally secretary, she seldom invited him to dine with her unless accompanied by his father. She had ordered for him his favourite meal of roast lamb, served, English fashion, with mint sauce from herbs grown in her garden. Although decrying all things English, she did adhere when possible to the food of her native land.

While she supervised the arrangement of her silver and delicate napery she wondered, as often before, if the prophecy foretold by Metta of the coming of the son in search of a father were already known. Against her will and the study of his horoscope that found him to be under the influence of the same stars as her own, doubt had crept in with the thought, never put into words, that old Loustenau might have been in communication with his son purposely to bring him here. But why not? It was natural that a father would wish to see the son from whom he had been parted for almost all his adult life.

Could she have overheard the talk between the two while she waited for her guest she might have had her suspicions verified.

'Why do you delay to make the advancement? Can you not see she is impassioned? You have only to offer so small a response and' – with his silver hook he pointed upward – 'you are elevated, isn't it? You are on what the English call "a good wicket".'

'Vicket?' the younger Loustenau grimaced. 'Pah! A language of the most impossible! What means it – vicket?'

'It is part of a game they play in England on a field with batons and balls – a game for schoolboys and that, mon cher, is a game you must play with her. For, look you, she is au fond a schoolboy, the monitor to command the younger boys. Until now she has been demi-vierge even though she was the mistress of this Bruce who quitted her. Me, I know women. I am more experienced than you for I have longer years to do with them. In effect, while you experiment with many women but none perhaps of this age of hers which is at a time of life that craves' – his cheeks, a trifle bloated with good living since, as a derelict exile, he had enjoyed the generous hospitality of his patronne, expanded in a lecherous grin – 'comme une chienne in her season for a dog. So have you now the sense of a dog to serve her and even to make an alliance with her.' He poured from a flagon at a table beside him a bumper of wine and drank lustily, smacking his lips. 'Drink then.' He offered the flagon. There was only one goblet. His son drank from and drained the bottle. His father nodded approval. 'Good! Be ready and warm for more when you dine with her tonight. A full head gives to a full heart. It is right you should think of your future. I, in the course of life, must die long before you, as so will she who has almost twenty more years than yours and can be of benefit in other ways than to satisfy a man.'

264

He chuckled slyly. 'You will not find her wanting. Eh well, then go to her. She is all prepared. She looks into the crystal and sees what she is told. Alors, bonne santé et bonne chance!'

'I shall need the good luck,' the son muttered.

They had dined between the day's slow death and the Arabian night's swift fall. Loustenau, replete with wine of the Levant, saw her face, a pale moon reflected in the table's polished wood. The last flicker of low burning wax in the silver candlesticks were like drowned stars in a lake of dark mahogany.

She was peeling a peach. Her fingers, long and slender, tapered to the points of her nails, henna dyed. She wore no turban, and her hair fell long and straight as rain about her shoulders. He had never seen her without a turban, and seeing her now she seemed more woman than he had thought her, for her rôle of masculinity repelled him, the accomplished womanizer. She selected a peach and offered it. He shook his head; his eyes were bold on hers, veiled before his appraising look. She spoke to the Arab servant to refill the glasses. They were drinking the wine of Portugal with the dessert.

Cognac and Turkish coffee in tiny cups was offered.

'Let us take our coffee and cognac on the patio,' she said. 'The moon is high and this room is too warm.'

The patio overlooked the garden whence came the subdued orchestra of cicadas, the hum of night flying insects, a sparkle seen of fireflies. The still, heavy air was full of the exotic scent of a myriad flowers. The staff's quarters were on the far side of the house, also the room occupied by Williams. Only Hester's own apartments gave out on to the patio where a divan draped with curtains was placed beneath the window of her bedroom. 'I sleep out here on warm nights,' she said, and seating herself on a pile of cushions bade him sit beside her.

They finished their coffee and the brandy, and when the servant had taken the table that held the cups and glasses a silence fell between them.

The moon shed a silver path across the lawn and lighted the branches of a palm tree as if, in the dimmed unearthly green, it were of a sea-bed garden. Above that incessant hum of insects and the rustle of some small wild creature in the long grass edging the shrub-lined lawn, could be heard the savage triumphant cry of a swift winged killer and the shriek of its captured prey; and in the high mountain forests the howl of hunting jackals.

'Nature,' Hester said, 'is thought to be kind. Why do the people call her "Mother"? She is not my idea of a mother. Not that I can remember mine. She died when I was four. I had a father who was a cruel and heartless tyrant. But as for "Mother Nature", there is no kindness in her, no pity, no care for her young. She gives nothing and takes all. She is merciless. What weak harmless little beast is even now being torn to pieces by some bird of prey? As for her mortal creatures, she instils into us a thirst and hunger for unexplained desires that unless satisfied lead us into God alone knows . . . what?'

She spoke in English, he now had a clear enough understanding of what she was saying.

The moon-flooded night, the perfume, not only of flowers but of some incense burning pastilles seeping through the open window of her bedroom, went to his head with the plentiful wine she had given him to drink. And in the moonshine which enwrapped them both he saw she had cast aside her outward garments and wore nothing but a thin transparent robe that bared her throat and partially her naked breasts. Her breath came fast upon the words:

'I have lost so much – so much of all I should have had of life. If the fates or my stars that are the same as yours according to our horoscopes, had been more favourable I could have been . . . married.'

266

She said this almost in the voice of a thwarted child; and still in that same little voice:

'He was killed fighting for my country, or what was once my country, against yours. The one man of the many who have wanted me as wife or – maybe not. But I loved him and would have been proud to marry him. I think I have never loved – not loved in the sense that I *would* have been loved – until now.'

He, who had enjoyed chiefly bought pleasures and whose encounters with women had been entirely casual, was strangely stirred. Never remarkable for perception, Loustenau realized that she, whose role of masculinity had at first repelled him, lived in a world created from her own wishful fantasies. Hitherto he had only responded to the crudest, basest instincts in his feminine relationships bought or taken. He had never sought to delve deeper than the surface of the sexual merchandise offered. That he could, however dimly, perceive the raison d'être of the part she played in this life of adventure – this game, as his father called it – a schoolboy's game which satisfied her folie de grandeur, Loustenau surprised himself to think her pathetic. In effect, a child who delights to make the fanfaronnade. She is more gamine brave than la femme desirée, was his summary.

Her hand stole out to his. 'Of what do you think?' she asked in French. 'You are quiet, isn't it?'

Taking the hand that caressed his he turned it palm upward to his lips.

'I think of you, so infinitely . . . young!'

'I? Young?'

Her eyes in that silvery light held a pleased childish expectancy. 'I am much older than you!' This she said in English and in English he answered her.

'Not so, Madame.' He fondled the hand he held. 'I believe – zat I do know you more zan do you know yourself. In effect what is old? We, what you call the creatures mortal of nature we have all in us the many ages. And

267

some who do think to be old are young as are you, Madame. Also we have in us many personnes. It is difficile always what is it to know veritably the personne who is the Me. . . . Excuse that I expliquer so bad in English, please.'

A rush of emotion overswept her. In that moment she believed him to be the epitome of all she had longed for, a man as John Moore with whom she could touch the heights beyond mere physical desire. She had thought to have found it in Michael but he failed her. That was her own fault striving for possession of him instead of his possession of her. Could this young Frenchman, commonplace, uncultivated, yet endowed with an intuitive insight, see beneath the false veneers of sham identity and show her to herself, the person who is Me? Was this the perfect love she had hungered for and lost?

They were islanded in the solitude of the moonlit dark that bound them each to each in a dangerously magic artifice. All shapes, the colours of flowers, pale in that translucent light, faded to ephemeral impermanence. A wisp of cloud passed across the staring moon whose face, blurred in a gossamer fairy-like mist, looked to wear a lop-sided grin as if to mock this miracle of love in which she was dissolved.

Hardly aware that she whispered: 'I love you,' she breathed. 'I need you. Take me.' She held out her hands to him.

He gathered her into his arms holding her close. His mouth hovered above hers, so eagerly offered. Drawing the curtains of the divan, she dragged him down with her into the unseeing dark. . . .

There was no carnal satisfaction in giving what she asked, only a queer urge to comfort this creature, neither woman, girl, nor man, and so to sweeten the bitter taste of life unloved.

Enfin! Let her have her dream, he might have said, not

268

to waken from this adventurous farcical comedy in which she plays the leading part to lead her – where?

As spring blossomed into summer, the house at Djoun, still in process of reconstruction, was of less interest now for Hester than this rejuvenating passion which absorbed her. Strange that Loustenau whose joy in life and living had been to seize each care-free moment, should detachedly give himself to her with no sexual enjoyment to be gained from it. That he could not respond to her, save by simulation, was a new experience for him and did not detract from, rather it enhanced, the curiously selfless pleasure he derived to indulge her desire as for a greedy child.

Although he knew she was no virgin after four years of a previous relationship and, as he gleaned from talk among the French consulates at Acre and Damascus, she had not repulsed the advances of at least one or two Arab chiefs who boasted of their conquests; nor did Nasar's tongue spare her to couple his name with hers. . . . Yet Loustenau found her refreshingly unschooled in the delights of erotic love play. Bruce had not much experience in anything more than the normal physical act. His Theophanie and his Parisian amourettes may have instructed him better.

'You are well placed,' his father told him, 'you have her in your hand. She has honoured you above everything to appoint you master of her horses – those two mares she regards as sacred, the highest compliment she can pay you. You have only to go so' – the old man beckoned with his hook – 'and she falls at your feet. You can have her to bed' – he sniggered – 'for wife or belle amie for ever if you will.'

'I will not have her for wife or belle amie for ever,' said his son. 'No, not if she would beg me on her knees. No, thank you! Would you have me to bed with a child?'

'By blue! A child, she? Pah! A rich old woman

insatiable, who will pay well for a young husband. She is ripe and over ripe, mon cher, and you are fresh and full of juice like this young orange.' He took one from a bowl on the table, newly plucked from the orchard of the convent.

'Shut you your mouth!' was his son's reply to that. 'I would not marry this type there, not on my life! She will have all she can take of me now, and my faith! that already is too much.' He mopped his forehead, beaded with sweat. The heat from the desert, even on these cooler slopes of Lebanon, was taking toll of him although he had been born and lived much of his twenty-five years in the south of France. 'When she has had enough of me, then will I go. But now I stay. It suits me to be here as I suit her, and when I quit she will be consoled with her horses, her new house, a new man – one of the Pasha's sons, perhaps. She has a fancy for their colour of café au lait and I have taught her how best she can enjoy him. They have the finesse with a woman, these Arabs, and she has learned from me to be more woman than ever she was with that Englishman of hers. She will finance and fight the battles of the sheiks until she grows too old to play the game of la grande aventure. Then the day will come when she wakes from her fantasies to see herself as she is and not as she dreams she is. So do I pity her.'

'Pity? That,' said the General, taking a spoon to scoop up the juice of the orange, 'is, as the English have it – how we say *apparent* – to love. Take care, then, or she will have you by the neck.'

'My neck, pouf!' he shrugged his splendid shoulders. Good living and hard riding on the mountains had developed his muscles; and he had not an ounce of superfluous flesh. 'Me, je m'en fiche de ça! I can take care of my neck and I will take care of her!'

*   *   *

Meryon having found himself very much *de trop* at Mar Elias with the two Frenchmen in highest favour, the one old the other young – in particular the young – was obliged 'with great reluctance,' he submitted to her ladyship, 'that I must return to England. My patient, Sir Gilbert Heathcote, is in more need of my medical attention than happily are you, praise be! I was agreeably surprised after Mr Barker's report on your condition, that brought me here as fast as ship and horse could bring me, to find you in such good health. The mountain air agrees with you, and this being so I feel you can dispense with my service at least, for —'

She cut him short.

'Spare me long winded excuses. If you want to go – go! I *am* well, thank God, and can do without a doctor and his physics, so don't you stay here on my account. You can leave me whenever you wish. I'll not detain you.'

Thankfully he left her. This latest liaison for the whole household to see and that old reprobate, the General, to encourage, living on the fat of her land, both the father and son too generously subsidized from his lady's apparently bottomless purse, had given the good doctor much anxiety. Yet he must admit she had regained her health, was more mentally balanced, less prone to violent outbursts of temper, looked years younger, and was certainly happier and more content than the woman he had known before she started off on her crazy adventures.

Summer passed and October winds swept down upon the convent and tore the leaves from the trees in Hester's garden that lay upon the lawns like heaps of newly minted copper coins. Yet she, who had dreaded these winter months on Lebanon that each year brought renewal of her distressing cough, the aftermath of plague, could now face joyously the icy winds and sandstorms of the desert on her daily rides with Loustenau. The

French consul at Sayda and the sons of Soliman Pasha who saw her accompanied by the handsome Frenchman, riding through the narrow streets or galloping across the desert, her long hair loosened from under the turban, may have wondered if this Loustenau, supposed to be her secretary, major-domo, head groom, or whatever she chose to call him in charge of her valuable mares was – something more?

That she had been the mistress of Bruce, all the consuls, French and English, were well aware; also that she had not entirely discarded the attentions of Emir Nasar. He it was who had presented her with one of those beautiful mares which she would allow no man to mount save this latest protégé.

'Let them talk!' she said when she heard all this from Barker at Aleppo in continuous correspondence with her, and would sometimes come for a brief visit to Mar Elias. 'My name is mud among the Europeans. I am the mistress or concubine of every aspiring sheik or his son. It is even said I am the wife of one of them.' She rippled into laughter. 'I have yet to see myself established in his harem. But that would never do. His women would all run for protection to the eunuchs, scared for their lives to see a man among them!'

Barker saw her, as did Meryon, transfigured. Her days were a joyous pageant filled with this love that encompassed her and was reflected in her eyes, more than ever a startling blue. Her nights when Loustenau came to her – how could she know with what reluctance – were yielded up to him with the ingenuous eager response of a girl bride. All that she had sought in dreams and the excitement of adventure since Michael had left her and whose love had led her only to a dead end, was found in this recurrence of her youth. That Loustenau had never voiced his love for her in words may sometimes have brought the shadow of a cloud, to be thrust aside with the reminder: What need of words between them when all

272

his thoughts were hers? Were they not born under the same stars?

He too may have wondered at himself since hitherto, in all his intimacies with women, brief enough, a night, a week, a month, he, when replete, had cast them off with no memory or emotion more than he would have felt after a satisfying meal. She could not know that for the first time in his life while he had no desire for her and leaving aside material benefit from her obsession for him, it pleasured him more to give than to take. That he could have married her – that she wished to marry him had been evident from the first – but sacred name! No, never that! To be legally tied to a woman for whom he had no regard more than for a gosse begging for sweets, revolted him.

'There is a fool you are!' his father said, 'not to wish to be legally tied to a fortune if she still has the fortune which I hear from Barker she is spending on this house at Djoun, and on any beggar who comes to her with tales – as did I and you!' He chuckled. 'But for you to refuse to marry her – to be "legally tied" – diable! And you without a sou as was I till I did hear of her interest in magic, and astrology, and so' – he waved his silver hook – 'I am here and well placed as you can be if you will take the chance. Why do you think I sent for you to see again a son I had not seen since you were an infant? A son who may not be mine? Your mother gave me half a dozen children – all may have been bastards. She had many men. You did not know this lady "Queen of the Desert" as they call her, when she was all bouleversée, mad as a cat for a man, but now she is content. Do not make me these bêtises. Take what the good God offers you!'

'Eh well,' his son grinned, 'I will take a holiday while I make my decision. I require a holiday. I have taught her much. She is too exigeante for me. I want a change of woman who will oblige me and not I to oblige her!'

His father cackled. 'Go then, to Aleppo, Damascus,

Acre, or where you will. In the Levant you will find change enough of women!.'

Although Hester was loth to be parted from her lover even for the good of his health which, according to General Loustenau, the stars had it as urgent, she could not but agree that the heat of the Syrian summer had told upon his energy. He certainly was paler, thinner, and the least exertion seemed to tire him. She regretted the absence of Meryon who she felt sure would, under the guidance of their stars, have given him a tonic without having to send him away – 'To Tiberius,' as suggested by the General, 'to drink the waters. He can also call upon the French consul at Acre who will advise him where the best accommodation can be found.'

So off went the son sped by the father and her ladyship, who sent him from her with two servants and enough cash to cover all expenses. He assured her he would only be away for a few weeks.

The few weeks lengthened into months before he returned, having sampled the delights of Beyruth, Damascus, Acre, and much entertainment in the houses of ladies of easiest virtue.

Yet when he had run through all that Hester had given him and more from other sources, he decided it were better to go back to the main source. Unfortunately no sooner had he arrived at Mar Elias, than he went down with an attack of acute gastritis. No doctor of any repute or medical skill could be obtained at short notice, and Hester, advised by the General who claimed inspiration from Hippocrates assisted by the now aged and almost senile Metta, treated him herself until an Italian doctor was sent for from Beyruth.

He advised bleeding, cupping, purging, gave laudanum for the pain – the poor man was doubled up in agony with frequent vomiting – but all to no avail.

Hester was frantic with anxiety, despite the avowal of

the crystal as seen by Metta that he would recover: 'This is but a test to try his faith and, as might be, a warning to discipline him against the self-indulgence of too good appetite. I eat but sparingly, as the *Sytt* well knows.'

Yes, the *Sytt* did well know, if 'sparingly' could be thought to cost her a formidable monthly account from the wine merchant at Damascus supplied at the order of the General and shared by her other 'wise man'.

The Italian doctor, who had served her as temporary physician after the departure of Newbury, left Hester in charge of the patient with full instructions to administer the various physics he prescribed, and went back after promising to call again within the week.

For three days and nights she nursed him, bathed his heated body with fragrant herb water, but still he weakened. Had medical science advanced at that time sufficiently to diagnose appendicitis he might have been saved; but it was not to be. On the third night he sank into merciful unconsciousness, and died in the dawn of the day.

*   *   *

The marble casket covered with flowers, soon withered, lay under a shroud of autumn leaves to be swept away each morning by her hands as the winds wrenched them from the branches of the trees in the convent garden where all that she loved lay buried.

He was gone from her as utterly as the joy that had consumed her with his coming, to leave her desolate in the months that followed his passing.

In the first weeks of her loss she had found some, if little, comfort in the semi-mystical philosophy propounded by the father who accepted with unimpassioned resignation that which had crippled her life.

'You must believe,' he told her, 'when I say that my son's death on earth was predestined.'

'You did not see his death in our stars,' she said in the flat toneless voice which had lost its buoyancy and youthful resonance; her voice was now that of an ageing woman. 'Why did you not tell me I am born to be cursed? That everyone I love must be taken from me?'

'No, miladi, no!' The silver hook was raised in a vehement denial. 'You – forgive me! – you blaspheme against the Powers who ordain our lives. You are not cursed, you are blessed as is he who has been spared much suffering on this purgatorial sphere. The stars have spoken.'

'He! Spared suffering with me were we married? How could he have suffered – with *me*?'

'Madame,' the General tactfully offered, 'my son would never have married you. He cared too much for you to take you in marriage. He has the same view as the Mohammedans whose faith, under my guidance, he would have embraced. He considered, as do I, that marriage as in the Christian Church is licentiousness made lawful by the hypocrisies of the theologians. This is proved by the word of Jehovah, God of the Jews, and as the wisdom of Solomon has testified with his wives and many concubines. In Europe not one man in one hundred – in effect – one thousand, is monogamous. But rest assured, Madame, I see only that which I am permitted to see. None of us goes until we are invited – that I do know – but I cannot see when the invitation will come. My son has been invited at an early age for some divine purpose beyond my visionary interpretation. You, miladi, who are still bound to this earth world, are given a purpose and you have not yet pursued that purpose to its end.'

'To what purpose is my life and to what end do I pursue it to find myself abandoned?' She covered her face, rocking herself to and fro on the divan while soundless sobs shook her slender – now too slender – frame. 'I am a failure in all my undertakings.'

'Not so, Madame. Your journey – your mortal journey to Mecca – is only just begun. Are you not crowned Queen of the Desert? Do not all men of these Arab tribes regard you with reverence? They recognize you are come to them on a divine mission. Do not grieve for my son's passing from this illusive vision which is called life to the ultimate reality of eternal consciousness, an awakening from the sleep which is called death. At present you are living apart from him on this lower sphere which is the purgatory of the Church of Rome, for I am led to believe that purgatory is the gateway from Gehenna to Paradise where all immortal spirits are conjoined. Every man or woman born under the same star is the counterpart of the other as in the heavenly twins, Castor and Pollux. So be of good cheer, Madame, for it grieves him to see you – as he can see you through the veil that divides the earthly body from its spiritual mate – sorrowing for that which should be your joy.'

Whether these consolatory ambiguities had the desired effect is doubtful. Certainly when Barker visited her, ostensibly to view the house at Djoun in its final stages of completion but actually to see how the death of Loustenau had affected her, he was shocked to see her a physical and mental wreck. It had come to him through the Levantine consulates, since gossip was the cream of their official lives, that 'crazy Hester Stanhope' had taken to herself a successor to Michael Bruce, and that he, her latest, had died from a surfeit of – hee-hee – the fleshpots, in consequence of which 'the Stanhope' had gone completely off her head.

'He'd been living on her money, he and his father, and now,' gleefully went the latest talk, 'she's up the spout, dead broke. . . .'

Barker was still more perturbed to hear how the General, known throughout the Pashalic as 'The Prophet', had turned to good account his spiritual counsel.

'He and that precious son of his must have drained her

dry,' Barker reported when back at Aleppo. 'The father with his balderdash and the son with his – well, and there it is.'

And there it was. And the General installed at Mar Elias for life, since Hester would not have him at Djoun, where she told Barker she intended to go into retreat.

FOUR

She could not have chosen a more isolated eyrie than the house at Djoun now that she had no lover to share it with her. The servants' quarters as well as her own were guarded by high walls, one within the other, like a Chinese puzzle. Any attempt on the part of her staff to escape would have been impossible. She had taken this precaution because at Mar Elias there had been a general exodus of the Negro servants whom she had severely chastised for some misdemeanour, and all of them fled in the night but returned chastened within a week.

Since Loustenau's death she had cut herself off from the world, received no visitors, was more than ever determined to fulfil the prophecy that ordained her to be the Bride of the Messiah on His second coming. She must live a life of the spirit, not the flesh. She would only leave her fortress to safeguard refugees from the tribal rebellions that were devastating Syria against the ruthless unscrupulous Emir Bechir, he who had welcomed her with such charming grace in his palace of Dayr-el-Kamar when she visited the Druses after leaving Nazareth – how long ago it seemed. And how she had been deceived in him! Living now in the heart of his territory she knew herself in danger of attack from the merciless Prince of the Mountain. She expected every day to be besieged. He was bent on the suppression of the rebels and had taken as his ally the nephew of her good old friend, Soliman Pasha, now dead. His successor, Abdullah, was as savagely cruel as the late Pasha, Soliman, was not.

There had been fierce guerrilla warfare in the Druse country instigated by the Emir's chief minister, Sheik

Bechir; the two identical names caused much confusion among the peasants. The Sheik, in the absence of the Emir who had gone to Egypt on a few months' mission, incited the Druses to rise in revolt against their lord and master, and proclaimed himself Prince of the Mountain.

No peaceful retreat was Hester's self-inflicted immolation on the rocky heights of Lebanon. Her pension from the British Government and the ten thousand legacy from Charles were all spent on the improvements of her house. The gardens alone had taken a whole year's income. She was up to her ears in debt and could no longer borrow from her old friend and banker Coutts who had died in the preceding year. Her only visitors in vain attempt to gain admittance were duns. They would wait in queues outside the walls of her fortress threatened by her guards unless they departed forthwith. She was forced to resort to Turkish moneylenders in Acre and Damascus who were demanding immediate payment of interest long overdue. She had pawned all her personal treasures collected on her travels through the Middle East. All her jewellery which would have paid off some of her creditors had been lost in the wreck off Rhodes at the start of her adventures.

The gardens that had cost her a fortune were magnificent with their labyrinthine walks, rare plants, and pergolas entwined with roses, jessamine, hibiscus – a glory of English and semi-tropical flowers; and in her private garden a marble urn marked the grave of Loustenau, brought from Mar Elias to lie where she would lie beside him.

Letters from England were few and far between. James wrote of his marriage to the daughter of Lord Mansfield and begged her to come back to live with them. She had no intention of returning to the land of her birth. And as the years raced on, for to those who tread the downward path time speeds ahead, while for the young time slowly limps – 'And for me,' she told the long-enduring Williams, 'there is no time, no life, but memory.' Yet there was life enough for her in the immediate future.

The war in the mountains had become an incessant menace. Abdullah Pasha had now joined forces with Emir Bechir in his struggle against the usurping Sheik. Day and night the mountains roared with the cannon fire from the Pashalic army brought up to quell the insurrection. Refugee Druses, wounded, homeless, sought shelter with their 'Queen'. She had taken several disused cottages in the village to house them and set her guards about their doors that they might not be seized by the Emir's scouts. Williams went in terror of her life. Hester had a couch put in her bedroom, for the poor little soul was afraid to sleep alone and was made to keep a pistol under her pillow although she would be terrified to use it.

No longer did Hester brood upon her past and all the loss of those she loved. When she heard how Sheik Bechir had been captured, cast into prison and, by order of the Emir beheaded, his body dismembered and thrown to the dogs, she was up in arms to avenge this monstrous crime. The Emir, having done away with his former minister, once his friend and adviser, fell upon his own two nephews who had rebelled against him and joined forces with the murdered Sheik. They in their turn were seized and tortured by their uncle, the Emir, at whose command their eyes were burnt out with red hot irons, and sent from him blinded and penniless beggars.

At once Hester rescued them, brought them to her house, cared for and nursed them as they might have been her brothers, till recovered from the horrors they had suffered – they were only boys scarcely out of their teens – and sent them forth with two of her own servants and money enough to get them safely to Acre and their relatives who would seek revenge on the murderous Emir.

In their hundreds Hester housed the refugees; they regarded her as a goddess sent by Mahomet as their

281

saviour. When the widow of the murdered sheik fled to the mountains with her child and took shelter in a cave, the Emir tracked her down with bloodhounds and ordered her child to be cut in pieces before her eyes – and then they slaughtered her.

Reports of the awful tortures perpetrated by the Prince of the Mountain decided Hester to take action. Guarded in her fortress she had already defied the Emir by harbouring his enemies and the wounded and homeless refugees who had escaped death in the rebellion. She now applied to Mr Abott, the British consul at Beyruth to intervene on behalf of the persecuted rebels and her refugees. But she could get no satisfaction from him or from his agent at Sayda, a defrocked Armenian bishop. He was in league with the Emir to be rid of the English-woman who caused so much trouble in the Mountain and whose influence with the Emir's subjects was an ever present danger. Bechir needed no reminder of that. His whole concern now that he had dealt with the sheik, his wife and child, his own two nephews, and all his enemies who had met with a like fate unless rescued by 'that woman in the guise of a man', was to be done with her. That he could not annihilate her by the same drastic measures he had employed against those others who dared defy him lest he incur investigation from the British Ambassador at the Porte, made him devise every cunning means, short of murder, to render her position intolerable. Her camels were stolen by his men to carry slabs of marble from Sayda to repair the damage done to his palace by the rebels.

The camels, passing through Djoun, were set upon by Hester's men, and every slab of marble smashed to bits as she had ordered the statue at Ascalon to be destroyed and the Emir's men hounded back to their master. There were many other incidents should any of the Bechir's minions come into contact with the servants of the *Sytt*.

Bechir was at his wits' end how to get her out of his

282

domain, for while she remained who could tell what devilment she would contrive? He had heard she dabbled in magic. Bechir, although born a Mussulman, had adopted Christianity which he never practised but firmly believed if not in Christ, in the devil and all his works, of which this woman, half man, must be one of Satan's most evil disciples. Of that he was convinced.

From the roofs of every village in his province, he ordered his criers to denounce the Englishwoman possessed of the Evil One who was bent on the destruction of himself, his territory and his people, and commanded that all her servants and the refugees she harboured should rise against her and return to their Emir, who would forgive and compensate them for any loss they had sustained.

Hester was virtually a prisoner in her mountain home, but not all Bechir's threats nor the thought of his merciless vengeance should she continue to defy him, weakened her decision to stay firm, even to her death.

Besides her brace of pistols she kept a dagger under her pillow and boasted that 'she slept like a top', while poor Williams, terrified out of her senses, slept not a wink.

'I'll not give in to that monster, never fear,' she assured the quaking Williams. 'Would I allow that bloodthirsty beast of hell to frighten me into submission? Let him try to drive me from my house and I'll strangle him with these.' She held out her still delicate white hands to the shrinking companion. 'Yes, I will! Let him come here and I'll kill him!'

Williams had no doubt of it.

When the Emir in desperation gave an order that his own men should be slaughtered at her very gates, thinking to scare her into submission, she came down from her fortress and stood among the bleeding wounded and the dead, and shouted at those who had obeyed their Emir's awful command, in fear of their own lives should they disobey him.

Standing in the shade of a palm to shield her from the sun's fierce glare: 'Tell your Emir,' she yelled at the leading officer in English, knowing that he understood a few words of her language – she did in fact remember him as one of Bechir's equerries when she visited that 'charming amiable gentleman' as she first had known him, in his palace of Dayr-el-Kamar – 'tell your dog of a master that there is not a more bloody tyrant on the face of the earth than he, and let him know I don't care a damn for his threats nor for what he would do to me as he has done to others if he dared – but he daren't. Tell him to come here – to me!' She thumped her chest. Her eyes were wild, blazing blue fire. The wall where she stood exposed her to capture despite that four of her men were on guard either side of her; two were Abyssinians, magnificent fellows, the rest her Syrian servants, but all as fearless as herself. 'Go then!' she continued in Arabic. 'I await him here.' She drew from her girdle the brace of pistols she always kept about her person, 'and I'll shoot him dead for all the tortured deaths he has done to the innocent and helpless. What of the child cut to pieces before his mother's eyes. What of her death and that of countless others? Let him come to me and meet *his* death – not mine!'

They believed her. They who feared no man save their Emir, feared this creature, neither man nor woman, who braved them and their bloodthirsty sovereign lord with what seemed to them to be superhuman courage.

With inward prayers to Allah for their safety from this devil incarnate, they returned to Bechir with her message, expurgated, but its meaning was clear enough, and all but lost them their heads in the telling, which reduced their master to so frantic a rage he looked to be on the verge of an apoplexy.

He was beside himself, but Hester held the trump card and played it with her usual consummate audacity. She appealed to the British Ambassador at Constantinople, no longer Liston; he would not have cared less about her part in the rebellion that had ravaged the Bechir's demesne. The recently appointed Ambassador at the Porte was her old friend Canning, whom she had offended over the de Maubourg affair of her passport which had long ago been amicably settled.

At once Canning made a report to the Sultan insisting in the name of the British Government that he should redress the wrongs of Lady Hester Stanhope. A secretary from the British Embassy landed at Sayda to warn both Bechir and the Pasha of Acre that her ladyship was under the protection not only of Britain but of the Sublime Porte, and that the Sultan commanded that her ladyship must never again have to undergo such shocking threats and maltreatment as she had suffered hitherto at the hands and the will of the Emir and his allies.

It was now Bechir who went in fear and trembling of his life having been severely threatened by the Sultan and the British Government. Hester had won hands down. Writing triumphantly to Dr Meryon, to whom was given a full account of her share in the war of the Mountain, she declared:

> The Emir Bechir is now become abjectly humble. . . . His unheard of insolence and outrages towards me were set to rights by our old friend Canning at Constantinople. . . . Finding that he (Bechir) had made a false calculation in displeasing great and small by his vile conduct he repents having given me the opportunity of showing them all an example of firmness and courage. I am thus become more popular than ever. . . .

That blast blown from her own trumpet echoed through the pashalic and came to the ears, growing slightly deaf, of old General Loustenau, her 'Prophet', as Hester chose to call him and as he came to be known throughout all Lebanon. Twice a year he would mount a mule and scale the heights of Djoun to visit his son's grave and hear all about Hester's conquest of Bechir which she never tired of recounting with much elaboration.

'You, Madame,' said the Prophet, stroking his long white beard with his hook, 'are the veritable David who defied the Giant. The stars foretold your conquest of this monster, born of the devil.'

'In effect,' said she speaking in French as she usually did with the 'Prophet', 'Bechir thinks *I* am of the devil. He had it cried from the housetops!'

'My dear son,' the General manufactured tears, 'recognized in you that which he so loved and —'

'He never said,' she interrupted, 'that he loved me.'

'Ah, yes, but love,' proclaimed the Prophet, 'asks no words. Love has many faces. The Greeks saw him as Eros, a boy, a child, and it is this quality which you possess of the child, the youth, which with your fearless courage makes of you a man to fight for the victims of oppression. But' – he spread his hook in a Gallic gesture – 'you, as my son did realize and which so engaged him, are as a maiden in love. For this rare charm all men must adore and worship you. Here in the desert lands they make you the homage as their *Sytt*, is it not?'

All this was honey to be taken at its worth to send him from her with a well-filled purse.

*   *   *

The years that followed her triumphant conquest of Bechir brought her much sorrow and personal loss. A recluse in her mountain home, she still refused to see any English visitors having cut herself off from all association with her former life. She became utterly immersed in the study of the occult and the necromantic charlatanism of her 'Prophet' Loustenau. She still firmly believed in her divine destiny as the 'Bride' chosen to lead the Messiah on His coming to Jerusalem, for which in her seclusion as the 'Nun of Lebanon' (self-named) she led a life of conventual chastity.

It was thought by all who heard of the fanatical Englishwoman in her mountain home that she was mad. Only one of the visitors from England with whose family she had been familiar in her Downing Street days and who called upon her, did she graciously receive.

This was Captain Yorke, R.N., whose ship, the *Alacrity*, put in at Sayda, and who braved a rebuff by sending a letter to her ladyship to ask if he might be accorded an interview.

She replied at once by sending an interpreter and mules to escort him to her fastness on the heights of Djoun.

He wrote a full account of his visit to his father, Lord Hardwicke, to whom he gave a glowing account of her ladyship's 'wit, her knowledge, and her beauty for she is still one of the finest specimens of a woman I ever saw!'

Yet, when conducted through several dark and gloomy passages, he was brought into a curtained apartment furnished in semi-Eastern and European style, its divans covered with threadbare cushions, there was evidence of poverty in the lack of amenities and earthenware pottery with which coffee was served to him. The tall Bedouin who rose in greeting gave no indication until she spoke that she was a woman. Nor did he at once see her as beautiful. He may have been taken aback to find himself face to face with the notorious Hester Stanhope in her orange coloured robe, embroidered shirt, her cloak of black and white stripes and her yellow boots. Her lance, topped with ostrich plumes and laid aside on a couch, she took up to lower in welcome according to the custom of the sheiks. But as soon as she bade him be seated and talked to him in her soft drawling voice, Captain Yorke was enchanted.

She had evidently lost none of the charm that had captivated men in her youth, and even now in her fiftieth

287

year entranced the Captain. She told him of the atrocities committed by Emir Bechir during the revolt in the mountain and her own share in the suppression of it as the hordes of refugees still harboured there by her did testify.

'So you see,' Hester told the Captain, all ears for her astonishing exploits, 'how my star has favoured me and brought to his knees this wicked, now repentant sinner, Bechir.'

Of the consuls – 'Those accursed rascals,' she called them, 'they deserve nothing better than a kennel. Imagine that swine of an Abbot and his Armenian familiar here at Sayda, refusing to lend me help in subduing the revolt! For all they cared I might have been torn to pieces like the other victims of the tyrant – a tyrant no longer.' She offered him Turkish delight and her fascinating smile, 'He now eats out of my hand.'

She was smoking her pipe – the hookah – seated cross-legged as always on her divan. York was enthralled. Had she the desire or inclination she could have had him as her lover, but physical love was nothing to her now. None the less she could not help but enjoy his voiced, and unvoiced, admiration.

She told him, coughing distressfully from the smoke of the hookah she inhaled and of which Yorke tactfully refused to partake, how her financial resources were at lowest ebb. Far be it to suggest that she hoped to enlist more than verbal sympathy from the captivated Captain, but he left her with the impression that she had rendered up all she possessed of worldly goods for the benefit of her homeless protegées who swarmed about her walls begging for alms, and that she starved herself for them.

So touched was he that when he sailed from the coast of Syria, he wrote to her uncle, Lord Chatham, with whom he was acquainted. His lordship had ignored the existence of his niece since her deplorable escapades in the Middle East and her shocking reputation as the mistress of Michael Bruce, to say nothing of her alleged

288

relations, or marriage, with an Arab chief. The chivalrous Yorke could scarcely have appealed to a less interested source than this second Earl of Chatham who, now elderly, reflected no glory from his illustrious father and brother, the two great Pitts. Lord Chatham entirely disregarded Yorke's appeal, in which he says:

My Lord,

I take the liberty of addressing you and I trust in so doing I shall not be thought impertinent. . . . (Damned impudence, was his lordship's likely comment before consigning the letter to the flames.) Particulars as to the mode of life of Lady Hester, your relation, you are well acquainted with, no doubt, so of that I shall not speak but of her distresses only. . . . She made me understand that her absolute want of money was a great source of uneasiness to her. The house she now lives in belongs to a Turk who threatens to turn her out if she does not pay him £500 for the purchase of the place. She told me she has not the money. . . .

An added source of anxiety to Hester, as confided to the sympathetic Yorke, was that she was being dunned for the rent of the house at Djoun with this threat of eviction unless she bought the leasehold, having already spent a fortune on it.

. . . But what would make her as happy as she could be in this world would be for you to purchase the house at Djoun for her. . . . (Of all the bloody nerve, was again the possible interjection of his lordship while he, fuming, perused the rest of the captain's well-intentioned letter.) You, my lord, who I know can make it known to her brother James of who (*sic*) she never ceases to talk and retains the warmest affection. . . .

Letters took so long to arrive in those days that not until some four months after Yorke's visit did she receive the shattering news that James was dead. Always ultra-sensitive and with the inherited Stanhope mental instability, he had taken so greatly to heart the death of the wife he adored and to whom he had only been married four years that, unable to endure life without her, he was found hanging from a tree in the grounds of Kenwood, his father-in-law's place where his wife had died.

He left two small children.

This was Hester's crowning sorrow. Not the death of Loustenau, nor the loss of Michael – he, too, had married, yet although she had expected him to marry she suffered some bitterness from that; but the death of James – her little brother as he always would be to her to whom the dying words of her uncle Pitt had given him into her care – left her broken-hearted. The thought that she had failed her uncle's trust; that this tragedy might have been averted had she stayed in England to be with James haunted her. Could she then have prevented this terrible revenge he had taken upon himself for the loss that had befallen him? Suicide! Her dear beloved James. . . .

Now was she utterly alone, thousands of miles from any of her own kind, even from Griselda with whom she had not corresponded in more than twenty years. But Griselda, hoping to heal the breach between them and knowing how much their youngest half-brother had meant to Hester, did write to her but received no answer.

From that time forth her whole life changed.

The house was now hers by deed of purchase. Having pawned or sold every available possession of worth, and borrowed from Damascan usurers to the hilt at highest rate of interest she had scraped up enough to pay the five hundred pounds demanded for the sale of the lease.

There, with Williams whose devotion never faltered, even when the few servants who were left deserted her having thieved and rifled everything they could lay hands on, she stayed, never stirring from her mountain fortress walled up within it like the bones of the Patriarch at Mar Elias.

There was no difficulty now for servants to scale the high walls for she had no guards left to prevent their escape, and none save Williams to care for her and on whom she could rely. But she could still care for and sacrifice herself for others who came to her for help when she was again besieged with refugees.

The battle of Navarino in which the English, Russians and French allied fleets blew the Turkish Navy out of Navarino Bay brought Hester once more to the rescue of the many who had fled from the Mediterranean coast to Djoun.

In forgetting her own sorrow she found comfort in comforting those who sought her charity and shelter. Yet when she had given more financial assistance than she could afford to house, feed and clothe them, leaving her almost penniless, they returned to their own homes not in the least grateful for what they considered their due from the *Sytt* of Lebanon whose fabulous wealth was fable indeed.

But her unceasing care of those who flung themselves upon her mercy had told on her failing health. Both she and Williams were exhausted with nursing the sick and injured who had suffered from the ravages of the Turks during the battles on land and sea.

First Hester and then Williams went down with an epidemical yellow fever that was devastating Syria. The refugees had luckily left before the fever had come to Djoun where Hester, deprived of her staff other than a few maid servants and two black slaves, was left to the unqualified attention of Arab medicine men and witch doctors. Her store rooms were rifled by thieving servants; the contents of her coffers, where she hoarded her scanty savings, stolen. Even the curtains of her rooms were ripped from the walls. Her bedding, cooking utensils, and the kitchens were filthy as were also the rooms. Williams, who could have put the house in some sort of order, was more desperately ill than herself.

As always, when others were in need, Hester managed to struggle out of bed and concoct a dose that she thought would help to allay the fever of poor little Williams who was delirious and trying to leave her own bed and attend to her mistress. Hester had to hold her down by force.

She left the dose with instructions to one of the maids to mix the right proportions and give it to Williams that evening at sundown.

The Arab and Syrian servants supervised by Williams in her capacity of housekeeper and favoured companion of the *Sytt*, were jealous of her authority and resented taking orders from her. Either from ignorance or with deliberate intent the dose administered was much in excess of the quantities so carefully prescribed and which Hester had made the woman repeat after her that there should be no mistake.

The effect was disastrous. Constant purging, vomiting and racking pains indicative, to Hester's horror, of poison were followed by total collapse, and finally, in the early hours of the morning, by death.

Hester was distraught. A rageful resentment against the fates, the stars, the prophecies that had foretold her glorification possessed her. She believed she was under the influence of some powerful ruthless adversary. Death! . . . All she had held most dear had been snatched from her. John Moore, James, Loustenau, and this humble, loving and loved being. . . . Yes, she had loved her although she was always chary of showing any demonstration to those who served her.

Kneeling beside the crumpled bed of Williams, no more now than a lifeless corpse, she was filled with anguish. . . . 'If you could only know how much you meant to me,' she whispered, taking the little cold hand in hers while her tears fell upon that pale placid face; no sign now of her agonized end. Only the look of a smitten child brought from turmoil into peace.

And Hester, to the God of the Christians, prayed: 'Dear Jesus, take her to Yourself, for she is a saint and worthy to be with you in life everlasting. . . . Am I?'

Fear seized her. What have I achieved? How have I been led astray thinking I am destined above all others for His grace? You, my little friend, are more worthy of Divine Love than ever I could be. I am nothing, a lost soul. Self-satisfied. *Vanitas vanitatum*. That should be my epitaph. The fates are revenged on me for my arrogance. . . . She was seeing herself for the first time as she held that small cold hand in hers.

'You,' she said below breath, 'are in heaven and I am in the hell of my own making – the hell of self-pride.'

Her few servants, thinking some evil was at work to kill those who served the *Sytt*, fled, leaving a couple of old men and an eight-year-old Negro child, the unwanted bastard of one of the women.

There was none to attend Hester, and the shock of that death, so cruelly sudden, brought about a recurrence of the fever from which she had barely recovered. She fell into delirium; her screams echoed throughout the deserted house and were heard by a peasant passing under the walls. He gained admittance by continuous pealing of the great iron bell that hung from the door of the main entrance. A scared child came, at last, to peer at him between the lattice of the portals. She could tell him nothing more than that the *Sytt* had run mad and was screaming. He had heard enough to convince him of that. He fetched his wife, and together they nursed her, cleaned her room, and when within twenty-four hours the fever had lessened to leave her still helplessly weak, she insisted on attending the burial of Williams who, before Hester's collapse had, at her order, been placed in a marble sarcophagus.

293

They laid her to rest under a tamarisk tree in Hester's private garden near to the grave of Loustenau, where, when her time came, she too would lie.

'How long, O God, how long must I be left alone?' was her heart-torn prayer.

But she was not to be left entirely alone. Word of her misfortunes and her desperate state reached her ex-dragoman, Beaudin, who had been appointed as French agent in Damascus. Hearing of her plight he at once came to her assistance, supplied her with money to pay her immediate necessities, and wrote to Dr Meryon who made all arrangements to come out to Syria with his wife and family. He now had been married some several years.

'I have no words to thank you,' she told Beaudin when he brought her the news that Meryon was on his way to her. 'I don't deserve all that you have done for me. I cannot thank you enough, but God will bless you. . . .'

*   *   *

Dr Meryon on a hired mule toiled up the steep incline from Mar Elias where he had lodged his wife and children, and was now visiting for the third and last time, Hester Stanhope. The urgent message in the year before from Beaudin had brought him with his wife and family to be received by Hester with effusive welcome accorded to him, but not to Mrs Meryon. Both she and the lady took an instant dislike to each other. Mrs Meryon was a hen-faced woman who bullied her docile husband and, between patient and wife, Meryon found conditions intolerable.

Having housed his appendages at Djoun he promised his much better half – at least in her own opinion – to return with her and the children to England. To this Hester agreed. She had quite enough of Mrs Meryon who gave her to understand, on the few occasions when her ladyship condescended to receive her, that she had married beneath her; and Hester was thankful to see the last of her and the hen-pecked doctor.

But when she wrote to him begging him to come to her again he answered her summons at once. This time he left his wife and children at Nice. She, full of complaints, was threatening to leave him if he went back to 'that woman' who had seduced him from his rightful spouse. Yet, Meryon at long last asserted himself, reminding her that for thirty years he had been her ladyship's medical adviser, and even when absent from her had corresponded and continued to advise as to her health and well-being. Would he now desert her in her hour of need?

He left in all haste, avoiding the volley of abuse and condemnation hurled after him.

He recalled the shock he had sustained when he had first come to Lady Hester in response to Beaudin's report, to find her living in dire poverty in spite of Beaudin's efforts to procure her some sort of staff, most of whom, as did their predecessors, deserted her since she could not afford to pay their wages. He found her the shadow of her former self, an ageing woman emaciated by illness, a victim of her incessant cough which she told him was asthma induced by the dry climate, and which his medical examination proved to be a consumption of the lungs.

And now that he was back again for the third time he remembered how she, with her amazing recuperative powers and strength of will, had fought against ill-health, penury, and persistent misfortune. She had managed to retain one or two of her dilapidated rooms in some semblance of the luxury and wealth which, during her years in the Middle East, she had been accustomed to live. Moth eaten coverings were concealed beneath faded brocades stored in the attics; her few remaining silver spoons and table appointments, not held in pawn or sold, she kept under her mattress safe from thieving hands, and were cleaned by herself ready for any visitors whom she would allow to call. We hear of only three in these latter lonely years. They gave glowing accounts of the extra-ordinary woman who had braved incredible adventures, and left their impressions of her compelling personality.

Lamartine, the poet, likening her to a 'Circe of the Desert', extolled her 'beauty, her purity of expression, her dignity, her majesty. . . .'

If these eulogies were repeated by her ladyship to Meryon, one might have doubted them as exaggeratedly embellished, if Lamartine had not recorded them in his travels for all to read.

After this French ultra-Romantic of the Parisian coterie of the Georges Sand, Chopin, Delacroix period, had scaled the heights from Djoun to see her of whom the whole civilized world – his world – talked, came another of less account, save to himself, than Lamartine. He, a Prussian princeling, handsome, debonair, sixtyish, led Hester to think him much younger than she which he wasn't. As Meryon remembered Prince Pückler Maukau, he had 'the air and demeanour of a man of high birth', which would have appealed to the doctor who had never lost his rever-ence for titles. The Prince, travelled in foreign countries in the hope of finding a rich heiress and, divorced from his wife, thought to maintain her and his mistresses on a second wife's fortune. He wrote for an interview in such emotional and deferential terms that Hester condescended to receive him.

She refused to see any visitors, and they were rare enough, before nightfall so that shaded candles would hide what the relentless sun revealed – the lines of age in the once perfect skin, the time worn eyes that still, in the careful candlelight, could shine with the sparks of former brilliance. The Prince was therefore announced to her in semi-darkness.

Meryon, as his hired mule picked its laggard way avoid-ing the boulders and loose stones which strewed the cactus-lined path, recalled that meeting with the Prince.

Hovering in the background, the doctor had heard the Prince's greetings as: 'This immense happiness afforded me of paying homage to the Queen of Palmyra and niece of the great Pitt.' He had come prepared with well-rehearsed flattery to ensure, he hoped, an equally flattering response from the enormously rich Lady Hester, as repute declared her to be and who would not reject, he hopefully judged, marriage in her elderly age with one so irresistible as he.

As Meryon records it, the Prince may have been disappointed in Hester's reply to this effusive gambit.

'Since my fortune has melted away,' she told him while they took coffee served by one small slave girl, 'I live here like a dervish and have no luxuries,' which was evident enough; and the Prince, who had arrived with a considerable cortège of attendants, realized he could not lodge them in the lady's reduced household.

'The older I grow,' as the doctor, discreetly inconspicuous, recounts this conversation, 'the fewer are my needs. My roses are my jewels. The sun, moon, the stars are my time-pieces, water and fruit my fare. From your countenance,' she continued with her whimsical grin, 'I see you are an epicure. How will you stand life here with me for a whole week?'

The Prince had invited himself for a stay of eight days at the minimum.

'And how am I to feed him and his servants, goodness knows,' she complained to Meryon who, anticipating that difficulty, had provided accommodation for the princely retinue at Djoun.

'And for which,' Hester said, 'he'll have to pay for I can't.'

None the less, and whether Prince Pückler Maukau's expectations of a wealthy wife were or were not to be attained with Lady Hester, 'she obtained an ascendancy over him,' Meryon observes, 'such as she never failed to do over those who came within her sphere of attraction.'

And which the doctor, for more than half his life, had come within that same fatal sphere.

The Prince, perhaps in the hope of cementing her ascendancy if not in a matrimonial but extra-marital relationship, tried to discover if there were any truth in the report that she had been married to a Sheik. The *affaire* Nasar had been well circulated to lend exaggeration to credulity. He went so far as to ask her outright if the son of Mahannah el Fadel had been her lover.

To this, which Hester received not as offence but as a compliment, she replied: 'No Arab has ever looked upon me either as a woman or a man but as a being apart.'

And very much apart from the Prince, who took his chagrined leave of her with the riddle of her marriage to an Arab chief unsolved.

There was yet another visitor to the 'Nun of Lebanon' in these last years of her life: the then young Kinglake whose mother and Hester had known each other as girls. . . . 'For hours and hours,' as Kinglake gives it us in his *Eothean*, 'this wondrous white woman poured forth her speech concerning sacred and profane mysteries.' He does not tell us if her speech also concerned sacred and profane love. Yet Kinglake might not have been averse to the subject if she had, since, from his own accounting and despite her age, he too had come within the 'sphere of her attraction'. . . .

Here Meryon's retrospective reflections halted and, hastening his lazy mule into a trot, he arrived at the walls of the Hermitage, as Hester called her mountain retreat. A small black slave girl answered his bell and was bidden to fetch one of the men. An ancient Syrian in ragged robes appeared. Meryon ordered the mule to be stabled and took himself unannounced to Hester.

He found her in her bedroom and was dismayed to see its extreme poverty and neglect. Dust lay everywhere, cobwebs festooned the walls and ceiling. She lay partially clothed on her bed, the coverlet and blankets were burnt with holes from the hot ashes of her pipe. The floor was littered with papers on which she had been writing and discarding: quantities of letters to England demanding redress of her wrongs, of which, that evening, she gave a full account non-stop, to Meryon.

As the doctor entered the pitiable room remembering it as once it was, beautifully kept and furnished with rare eastern rugs and rich curtains, all sold now or stolen, the doctor could not speak for the tears that choked his voice as she stretched out her arms to greet him. . . . So thin were those arms the bones almost protruded through the skin.

'Thank God you are come!' she cried. 'I was afraid your wife who detests me would not have allowed you to return even for the little time that is left to me here . . .' her voice faltered. 'You see how I am. But,' with a gallant attempt to disdain self-pity, 'I'll be well again in the spring. These winters and the icy mountain winds always bring on my cough.'

'Madam,' Meryon found voice to expostulate, 'my wife honours and respects you and,' he lied, 'she sends you her warmest regards and – and affection.'

'My good Meryon,' she grinned up at him, 'have you ever known any woman other than my dear Ann Fry and Williams of blessed memory who have had any affection for me? I have always been hated by women, maybe because men have loved me too much. Yet . . . not enough. As for the women who have served me – you see how I am left? With only two decrepit old men and the child who admitted you. And here am I and none to . . .'

A fit of coughing seized her, and with a heart pang he saw how she had wasted since his last sight of her. The enemy, he thought, is eating her away. She'll not live through another winter.

Miraculously she did live through another winter with Meryon beside her to fight the destroyer that had not yet gained its deadliest hold upon her perished lungs.

A letter from Colonel Campbell, the Consul General at Alexandria, had informed her that her Government pension was in danger of being confiscated in payment of her debts to Turkish creditors for which the British Foreign Office would be held responsible. While Wellington was Foreign Secretary – for her creditors had been dunning her for payment these three years – he would not have allowed any such action to be taken; but when Palmerston became Secretary of State for Foreign Affairs, he wrote commanding Campbell that if Lady Hester did not pay her debtors and a thousand pounds to a moneylender who was threatening to sue, not only her but the British Government, Palmerston would approach Her Majesty, the young Queen Victoria, to stop payment of her pension.

Hester was in the throes of this calamity when Meryon for the third and last time arrived on the scene. Yet although she knew she was dying, her courage defied those bent on pursuing their ruthless action against the woman whom the British Government and George III, the young Queen's grandfather, had pensioned in gratitude and in memory of her uncle, the deceased Prime Minister, who had steered his country through cataclysmic war.

Faced with bankruptcy, since a small annuity from James and the legacy from Charles had long been dissipated in housing and subsidizing those in need, regardless of her own necessities, she still could summon strength to fight for her rights. She who had commanded and quelled hordes of fanatical rebels and the merciless tyrant, Prince of the Mountain, Emir Bechir, was not to be cowed by cruel intimidations imposed on her by the Ministers of the girl who had recently stepped from the schoolroom to a Throne, and whom Hester realized had no part nor voice in these proceedings.

She who could rage at and beat recalcitrant servants for the least minor fault took this latest and fatal misfortune with a stony calm. The piles of letters Meryon had seen littering the floor of her room on his arrival, were copies of the many she had sent in protest to those who dared to treat her as a common debtor with threats to seize her pension, a Government grant.

Lying on her miserable bed, devoured by disease, racked with persistent paroxysms of coughing, she still could summon her unconquerable spirit to dictate to Meryon this letter to the young girl Queen:

> Djoun, Mount Lebanon
> *February 12th 1838*
>
> Madam,
>
> You will allow me to say that few things are more disgraceful and inimical to Royalty than giving commands without examining all their different bearings, and casting without reason aspersion upon the integrity of any branch of a family who had faithfully served their country and the House of Hanover. . . .
>
> As no inquiries have been made as to what circumstances induce me to incur the debts alluded to I shall not allow my pension given to me by your Royal Grandfather, to be stopped by force but I shall resign it for the repayment of my debts and with it the name of English subject and the slavery that is at present attached to it.

It was typical of her indomitable courage that she could write so proud and insolent a letter to the Queen of England, but it is unlikely her young Majesty ever saw the letter which was eventually answered by the Foreign Secretary who dealt Hester the final shattering blow. The renunciation of her pension was accepted and all payment finally, irrevocably, stopped.

And there in her wretched room with Meryon watchfully beside her, she waited for the long delayed reply to her appeal while winter dragged on into spring and with it the first glorious blossoms in her neglected orchard where the grass, unscythed, had grown knee-high, all hope of justice and redress for her wrongs vanished with Palmerston's ultimatum.

On a golden day when spears of sunlight pierced the jalousies at her window to stab at her weakened eyes, she raised herself from her pillows to tell Meryon with that same stoical calm in which she had faced bankruptcy and this culminating disaster:

'So! The die is cast. The sooner you take yourself off the better. I have no money. I cannot pay your salary. Go back to England where you belong and I do – not . . .'

Her breathing became difficult but she mustered strength to tell him:

'This is what you can do for me though I can do . . . nothing for you . . . Yes! I can. I *can*!' She paused for breath. 'I want you to publish my letters to the British Government in the English Press. Let them know . . . how I have been served by those who dictate to that child on the Throne. And also,' she pointed a long skeletal finger; a hectic flush suffused her hollow cheeks, her eyes shone with a spark, not of fever, of inspiration. Even at this eleventh hour she could be of help to him who for so long and selflessly had helped and served her. 'Since you have been here with me in my solitude and poverty, I have kept you writing for hours through the nights while you wrote to my dictation all about my early life, my hopes, and my adventures which you shared with me. Write it. . . . Write every word of it that it may be given to the world and let them be your memoirs . . . *yours* to publish in memory of your most grateful and . . .' A distressing cough stayed her words. A trickle of blood oozed from her shrunken lips. Again she pushed his proffered hand aside. 'Do not pity me. I have no pity for myself and none can say for all my faults that I'm a coward. I have faith in my star – my name means a star, did you know that? *My* star of destiny which has shaped my ends not as I had willed it but as yet to be . . . fulfilled.'

Again she mustered her last remaining strength to let him know that which must be said. . . . 'I wish you to return with your wife and children to England and to

302

leave me with no regret and no self reproach. . . . No, hear me and grant me this. You must let the world know it is *my* wish, not yours, that you should leave me. . . . None will blame you . . . none will ever blame you.'

That broke him.

He knelt beside her taking her hot dry hand in his, earnestly to beg her:

'Do not ask this of me. How can I leave you here alone with none to care for you? With no European near you – left to wanton rascally servants? You must not sacrifice yourself for me, I cannot . . .' He bowed his head on her hands. She felt his tears. And releasing that hand she laid it on the bald patch of his bent head from where the hair had thinned.

'Please, for my sake, do not grieve for me. I have lived my life to the full and of my choice even to this last bitter disillusionment which is my fault . . . *my* fault,' she repeated. 'I allowed myself to believe too much in what I thought to be my . . . ordination. Maybe it was that I should learn the truth of me . . . myself, if we can ever know ourselves until . . .' her voice failed her, but yet she found breath enough to ask:

'Just this one thing more. Before you go tell Beaudin . . . he is at Damascus, that he may come to me when I am gone and take my poor precious mares, grown fat for want of exercise, and old . . . so old as I . . . and let him see that they are painlessly put to sleep. As I too hope painlessly . . . to sleep.'

He went from her tear-blinded.

*   *   *

The roses in Hester's neglected garden, wilting in the heat of the June day, lifted their drooped petals to the grateful fall of evening dew. On these hot summer nights she slept on the divan beneath the faded canopy where she first gave herself to Loustenau. Her distressful cough

303

had quietened under the beneficent sun that followed the winter's winds. Yet her nights were feverishly restless.

It was moonrise, and the mountain wrapped in silence save for the sweet intermittent tremulo of birds' late evensong. Rising from her cushions she went with lagging steps to lean against the parapet inhaling the fragrant cool night air.

Lifting her face to the purple-mantled sky she saw one lone star detached from the blossoming galaxy that glorified the heavens. As she watched, it seemed to burn with silver flame in the dark river of the night. A moth flew past her, a fairy thing, its wings glistening diamond bright in the lovely light which shone upon her where she stood with arms upraised to that one lone star.

'My star,' she whispered, 'and yours, Loustenau, together now ... for ever.'

In the heat of early day, a little black girl came out upon the patio calling softly: '*Sytt.*' She brought the cup of coffee with which she would waken the *Sytt* each morning. And again she called more loudly: '*Sytt.*'

There was no movement, not a sound other than the joyous chorus of bird song. The child saw her lady where she lay on the flagstones with her white robes spread about her, and was suddenly afraid.

Turning, she ran into the house and fetched the old grey servant. 'The *Sytt*,' she told him, 'sleeps and does not wake. Come and see.'

The old man came, saw, and seeing, knelt to lower his head on the stone floor beside that quiet whiteness. . . . 'Yes,' he said, 'the *Sytt* she sleeps, nor will she wake until she enters the Garden of Allah.'

They buried her at night beside the grave of Loustenau. An American missionary performed the service at the request of one of the consuls whom she had despised as 'fit only for a kennel'. Her three remaining servants

304

straggled behind the plain deal coffin draped with the British flag of the country she had renounced. Torch flares flickered along the winding weed-grown paths and on the earth shovelled on to that humble resting place.

And none but a little black slave girl wept for her who had followed a star.